I0816849

PUBLICATIONS OF THE ISRAEL ACADEMY

OF SCIENCES AND HUMANITIES

SECTION OF HUMANITIES

ROYAL ASSYRIAN INSCRIPTIONS

Royal Assyrian Inscriptions
History, Historiography and Ideology

A Conference in Honour of

Hayim Tadmor

on the Occasion of His Eightieth Birthday

20 November 2003

Edited by

Israel Eph'al and Nadav Na'aman

Jerusalem 2009
The Israel Academy of Sciences and Humanities

We are grateful to the following individuals and institutions for graciously permitting us to reprint illustrations appearing in the article by Tallay Ornan (pp. 70–96):
Orbis Biblicus et Orientalis (OBO series), Academic Press Fribourg, Switzerland (Figs. 1, 7, 8, 9, 10, 12, 15, 16, 18 and 19); the British Institute for the Study of Iraq (BISI), London (Fig. 5); the Museum of Fine Arts, Boston (Fig. 14); Prof. David Hawkins, London (Fig. 17); Prof. Dr. Dominique Parayre, France (Fig. 23); Prof. Othmar Keel and Prof. Christoph Uehlinger, Switzerland (Figs. 24, 25).
Fig. 3 is reprinted by permission of Princeton University Press from: J.B. Pritchard, *The Ancient Near East in Pictures Relating to the Old Testament*, © 1954 Princeton University Press, 1982 renewed PUP Princeton University Press.

Should any rightsholders be found missing from this list, the errors will be corrected in any subsequent printing of this book.

Copy editors: Esther Goldenberg (Hebrew); Deborah Greniman (English)

Executive editor: Zofia Lasman

ISBN 978–965–208–178–0

Typeset by Art Plus, Jerusalem
Printed in Israel at Keterpress Enterprises, Jerusalem

CONTENTS

History and Ideology in the Inscriptions of Shalmaneser III

An Analysis of Stylistic Changes in the Assyrian Annals

by

SHIGEO YAMADA

1. INTRODUCTION

With the rise of military expansionism in Assyria in the ninth century BCE, many texts were composed in various annalistic styles to record the numerous military campaigns, chronologically and in considerable detail. Thus were the annals eventually, during this period, established as a standard type of Assyrian royal inscription. An especially large number of annalistic inscriptions has survived from the reign of Shalmaneser III (859–824 BCE). This paper examines them with regard to stylistic changes and related issues, and with regard to their historical-ideological background.[1] In 1991, T.J. Schneider undertook a literary analysis of the annals of Shalmaneser III and examined their structure in comparison with those of previous Assyrian rulers.[2] Since then, editions of four additional texts (Annals 1, 2, 12 and 14 in Table 1) have been

1 The main points of this article were stated in my Japanese article, 'Stylistic Changes in Assyrian Annals of the Ninth Century B.C. and Their Historical-Ideological Background', *Bulletin of the Society for Near Eastern Studies in Japan*, 46/2 (2003), pp. 71–91 (with an English summary), which dealt with the annals of Ashurnasirpal II and Shalmaneser III. The present article, dealing specifically with the annals of Shalmaneser III, includes some modifications and additions.

2 T.J. Schneider, 'A New Analysis of the Royal Annals of Shalmaneser III', Ph.D. Dissertation, University of Pennsylvania, 1991. Earlier fundamental studies of the Assyrian annals include: A.T. Olmstead, *Assyrian Historiography: A Source Study*, New York 1916; H. Tadmor, 'The Campaigns of Sargon II of Assur: A Chronological-Historical Study', *JCS*, 12 (1958), pp. 22–40, 77–100; idem, 'Observations on Assyrian Historiography', in M. de Jong Ellis (ed.), *Essays on the Ancient Near East in Memory of J.J. Finkelstein*, Hamden, Conn. 1977, pp. 209–213; idem, 'History and Ideology in the Assyrian Royal Inscriptions', in F.M. Fales (ed.), *Assyrian Royal Inscriptions: New Horizons in Literary, Ideological and Historical*

published in Grayson's RIMA 3, and I have treated them in my own previous studies.[3]

TABLE 1. ANNALISTIC TEXTS OF SHALMANESER III AND THEIR COMPOSITION DATES

Date of composition	Name of Text (Text number in RIMA 3)
Year 1 (858 BCE)	Annals 1*: Calah Nabu Temple Stone Tablet = The One Year Annals (A.0.102.3)
Year 2 (857 BCE)	Annals 2: Calah Fort Shalmaneser Stone Tablet = The Two Year Annals (A.0.102.1)
Year 6 (853 BCE)	Annals 3: Kurkh Monolith (A.0.102.2)
Year 9 (850 BCE) or later	Annals 4: Balawat Gate Inscription (A.0.102.5)
Year 16 (843 BCE)	Annals 5: Ashur Clay Tablet = The 16 Year Annals (A.0.102.6)
Year 18 (841 BCE)	Annals 6: Calah Bull Inscription = The 18 Year Annals (A.0.102.8)
Year 20 (839 BCE)	Annals 7: Ashur Stone Tablet = The 20 Year Annals (A.0.102.10) Annals 8: Ashur Stone Fragment (A.0.102.11) Annals 9: Kurbail Statue (A.0.102.12)
c. Year 20 (839 BCE)	Annals 10: Stone Fragment III R 5, 6 (A.0.102.8) Annals 11: Ashur Stone Fragment (A.0.102.15)
Year 28 (831 BCE)	Annals 12: Ashur Stone Fragment (A.0.102.13)
Year 33 (826 BCE)	Annals 13: Black Obelisk (A.0.102.14) Annals 14: Calah Statue (A.0.102.16)

* I use the plural term 'annals' for a record of events arranged in yearly sequence, thus applying it also to a single annalistic text.

Analysis, Rome 1981, pp. 12–33; A.K. Grayson, 'History and Historians of the Ancient Near East: Assyria and Babylonia', *Orientalia*, 49 (1980), pp. 140–194.

3 S. Yamada, *The Construction of the Assyrian Empire: A Historical Study of the Inscriptions of Shalmaneser III (859–824 BC) Relating to His Campaigns to the West*, Leiden 2000. Cf. idem, 'Peter Hulin's Hand Copies of Shalmaneser III's Inscriptions', *Iraq*, 62 (2000), pp. 65–87.

The addition of this source material, I believe, justifies a further analysis of Shalmaneser III's inscriptions. In what follows, then, I shall partly follow Schneider's analysis, but I shall present my own analysis of the expanded group of texts.

2. Annalistic Texts with Eponym Designations

In my accounting, the inscriptions of Shalmaneser III include 14 known texts of the annalistic type (see Table 1).[4] The earlier annalistic texts, composed up to and including his sixth regnal year (Annals 1, 2 and 3), were written in a style similar to that of the annals of his father, Ashurnasirpal II (884–859 BCE; RIMA 2, A.0.101.1), in which the dates of the campaigns were often given according to the *limmu/līmu* (the eponym), following the traditional dating system in use in Assyria from the Old Assyrian period onward. These texts are henceforth referred to as the *limmu* annals.

A brief history of the *limmu* annals is in place. At the end of the second millennium BCE, a lengthy text of Tiglath-pileser I (1115–1076 BCE), composed in an annalistic style, was inscribed on a number of clay prisms buried in the city of Ashur (RIMA 2, A.0.87.1). It presents six campaign accounts, separated from each other by short passages giving the royal name, titles, and epithets. At the end of the final campaign account, the military accounts are described as covering the period 'from the beginning of my kingship until my fifth regnal year' (*ištu rēš šarrūtīya adi* 5 *palêya*; vi 44–45). Similar annalistic texts were again compiled later in the reign of Tiglath-pileser I, as well as in that of Ashur-bel-kala (1074–1056 BCE; RIMA 2, A.0.87.2–4 and A.0.89.1–9). In these texts, however, no consistent use of eponym dates is detectable.[5]

The clearest examples of *limmu* annals have survived from the beginning of the first millennium BCE, with the onset of the pre-imperial military expansion after a period of decline. Especially striking in this regard are the annals of Adad-nerari II (912–891 BCE),

4 See Yamada, *Construction* (above, note 3), pp. 11–28 and 54–55 (Table 2).

5 Occasional use of the eponym date is attested in the annals of Ashur-bel-kala (RIMA 2, A.0.89.7, iii 20); e.g.: 'in the month Kislev, eponym of Ili-iddina' ([...] ITI.GAN *li-me* [m]DINGIR-SUM-*na*). The text is fragmentary and may originally have included more eponyms.

inscribed on a clay tablet from Ashur (RIMA 2, A.0.99.2). The text records eight annual campaigns undertaken during the latter part of his reign (ll. 39–119), each designated as having taken place 'in the eponym (*ina līme*) of so and so'. The campaign accounts are arranged chronologically, with no gaps, from the eponyms Dur-mati-Ashur (901 BCE) to Shamash-abua (894 BCE). The custom of designating eponyms was thereafter adopted in the inscriptions of Tukulti-Ninurta II (891–884 BCE) and Ashurnasirpal II (884–859 BCE).[6]

The Annals of Ashurnasirpal II, inscribed on the pavement and inner walls of the Ninurta temple in Calah (RIMA 2, A.0.101.1), comprise the lengthiest text, including an annalistic record dated by eponyms. The heading preceding the account of the first campaign reads: 'In the beginning of my kingship, in the start of my reign, when Shamash, judge of the quarters, spread his beneficial protection over me, (and) I nobly ascended the royal throne'(*ina šurrât šarrūtīya ina maḫrî palêya ša Šamaš dayyān kibrāti ṣulūlšu ṭābu elīya iškunu ina kussî šarrūti rabîš ūšibu*; i 43–44).[7] This seems to refer loosely to the beginning of Ashurnasirpal's reign, the entire period covered by his accession year (884 BCE), and his first regnal year (883 BCE). The account of the next campaign, probably undertaken in the first regnal year, opens with the heading 'in the same eponym year, in the month Abu, the 24th day' (*ina līme annīma ina* ITI.NE UD 24 KÁM; i 69). The third campaign account bears the heading: 'in the eponym year of my name' (*ina līme zikir*[MU] *šumīyāma*[MU-*a-ma*]; i 99) corresponding to the second regnal year (882 BCE).[8] The account of the third regnal year (881 BCE) comes with the normal eponym

6 RIMA 2, A.0.100.5; A.0.101.1, ll. 17 and 19.

7 The first campaign of Ashurnasirpal II, described after this heading, likely took place in his first regnal year (883) rather than in his accession year (884); see A. K. Grayson, 'Studies in Neo-Assyrian History: The Ninth Century B. C.', *Bibliotheca Orientalis*, 33 (1976), p. 138. The formula *ina šurrât šarrūtīya ina maḫrê palêya* and similar expressions were occasionally used in the inscriptions of earlier Assyrian rulers; see Tadmor, 'Campaigns of Sargon II' (above, note 2), pp. 27–29. Cf. also Yamada, 'Peter Hulin's Hand Copies' (above, note 3), p. 72, note 8.

8 Or 'in the eponym, the year of my name' (*ina līme šanat šumīyāma*); Tadmor, 'Campaigns of Sargon II' (above, note 2), p. 25, note 26; CAD, L, s. v. *līmu* A, p. 195b. In the period from Adad-nerari II (912–891 BCE) to Tiglath-pileser III (745–727 BCE), the king regularly assumed the office of eponym in his second regnal year; see A. Poebel, 'The Assyrian King List from Khorsabad', *JNES*, 2 (1943), pp. 76–78; and cf. Tadmor, 'Campaigns of Sargon II', p. 28; and A. Millard, *The Eponyms of the Assyrian Empire 910–612 BC*, Helsinki 1994, p. 13.

date: 'in the eponym of Ashur-iddin' (*ina līme Aššur-iddin*; ii 23), and the subsequent accounts largely continue in this manner. Notably, this series of chronological headings elegantly sets the king himself as the point of departure for its dating system.

The scribes of Shalmaneser III followed this style of composition in editing the annals of his first, second, and sixth regnal years, as preserved on the two stone tablets from Calah (Annals 1 and 2) and the Kurkh Monolith (Annals 3). Following the introduction (royal name, titles, epithets, genealogy, and the statement of royal nomination by the god Ashur), these texts record the yearly campaigns up to the date of composition. All three open the account of the first campaign – against Urartu, probably undertaken in the accession year (859 BCE) – with the heading 'In the beginning of my kingship, in the start of my reign, when I nobly ascended the royal throne' (*ina šurrât šarrūtīya ina maḫrê palêya ša ina kussî šarrrūtī(ya) rabîš ūšibu*; see Table 2). The next campaign was to the Mediterranean Sea; its account, assigned to the first regnal year (858 BCE), is introduced in Annals 1 and 3 with the date of the king's departure, recorded only by the month and the day: 'in the month Ayyaru on the 13th day' (*ina* ITI.GU$_4$ UD 13 KÁM). The account of the same campaign opens differently in Annals 2, with the heading 'in that very year' (*ina šattimma* [MU.1.KÁM-*ma*] *šuāti*),[9] with no indication of the month and day. The paraphrasing here of *ina šurrât šarrūtīya ina maḫrê palêya* as *šattimma šuāti* implies that the former expression, representing the entire period of the accession year and the first regnal year, was loosely equated with the year of the next campaign, i.e., the first regnal year. The account of the next campaign in the second regnal year (857 BCE), against Bit-Adini in Syria, is introduced in Annals 3 by the heading 'in the eponym year of my name' (*ina līme zikir šumīya*; the line is broken in Annals 2, and Annals 1 ends before this year), as in the Annals of Ashurnasirpal II[10]; in the following years, dealt with only in Annals 3, the headings refer to the eponym year: 'in the eponym (*ina līme*) of so and so'.[11]

9 Read thus (MU.1.KÁM = *šattu*) rather than 'in this first year' (RIMA 3). Cf. Yamada, 'Peter Hulin's Hand Copies' (above, note 3), pp. 70–73; and idem, *Construction* (above, note 3), p. 13, note 9, and the references there.

10 Grayson restores [... *ina līme* MU MU]-*ia-ma* [...] in Annals 2, l. 82' (RIMA 3, p. 10).

11 The heading for the subsequent years are as follows: Year 3: *ina līme* [m]*Aššur-bēlu-ka'in ina* ITI.G[U$_4$] UD 13 KÁM (ii 30); Year 4: *ina līme* [m]*Aššur-būnāya-uṣur* (ii 69);

TABLE 2. DATE YEAR FORMULAE IN THE *LIMMU* ANNALS AND THE *PALÛ* ANNALS

Year	Annals of Ashurnasirpal II	*limmu* Annals of Shalmaneser III (Annals 1, 2, 3)	*palû* Annals
Years 0/1	*ina šurrât šarrūtīya ina maḫrê palêya ša Šamaš dayyān kibrāti ṣulūlšu ṭābu elīya iškunu ina kussî šarrūti rabîš ūšibu* (i 43–44) ... (followed by the campaign account of Year 1)	*ina šurrât šarrūtīya ina maḫrê/î palêya ša ina kussî šarrūtī(ya) rabîš ūšibu* (Annals 1, ll. 18–19; Annals 2, l. 14; Annals 3, i 14–15) ... (followed by the campaign account of Year 0)	*ina šurrât šarrūtīya*
	ina līme annīma ina ITI.NE UD 24 KÁM (i 69) ... (followed by the campaign account of Year 1)	*ina* ITI.GU$_4$ UD 13 KÁM (Annals 1, obv. 42; Annals 3, i 29) ... (followed by the campaign account of Year 1) *ina šattimma* (MU.1.KÁM-*ma*) *šuāti* (Annals 2) ... (followed by the campaign account of Year 1)	*ina* 1 *palêya*
Year 2	*ina līme zikir šumīyāma* (i 99)	*ina līme zikir šumīyāma ina* ITI.GU$_4$ UD 13 KÁM (Annals 3, ii 13; broken in Annals 2)	*ina* 2 *palêya*
Year 3	*ina līme Aššur-iddin* (ii 23)	*ina līme Aššur-bēlu-kaʾin ina* ITI. G[U$_4$] UD 13 KÁM (Annals 3, ii 30)	*ina* 3 *palêya*

Year 5 is skipped (see below); Year 6: *ina līme Dayyān-Aššur ina* ITI.GU$_4$ UD 14 KÁM (ii 78). On the special structure of the episode of Ahuni, which covers the period from the second to the fourth regnal years (857–855 BCE), see Yamada, 'The Conquest of Til-barsip by Shalmaneser III: History and Historiography', *ASJ*, 20 (1998), pp. 217–225.

3. Adoption of a New Style in the Inscriptions of Shalmaneser III

The Balawat Gate Inscription (Annals 4), inscribed in duplicate on the bronze sheathing that covered the free edges of each of the gate doors, was composed in Shalmaneser III's ninth regnal year, or slightly later. This text cannot be regarded as genuinely of the annalistic type. Though the narration of the events from the first to the fourth years is arranged roughly in chronological order, there are no chronological headings, and the strict chronological order of the events in these years does not seem to have been the editor's main concern.[12] The inscription includes the record of the Babylonian campaigns in the eighth and ninth regnal years (851 and 850 BCE), with the chronological heading by the eponym for each of the campaigns (iv 1–vi 8). In this respect, the text still followed the preceding *limmu* annals (Annals 1, 2, and 3).

However, the subsequent annalistic text (Annals 5), edited in the sixteenth regnal year and inscribed on clay tablets buried in several places in the city of Ashur, was compiled in an entirely new style. Following the introduction (invocation of gods, royal name, titles, epithets and genealogy; i 1–27), the account of the campaign in the accession year is introduced by the heading 'in the beginning of my kingship' (*ina šurrât šarrūtīya*). The account of the first regnal year is then headed 'in my first *palû*' (*ina* 1 *palêya*), and thereafter each subsequent regnal year, up to and including the sixteenth, is indicated in the heading of the campaign account with the words 'in my *x*th *palû*' (*ina* x *palêya*; see below, Table 4). With the adoption of this style, the accession year and the first regnal year were clearly differentiated from each other. The campaign undertaken in each year was reported within an independent chronological framework assigned to a single calendar year. I will refer to this new type of annals as the *palû* annals.

The Akkadian *palû*, like its Sumerian counterpart, the BALA, originally meant 'term of office, turn', etc. It was used in southern Mesopotamia specifically in the political-chronological sense of

12 Apart from the absence of dating, the lack of chronological precision may be seen in the third year, in the placement of the episode of Ahuni's escape (iii 3b–6) after the Urartian campaign (ii 5b–iii 3a), though it actually occurred beforehand in the same year.

'reign' or 'dynasty'.[13] In Assyria, it started being used in the sense of 'the reign as a whole' or 'a single year of the reign' from the Middle Assyrian period. As we have seen, the first example of the expression x *palêya*, meaning 'the *x*th year of my reign', is attested in the inscriptions of Tiglath-pileser I,[14] while in the *palû* annals of Shalmaneser III, the expression *ina* x *palêya* is placed at the head of each consecutive yearly account. This systematic presentation emphasized that the king went out on a campaign annually, never missing a year.[15] In the old style of the *limmu* annals, by contrast, it remained unclear whether the recorded campaigns took place every year without interruption. Even a contemporaneous ancient reader must have felt this chronological uncertainty, unless he remembered the exact order of *limmu*s or checked the chronologically arranged lists of *limmu*s for reference.

No known text of *limmu* annals includes accounts of all the years up to the year of its composition. The yearly campaign account in the annals of Adad-nerari II (see above) does not include the beginning of the reign but starts only from the eleventh regnal year. The annals of Ashurnasirpal II also lack a record of the many years after his seventh regnal year. Similarly, the Kurkh Monolith of Shalmaneser III (Annals 3), recording events from his accession year up to and including his sixth regnal year, skips the fifth regnal year. It appears that the compilers of these texts felt free to skip years, choosing to record only those in which the events they considered important took place. That is, they did not regard the omission of several years as a structural defect, as long as the campaign records

13 PSD, B, s.v. BALA B, pp. 65–71; *AHw*, s.v. *palû*, p. 817; CAD, P, s.v. *palû* A, pp. 70–74.

14 The annals of Tiglath-pileser I (RIMA 2, A.0.87.1) describe the campaigns undertaken following his accession and conclude the account by stating: 'from the beginning of my kingship until my fifth regnal year, I conquered ...' (*ištu rēš šarrūtīya adi* 5 *palêya*; vi 44–45). The text of another inscription (A.0.87.2) states: 'my hands [conquered] ... in [my] ten regnal years' (... *ina* 10 BALA.M[EŠ-*ia* *q*]*a-ti* [*lu ikšud*]; l. 6'). Here, too, the *palû* appears to indicate a year of the reign. The usage of the word *palû* in Assyria from the Middle Assyrian period onward was investigated in detail by Tadmor, 'Campaigns of Sargon II' (above, note 2), pp. 26–32. Cf. also *AHw*, p. 817; Tadmor, 'History and Ideology' (above, note 2), pp. 15–16; Schneider, 'A New Analysis' (above, note 2), pp. 73–75.

15 Schneider, 'A New Analysis' (above, note 2), pp. 231–234; M. de Odorico, *The Use of Numbers and Quantifications in the Assyrian Royal Inscriptions*, Helsinki 1995, pp. 163–166.

were arranged chronologically. It seems that until the yearly royal campaign became customary or was even institutionalized in the reign of Shalmaneser III, no one attempted to record all the royal campaigns, without exception, in a single text. Only after the annual royal campaigns had actually been undertaken consecutively for over ten years did the scribes of Shalmaneser III start to compile the *palû* annals, with the intention of recording all of them.

4. Literary Characteristics of the *Palû* Annals and the Image of the King

In the *limmu* annals of Shalmaneser III, as well as those of Ashurnasirpal II, the campaign account of each single year was highly detailed. It indicated meticulously the course of the king's march, using the standard itinerary formulae: 'departed from ... approached ...' (*ištu ... attumuš ana ... aqṭirib*, etc.). Poetic imagery was used to describe the king's heroic advance, and the booty taken and tribute received during the campaign were often itemized. In comparison, the account of each year in the *palû* annals is much briefer, contenting itself with selected topics from among those dealt with in the *limmu* annals. The description of the course of the campaign was relatively general, omitting many of the itinerary formulae and largely abandoning the poetic imagery.[16]

After the compilation of Annals 5 in the 16th regnal year of Shalmaneser III, the *palû* form became the standard form of the annalistic texts. Subsequent revised versions were compiled periodically on the basis of the older versions, to which the record of new events was added (Annals 6–14). The composition of a new version was a straightforward programmatic process, in which the previous version was incorporated almost verbatim, with some omissions, additions, and word replacements. The campaign account in the earlier version was often shortened in the revised version. As the king's reign lengthened, his deeds accumulated, and his *res gestae* became more voluminous, it was not easy to find a

16 For a detailed analysis of the campaign accounts of the *limmu* annals (Annals 1, 2, and 3) and of the *palû* annals (Annals 5 and subsequent editions) see Yamada, *Construction* (above, note 3), pp. 77–85 (Year 1), 108–113 (Year 2), 120–123 (Year 3), 130–136 (Year 4), and 143–148 (Year 6).

medium and a place to inscribe all of the king's deeds in great detail. The style of the *palû* annals enabled the scribes to simplify the record of each single year and thus to include the king's achievements over all the years of his reign in a relatively limited space, on the surface of a single clay or stone tablet, or on a monument such as a statue or an obelisk.

The new structure, emphasizing the image of the king as a restless military leader who went out to fight in distant lands every year without interruption, changed the narrative focus of the annals and brought secondary literary phenomena into the text. First, since all the years of the reign had to be included, the editor had to fill each one with some record, even if no remarkable event had taken place. Thus, in the 17th and 19th *palû*s of Shalmaneser III, we have accounts of timber cutting in Mt. Amanus and of the royal hunt in Syria, in compensation for the lack of military campaigns. In his predecessors' inscriptions, such details were reported in a special section at the end, separated from the main body of the text.[17] In the *palû* annals, however, these events were treated as belonging to a specific year in the main part of the text, alongside military campaigns.[18]

Another new phenomenon is the frequent notation of the number of Euphrates crossings in the king's campaigns to Syria. All the major versions of the *palû* annals, edited in the 16th regnal year and thereafter (Annals 5, 6, 7, 9, 13, 14), include chronologically headed formulae of the format: 'In my *x*th *palû*, I crossed the Euphrates (in its flood) for the *y*th-time' (*ina* x *palêya* y-*šu Puratta* (*ina mīlīša*) *ē*(*te*)*bir*). As shown in Table 3, the first such notation records the eighth crossing, in the tenth *palû*; then similar notations are added frequently until the 22nd *palû*. As I have discussed in a separate article, all of these numbers were larger than the real one.[19] By the 20th *palû* and thereafter, the number of crossings was made equal to that of the *palû*, though there were several years in which the king

17 For example, RIMA 2, A.0.87.1, vi 58–vii 27 (Tiglath-pileser I); A.0.89.2, iii 29'–35' and A.0.89.7, iv 1–34a (Ashur-bel-kala); A.0.98.1, ll. 68–72 (Ashur-dan II); A.0.99.2, ll. 122–127 (Adad-nerari II); A.0.100.3, r. 5'–6' and A.0.100.5, ll. 134f. (Tukulti-Ninurta II).

18 Schneider, 'A New Analysis' (above, note 2), p. 87; de Odorico, *The Use of Numbers* (above, note 15), p. 164; cf. Yamada, *Construction* (above, note 3), p. 67.

19 Yamada, 'The Manipulative Counting of the Euphrates Crossings in the Later Inscriptions of Shalmaneser III', *JCS*, 50 (1998), pp. 87–94; cf. idem, *Construction* (above, note 3), pp. 335–341.

did not reach the lands west of the Euphrates. This phenomenon should be regarded as a literary hyperbole, forged to serve the claim that the king had conquered countries in the west by virtue of his unremitting yearly campaigns.

Table 3. Euphrates Crossings Noted in the Texts of Shalmaneser III

Text / *palû*	16 Y. Annals (Annals 5)	18 Y. Annals (Annals 6)	20 Y. Annals (Annals 7)	Kurbail (Annals 9)	Black Ob. (Annals 13)	Calah St. (Annals 14)
10	8-šu	8-šu	8-šu		8-šu	[8-šu]
11	9-šu	9-šu	9-šu		9-šu	9-šu
12	10-šu	10-šu	10-šu		10-[šu]	10-[šu]
18		16-šu	16-šu	16-šu	16-šu	[16-šu]
19			17-šu		18-šu	[1]7-šu
20			20-šu	20-šu	20-šu	[20-šu]
21				21-šu*	21-<šu>	21-[šu]
22					22-<šu>	22-<šu>

[ ] indicates a break in the text.

* The Kurbail Statue inscription erroneously assigns the heading of the 21st *palû* as well as the notation of the 21st crossing to the account of the campaign that was actually undertaken in the 20th *palû*.

There is thus a functional similarity between the counting of the Euphrates crossings and the *palû* dating, both of which emphasized the king's constant military activities. It is hardly accidental that the notations of the number of Euphrates crossings appear in exactly the same group of texts in which the *palû* pattern is used. These two features apparently were introduced simultaneously into the annals of Shalmaneser III. To be sure, occasional notes on the number of times the king travelled to distant lands are also attested in the inscriptions of Shalmaneser III's predecessors.[20] However,

20 For example, Tiglath-pileser I is said in his inscription to have crossed the Euphrates 28 times in pursuit of Aḫlamû-Aramaeans, twice for each year

the counting of the Euphrates crossings in his annals should be regarded as a unique phenomenon, as the numbers were purposely manipulated in combination with the systematic *palû* datings to buttress the same political-ideological claim.

5. The *Palû* Annals and the Eponym Chronicle

The desire to record every annual campaign appears to have led the Assyrian scribes to compile a different type of historical document – the Eponym Chronicle. From the Old Assyrian period onwards, Assyrians compiled the eponym lists, in which the eponyms (*limmus*) by which the years were known were recorded in their chronological order, certainly for practical purposes.[21] The Eponym Chronicle is a variant of the eponym lists, adding to the names of the eponyms short notes indicating the annual military targets of the royal army. Of the ten fragmentary surviving copies of the Eponym Chronicle, none includes years before the reign of Shalmaneser III.[22] An interesting example is the small fragment BM 82-5-22, 526, on which only part of the first twelve lines remains.[23] In the first line, the text reads: [*x*] *ša* [md]*Salmānu-ašarēd mār* [m]*Aššur-nāṣir-apli* LU[GAL *māt Aššur*]. After a dividing line, there follow the names of the eponyms for the first years of Shalmaneser III's reign. It appears that the broken sign at the beginning of the first line is to be restored as BALA (= *palû*), and that the tablet thus began with the heading:

(RIMA 2, A.0.87.4, l. 34). Adad-nerari II adds the numerical notations of the times of his campaigns against Hanigalbat to the chronological headings by *limmu* (RIMA 2, A.0.99.2), e.g.: 'I went again to Hanigalbat' (l. 42), 'I went to Hanigalbat for the third time', and so forth until the seventh time (l. 98, written erroneously as 'the fifth time'). This document, which also records the numbers of campaigns in other lands, may have served as a literary model for the similar numerical notes in later Assyrian royal inscriptions.

21 K.R. Veenhof, *The Old Assyrian List of Year Eponyms from Karum Kanish*, Ankara 2003. Later eponym lists of various sorts are edited in Millard, *Eponyms* (above, note 8).

22 Millard, *Eponyms* (above, note 8), Manuscripts B 1–10.

23 Though the right half, on which the military targets must originally have been inscribed, is broken off, the remaining features show that it is a fragment of the Eponym Chronicle. A. Ungnad, 'Eponymen', *RLA*, 2, 1938, p. 413 (Cb 5); Millard, *Eponyms* (above, note 8), pp. 20, 27 and Pl. 16 (B5).

'[The reign of] Shalmaneser (III), son of Ashurnasirpal (II)'. Two other fragments, Rm 2.97 (= B4) and SU 52/18 + (= B10), also seem to have started with the beginning of Shalmaneser III's reign.[24] If this is not accidental, it suggests that it was in his reign that the Eponym Chronicle was first composed.

Several fragmentary documents of the chronicle type, in which events are recorded in the third person with the dates indicated by eponyms, are known from Assyria in the second millennium BCE.[25] It is not impossible that the tradition of these chronicle-type documents gave some inspiration to the scribes of Shalmaneser III for the compilation of the Eponym Chronicle. Be that as it may, the Eponym Chronicle must have taken its form in response to a new demand, after the annual expedition of the royal army had been institutionalized. As I mentioned above, its purpose seems to be that of recording all the royal campaigns chronologically, just as the *palû* annals do. These two types of chronographical writing thus appear to have been produced simultaneously, with the same motive. The style of the Eponym Chronicle was later to change; starting in the second half of the eighth century BCE, it recorded not only military targets but also a variety of other events, sometimes at considerable length. But this was a deviation from the original formula, probably influenced by the Babylonian Chronicle.[26]

24 J.E. Reade, 'Neo-Assyrian Monuments in Their Historical Context', in Fales (ed.), *Assyrian Royal Inscriptions* (above, note 2), p. 155; cf. Millard, *Eponyms* (above, note 8), p. 6.

25 The oldest type of Eponym Chronicle is known from the time of Shamshi-Adad I in the eighteenth century BCE (M. Birot, 'Les chroniques "Assyriennes" de Mari', *MARI*, 4 [1985], pp. 219–242). The chronicle-like account of the deeds of Shamshi-Adad I, with their dates, in the Assyrian King List (A.K. Grayson, 'Königslisten und Chroniken', *RLA*, 6, 1980–1983, p. 105, § 11) was probably cited from a similar type of Eponym Chronicle. From the middle Assyrian period, several fragments bearing the chronographic third person account have survived (A.K. Grayson, *Assyrian and Babylonian Chronicles*, Locust Valley, N.Y. 1975, pp. 184–189).

26 For the stylistic interchange between the Eponym Chronicle and the Babylonian Chronicle, see E. Weissert, 'Interrelated Chronographic Patterns in the Assyrian Eponym Chronicle and the Babylonian Chronicle: A Comparative View', in D. Charpin & F. Joannès (eds.), *La circulation de biens, des personnes et des idées dans le Proche-Orient ancien*, *RAI XXXVIII*, Paris 1992, pp. 273–282.

6. BABYLONIAN INFLUENCE ON THE *PALÛ* ANNALS

An exceptional dating formula appears in the colophon inscribed on Shalmaneser III's clay cone (RIMA 3, A.0.102.44): *līmu* MU 23 KÁM *palêya*. Interpreted as 'the eponym of the 23rd year of my reign', it appears to combine the Babylonian regnal year dating (MU x KÁM ... [royal name]) with the Assyrian eponym dating (*līmu* ... [name of the eponym holder]). This finding supports the suggestion that the numerical designation of the year, x *palêya*, was formulated in imitation of the Babylonian presentation of the regnal year, used from the Kassite period onward. Indeed, it has already been suggested that the *palû* pattern was devised under Babylonian influence.[27] In keeping with this hypothesis, I will review some evidence concerning the cultural contacts between Assyria and Babylonia in the time of Shalmaneser III.

Babylonian cultural influence flowed into Assyria on many occasions from the beginning of the second millennium BCE onward and is attested in the period just preceding the reign of Shalmaneser III. According to the Synchronistic History, Adad-nerari II, grandfather of Shalmaneser III, concluded a peace pact with Nabu-shuma-ishkun, king of Babylon, after the battle between them,[28] and 'the people of Assyria and Babylonia (lit. Akkad) joined together'. In the reign of Shalmaneser III, too, close relations were maintained between Assyria and Babylonia. According to the same chronicle, Shalmaneser III was bound by a peace treaty with Nabu-apla-iddina, king of Babylon. Following the death of the latter, the chronicle reports, there was an internal revolt in Babylonia, and Shalmaneser III went forth to suppress it, supporting Marduk-zakir-shumi I, the nominated heir to the Babylonian throne.[29] According to the inscriptions of Shalmaneser III, he succeeded in his Babylonian campaigns, undertaken in his eighth and ninth regnal years (851–850 BCE),[30] in defeating the rebels, and he visited the Babylonian holy cities of Babylon, Borsippa, Cutha, and others. The relief incised on

27 Tadmor, 'Campaigns of Sargon II' (above, note 2), p. 29, note 60; Schneider, 'A New Analysis' (above, note 2), pp. 80–83.

28 Grayson, *Assyrian and Babylonian Chronicles* (above, note 25), p. 166, Chron. 21 iii 17–19.

29 *Ibid.*, p. 167, iii 22–35.

30 RIMA 3, A.102.5, iv 1–vi 7; A.0.102.6, ii 41–54.

the front face of the throne-base found in Fort Shalmaneser of Calah bears the images of Shalmaneser III and Marduk-zakir-shumi I shaking hands.[31] The scene, prominently displayed where anyone facing the king would have seen it, may reflect the importance that Shalmaneser III placed on good diplomatic relations with Babylonia.

Possible evidence for Assyrian importation of Babylonian scribal tradition appears in a copy, inscribed on an Assyrian tablet, of a ritual text for the cure of illness (*udug-ḫul*), originating in Nineveh (K 3054), which bears the following colophon:[32]

17 [*x x x x*] ḪA.LA BA.AN.UŠ *x* [*x x x x*].BI NU.ŠA$_6$
18 [DUB *x* KÁM UDU]G.ḪUL.A.KÁM *ki-*⸢*i*⸣ [*pî lēʾi*/*ṭuppi* (?)] URI.KI *gab-ri* KÁ.MIN.KI
19 [*ša x x* -AMAR].UD DUMU ^{m}MU-*líb-ši* LÚ.A.[B]A ^{d}AMAR.UTU
20 [*x* (*x*) ^{md}SILIM-*ma*]-*nu*-MAŠ LUGAL KUR *Aš+šur u* ^{md}AG-A-S[UM-*n*]*a* LUGAL KÁ.DINGIR.RA.KI
21 [*x x x x i*]*š-ṭu-ru šà-ṭir-ma sa-ni*[*q ba*]*-rì* GÙ.GÚ.SUM *up-pu-uš*
22 [*ṭuppi* (?) *x x x* L]Ú.GAL-DUB.SAR.MEŠ *šá* ^{m}*Aš+šur*-[DÙ]-A LUGAL KUR *Aš+šur*
23 [*mār* (?) *x x* LÚ.G]AL-DUB.SAR.MEŠ *ù* ⸢DUB.SAR É⸣.[M]EŠ (?) *šá qé-reb* URU LÍMMU-DINGIR
(break)

17 (catch line)
18 [The *x*th tablet of] *udug-ḫul*. According [to a writing board/tablet (?)] of Akkad, an exemplar of Babylon.
19 [which… -Mar]duk son of Shumu-libshi, scribe of the god Marduk,

31 M. Mallowan, *Nimrud and Its Remains*, II, London 1966, pp. 447–449; J. Oates & D. Oates, *Nimrud: An Assyrian Imperial City Revealed*, London 2001, pp. 175–176, Figs. 109–110.

32 CT 16, Pl. 38; cf. O. R. Gurney, 'Babylonian Prophylactic Figures and Their Rituals', *Annals of Archaeology and Anthropology*, 22 (1935), pp. 94–95 (transliteration and translation); W. G. Lambert, 'Ancestors, Authors, and Canonicity', *JCS*, 11 (1957), p. 5, note 21 (transliteration); H. Hunger, *Babylonische und assyrische Kolophone*, Neukirchen-Vluyn 1968, p. 136, No. 502 (transliteration and translation). I am grateful to Daisuke Shibata (formerly of Heidelberg and now of Tsukuba) for his valuable comments on the interpretation of the colophon.

20 [... Shalma]neser (III), king of Assyria, and Nabu-apla-iddina, king of Babylon
21 [...] wrote. Copied, checked, collated, ... (and) completed.
22 [Tablet of (?) ...] chief scribe of Ashurbanipal, king of Assyria,
23 [son of (?) ...] chief scribe and scribe of te[mples (?)] in Arbail (break)

The absence of approximately four signs in each line, broken at the left edge of the tablet, leaves the intent of the colophon not entirely clear. However, the text manifestly refers to a scribe of Marduk, whose name probably included the name of the god himself as its last element, and then mentions the names of both Shalmaneser III and his contemporary Babylonian counterpart, Nabu-apla-iddina. The colophon appears to have noted that the tablet belonged to the chief scribe of Ashurbanipal, whose name is broken off in line 22, and it apparently recorded that this text was copied from the Babylonian original written by '[... -Mar]duk son of Shumu-libshi (alias Mukallim), scribe of the god Marduk' in the time of Shalmaneser III and Nabu-apla-iddina.

The Shumu-libshi family was a well-known Babylonian scribal family in that period. The scribe called Shumu-uṣur son of Shumu-libshi, mentioned in a land grant document written in the time of Marduk-zakir-shumi I, son of Nabu-apla-iddina,[33] was probably a relative of the [... -Mar]duk son of Shumu-libshi mentioned in our colophon. The reference to the Assyrian king, Shalmaneser III, may have been added to the Assyrian tablet purely in order to note the date of the original by invoking his name. Thus, it may be farfetched to assume from the colophon that a member of the famous Babylonian scribal family came to Assyria to serve Shalmaneser III, as previously suggested.[34] It is, however, not impossible that the Babylonian tablet was brought to Assyria during the reign of Shalmaneser III.

Another source relating to the scribes of Shalmaneser III is the Synchronistic King List. It records the name of Shalmaneser III's

33 F. Thureau-Dangin, 'Un acte de donation de Marduk-Zakir-Šumi', *RA*, 16 (1919), pp. 117–156, iv 23. On the scribal family of Shumu-libshi (alias Mukallim) see Lambert, 'Ancestors, Authors' (above, note 32), p. 5.

34 J.A. Brinkman, *A Political History of Post-Kassite Babylonia: 1158–722 B.C.*, Rome 1968, p. 191, note 1176; Schneider, 'A New Analysis' (above, note 2), p. 81.

ummanû, [m]*x-ḫa-a-a*.[35] The *ummanû* was the highest-ranking master of the scribal art, who served as adviser to the king regarding various political or religious problems.[36] As suggested by H. Tadmor, following O. Schroeder, the *ummanû* may also have been responsible for the composition of the major royal inscriptions.[37] According to the same king list, the *ummanû* who served Tukulti-Ninurta II and Ashurnasirpal II was Gabbi-ilani-eresh, and so *x-ḫa-a-a* must have replaced him in the reign of Shalmaneser III or immediately before. This very new *ummanû* was perhaps responsible for the compilation of the new type of annals that used the *palû* pattern. Though the evidence is again far from compelling, the participation of new scribes strongly influenced by the Babylonian scribal tradition may have affected the major stylistic change in the Assyrian annals made during the reign of Shalmaneser III. If so, we may infer that the *palû* annals were most likely compiled as a result of the newly activated cultural flow from Babylonia, following Shalmaneser III's Babylonian campaigns.[38]

7. UPDATING OF THE ANNALS AND NEW PROBLEMS: THE BLACK OBELISK AND THE CALAH STATUE

After the compilation of the *palû* annals in the 16th regnal year (Annals 5) of Shalmaneser III, the scribes periodically edited

35 E. Weidner, 'Die grosse Königsliste aus Assur', *AfO*, 3 (1926), pp. 66–77, esp. p. 71, iii 21; cf. A.K. Grayson, 'Königslisten und Chroniken, B: Akkadisch', *RLA*, 6, 1980–1983, p. 119 (transliteration).

36 S. Parpola, *Letters from Assyrian Scholars to the Kings Esarhaddon and Assurbanipal*, I, Neukirchen-Vluyn 1971, pp. 6–10.

37 H. Tadmor, 'Propaganda, Literature, Historiography: Cracking the Code of the Assyrian Royal Inscriptions', in S. Parpola & R.M. Whiting (eds.), *Assyria 1995*, Helsinki 1997, p. 328.

38 Though the extant earliest version of the *palû* annals is that from the 16th regnal year (Annals 5), an older version may have been compiled. The chronological designation MU 10 *palêya*, 'the tenth year of my reign', on the clay cone Assur 13215, which Tadmor noted as possible evidence for the start of the *palû* dating ('Campaigns of Sargon II' [above, note 2], p. 29, note 60), must be dismissed, since it is now apparent that it must be read 'MU 20(!) *palêya*' (RIMA 3, p. 116, footnote). However, the counting of the Euphrates crossings beginning with the tenth *palû* (see above) may be a trace of the first version of the *palû* annals having been edited in the tenth regnal year. On this see Yamada, 'Manipulative Counting' (above, note 19), p. 89; idem. *Construction* (above, note 3), p. 338.

revised versions in the *palû* style. The chronographic format of the *palû* annals, so consistent and easy to maintain, must have been extremely convenient for the royal scribe to use in updating and revising the king's *res gestae*. All he needed to do was arrange the numbered *palû* datings up to his time of writing, with much recourse to the *Vorlage*, and add an account of new campaigns. With the prolongation of the reign, however, the scribes faced new problems, unanticipated when the *palû* pattern was first devised. Evidence of such problems is detectable in two texts edited toward the end of Shalmaneser III's reign: the Black Obelisk (Annals 13) and the Calah Statue (Annals 14).

The first problem is evinced in the deviation of the *palû* number, in the formula *ina* x *palêya*, from the real number of the regnal year, as revealed by a comparison between the annals and the chronological data of the Eponym Chronicle. The deviations start from the 21st regnal year/*palû* (Table 4).[39]

TABLE 4. CHRONOLOGY OF SHALMANESER III'S CAMPAIGNS

Year	*palû* in Annals	(*līmu* / *limmu*)	Military targets
Year 0 (859 BCE)	*šurrat šarrūtīya*	Tab-belu	Ḫubuškia, Urartu
Year 1 (858)	1 *palêya*	Šarru-balti-niši	Mediterranean Sea
Year 2 (857)	2 *palêya*	Salmanu-ašared (king)	Bit-Adini, Carchemish
Year 3 (856)	3 *palêya*	Aššur-belu-ka'in	Bit-Adini, Urartu
Year 4 (855)	4 *palêya*	Aššur-bunaya-uṣur	Bit-Adini, Urartu
Year 5 (854)	5 *palêya*	Abi-ina-ekalli-lilbur	Šubria
Year 6 (853)	6 *palêya*	Dayyan-Aššur	Ḫamath
Year 7 (852)	7 *palêya*	Šamaš-abua	Til-abne, source of the Tigris
Year 8 (851)	8 *palêya*	Šamaš-bel-uṣur	Babylonia
Year 9 (850)	9 *palêya*	Bel-bunaya	Babylonia

39 J.E. Reade, 'Assyrian Campaigns, 840–811 B.C., and the Babylonian Frontier', *ZA*, 68 (1978), pp. 251–260; A. Fuchs, *Die Annalen des Jahres 711 v. Chr. nach Prismenfragmenten aus Ninive und Assur*, Helsinki 1998, pp. 89–95; Yamada, *Construction* (above, note 3), pp. 59–67, 321–334.

Year	*palû* in Annals	(*līmu / limmu*)	Military targets
Year 10 (849)	10 *palêya*	Ḫadi-lipušu	Carchemish, Bit-Agusi
Year 11 (848)	11 *palêya*	Nergal-alik-pani	Ḫamath
Year 12 (847)	12 *palêya*	Bur-Ramman	Paqarḫubuni
Year 13 (846)	13 *palêya*	Ninurta-mukin-niši	Matyati
Year 14 (845)	14 *palêya*	Ninurta-nadin-šumi	Central Syria
Year 15 (844)	15 *palêya*	Aššur-bunaya	Nairi, source of the Euphrates
Year 16 (843)	16 *palêya*	Tab-Ninurta	Namri
Year 17 (842)	17 *palêya*	Taklak-ana-šarri	Mt. Amanus
Year 18 (841)	18 *palêya*	Adad-remanni	Damascus
Year 19 (840)	19 *palêya*	Šamaš-abua	Mt. Amanus
Year 20 (839)	20 *palêya*	Šulmu-beli-lamur	Que
Year 21 (838)	21 *palêya*	Ninurta-kibsi-uṣur	Malaḫi, Damascus
Year 22 (837)		Ninurta-ilaya	Danabi, Damascus
Year 23 (836)	22 *palêya*	Qurdi-Aššur	Tabal
Year 24 (835)	23 *palêya*	Šep-šarri	Melid
Year 25 (834)	24 *palêya*	Nergal-mudammiq	Namri
Year 26 (833)	25 *palêya*	Yaḫalu	Que
Year 27 (832)		Ululaya	Que
Year 28 (831)	26 *palêya*	Šarru-ḫatti-ipel	Que
Year 29 (830)	27 *palêya*	Nergal-ilaya	Urartu
Year 30 (829)	28 *palêya*	Ḫubayu	Unqi (Patin)
Year 31 (828)	29 *palêya*	Ilu-mukin-aḫi	Ulluba (Ḫabḫu)
Year 32 (827)	30 *palêya*	Salmanu-ašared (king)	Mannai
Year 33 (826)	31 *palêya*	Dayyan-Aššur	Parsua, Namri; rebellion
Year 34 (825)	no record	Aššur-bunaya-uṣur	rebellion
Year 35 (824)	no record	Yaḫalu	rebellion (death of the king)

As we have seen, the formula *ina* x *palêya* probably imitated the regnal year formula used in Babylonia; accordingly, the numbered *palû* was surely intended to correspond to the regnal year, justifying the accepted translation of *ina* x *palêya* as 'in my xth regnal year'. Originally, however, the word *palû* did not have the specific meaning of 'one year'; it was a chronologically loose concept referring to a term or turn, an ambiguity that was exploited by the scribes. When the 21st and 22nd years were spent in a continuous series of military campaigns against Damascus, the scribe referred to this series of operations as a single 'term', namely, the 21st *palû*. Similarly, he telescoped the three successive years of the Que campaigns in the 26–28th years into two *palû*s, the 25th and 26th. Thus, the compiler(s) of the later annals took the formula *ina* x *palêya* not as an exact year designation, but in the looser meaning of 'in my xth military term', which could be longer than a year. As a result, the *palû* dating is one less than the regnal year in the 22nd–25th *palû*s and two less in the 26th–31st *palû*s. This deviation was difficult for later scribes to discern, since, in Assyria, years were recorded by their eponyms, and regnal year dating was not widely used.[40]

Another problem is the intrusion of the deeds of high officials into the royal annals. We may assume that throughout Assyria's military campaigns, not only the king but also other, subordinate commanders fought for the kingdom on its various frontiers. However, the Assyrian annals, composed as the king's *res gestae*, in principle recorded only the campaigns conducted by the king himself, glorifying his achievements at the expense of those of his subordinates and emphasizing his unremitting military activities by

40 The complication with some date formulae found in the Black Obelisk shows that the editor actually overlooked the disagreement between the regnal year and the *palû* dating in his text. The Black Obelisk, though it constantly uses the *palû* dating, deviates from the practice by replacing the fourth *palû* with the eponymate of the *turtānu* Dayyan-Ashur. However, this position is erroneous, as Dayyan-Ashur took the office of eponym in the sixth *palû* (RIMA 3, A.0.102.14, l. 45). It could be that the editor, failing to notice the two-year discrepancy between the 31st *palû*, which was the second eponymate of Dayyan-Ashur (see the next note), and the actual regnal year, assigned the 31st *palû* to the 31st regnal year and then counted back on the eponym list the interval of 27 eponyms from the second to the first eponymate of Dayyan-Ashur, thus reaching the position of the fourth *palû* (= the fourth regnal year), two years earlier than the actual date. For a detailed analysis see Fuchs, *Die Annalen des Jahres 711* (above, note 39), pp. 91–93; and Yamada, *Construction* (above, note 3), pp. 325–327.

presenting annual campaign accounts. This format, however, must have presented difficulties when the king himself was not able to go out to fight.

The inscriptions of the Black Obelisk and the Calah Statue (Annals 13 and 14) record in the account of the 27th–31st *palû*s that the king stayed home and dispatched the *turtānu* Dayyan-Ashur to lead the army. As has often been pointed out, the exceptionally bold reference to the deeds of Dayyan-Ashur in the royal inscriptions must attest to the unusual rise of his political power in the kingdom. However, it may well also have been a consequence of the format imposed by the *palû* annals. Originally intended to emphasize the heroic prerogative of the king in leading the nation's army on its annual campaigns, that format now ironically compelled the scribe to include the deeds of somebody other than the king in the royal annals.

A close examination of the campaign account in the 27th to 31st *palû*s on the Black Obelisk and the Calah Statue reveals that the scribe was in trouble. The verbs alternate between the first and third person, apparently because of the involvement of Dayyan-Ashur as a real actor alongside the king, who stayed in the capital of Calah. The verbs are in the first person, reserved for the king, until the point at which he sends the army off with Dayyan-Ashur, the actual commander. In the accounts of the 27th to 30th *palû*s, the verbs for the commander's itinerary actions are largely in the third person, while those of fighting and achievement (destruction, conquest, receiving tribute, etc.) remain in the first person, still reserved for the king, thus creating a *modus vivendi* between the king and the *turtānu* that acknowledges the latter's actual conduct of the campaign. In the account of the 31st *palû*, by contrast, not only the verbs of fighting and achievement but also most (though not all) of the itinerary actions appear in the first person. This clumsy composition, leaving the reader unsure as to whether the subject is the king or Dayyan-Ashur, bears witness to the dilemma encountered by the scribe in endeavoring to fulfill two conflicting demands: maintaining the king's prerogative, and filling the *palû*s with an account of the expedition, which was led by Dayyan-Ashur.[41] This phenomenon

41 For a detailed analysis of the alternation of the persons, see Yamada, *Construction* (above, note 3), pp. 328–331 (with collaboration of E. Weissert); cf. also Schneider, 'A New Analysis' (above, note 2), pp. 132–135. The introduction to the 31st *palû*

may be regarded as a stylistic breakdown of the *palû* annals in the face of a complex reality.

8. CONCLUSION: AFTER SHALMANESER III

In conclusion, I shall consider the influence of Shalmaneser III's texts on later Assyrian royal inscriptions. Two trends apparent in the aftermath of the reign of Shalmaneser III may be cited in this regard. The first was the search for a new annalistic style to replace that of the *palû* annals. The problem faced by scribes towards the end of the reign in editing the *palû* annals became even more critical in the reign of the next king, Shamshi-Adad V (824–811 BCE). The great internal revolt that had begun in the 33rd year of Shalmaneser III (826 BCE) continued for seven years, until Shamshi-Adad V's fourth regnal year (820 BCE). The latter, obliged first to establish his kingship, could not go out on campaigns against distant lands until his fifth regnal year (819 BCE).[42] For such a ruler, unable to fill the first years of his reign with accounts of yearly campaigns, the pre-determined, chronologically rigid format of the *palû* annals was inconvenient. The scribe avoided its restrictions by replacing the term *palû* with *girru*, 'campaign', setting the phrase 'in my *x*th campaign' (*ina* x *girrīya*) as the heading of each of the recorded campaigns in the royal annals (RIMA 3, A.0.103.1–2).[43]
The second trend, attested already at the end of Shalmaneser III's reign in the texts on the Black Obelisk and the Calah Statue, is that of reference to the names and deeds of Assyrian high officials in the royal commemorative inscriptions. Following the reign of Shalmaneser III, from the end of the ninth to the first half of the eighth

---

account in the Black Obelisk and the Calah Statue (Annals 13, ll. 174f., and 14, ll. 320' f.) reads *ina* 31 *palêya šanūtēšu pūru in pān Aššur Adad akruru*, 'in my 31st *palû*, I placed the lot for the second time in front of Ashur and Adad'. In my opinion, this is a reference to the second eponymate of Dayyan-Ashur, but not of the king, as long believed. See Yamada, *ibid.*, pp. 321–334; cf. also Fuchs, *Die Annalen des Jahres 711* (above, note 39), pp. 91–93. For the confusion between the third and first persons in the royal inscriptions in general, see Grayson, 'History and Historians' (above, note 2), pp. 165f.

42 Millard, *Eponyms* (above, note 8), pp. 30–31, 57; RIMA 3, A.0.103.1 (= 1R 29–34), i 39ff.

43 Tadmor, 'Campaigns of Sargon II' (above, note 2), p. 30.

century BCE, royal inscriptions were compiled that mentioned the names of provincial governors and in some cases recorded their deeds. These were found mainly in provincial sites, as exemplified by the two stelae of Adad-nerari III (811–783 BCE) from Tell el-Rimah and Sabaʾ, referring to Nergal (or Palil)-eresh, governor of Raṣappa (RIMA 3, A.0.104, 6 and 7), and by the inscription of Shalmaneser IV (783–773 BCE) inscribed on the Pazarcik Stele, mentioning the *turtānu* Shamshi-ilu (RIMA 3, A.0.105.1).[44]

With the reign of Tiglath-pileser III (745–727 BCE), who resumed annual campaigns from the beginning of his reign, the *palû* annals were revived and inscribed on the walls of his palace at Calah.[45] Sargon II (722–705 BCE) also used the *palû* format to record his numerous campaigns, though he used the term *palû* in a chronologically looser sense.[46] Thereafter, Sennacherib and Ashurbanipal adopted the *girru* pattern as the basic style of their historical texts.[47]

In light of this general picture, we may regard the reign of Shalmaneser III as the most significant turning point in the transformation of the style of the Assyrian annals. In his reign, the annals definitively became the major type of Assyrian royal inscriptions. Most of the basic characteristics of the annals, which would be reproduced with some variations in the following centuries of Assyria's imperial phase, were also set during this period. The stylistic transformation attested in the texts of Shalmaneser III was influenced by historical reality, and in particular by the circumstances of his long, campaign-filled reign.

44 From the same period, there are also the commemorative inscriptions definitely known to have been commissioned by provincial governors for themselves: RIMA 3, A.0.104.2010 (Shamshi-ilu's lion inscription from Til-barsip); RIMA 3, A.0.105.2 (Bel-Ḫarran-beli-uṣur's stele from Tel-Abta). These inscriptions include the account of the governors' own constructive or military deeds and mention the name of the king only in their titles, or not at all.

45 H. Tadmor, *The Inscriptions of Tiglath-pileser III, King of Assyria*, Jerusalem 1994, pp. 27–89. The first *palû* is assigned to the accession year.

46 A. Fuchs, *Die Inschriften Sargons II. aus Khorsabad*, Göttingen 1994, pp. 82–188; idem, *Die Annalen des Jahres 711* (above, note 39). For the distinct problems of the *palû* pattern involved in the annals of Sargon II, see *ibid.*, pp. 81–88; Tadmor, 'Campaigns of Sargon II' (above, note 2).

47 About this transformation from *palû* to *girru*, and the arrangement of incidents in the *girru* pattern, see Tadmor, 'Campaigns of Sargon II' (above, note 2), pp. 30–32; idem, 'History and Ideology' (above, note 2), pp. 20–21.

POSTSCRIPT

It was only after the final manuscript of this article was completed in 2004 that I became aware of G.B. Lanfranchi's article, 'Chronology in the Inscriptions of Shalmaneser III and in the Eponym Chronicle: The Number of the Campaigns against Que', in S. de Martino et al. (eds.), *Anatolia Antica: Studi in memoria di Fiorella Imparatti*, Firenze 2002, pp. 453–469. Lanfranchi suggests an original historical reconstruction of Shalmaneser III's campaigns against Que, while retaining his trust in the chronological accuracy of the *palû* datings of the Annals, which he takes as preceding the data given in the Eponym Chronicle. Thus, he regards the Eponym Chronicle as a secondarily formulated source, dependent upon the royal annals. His approach is diametrically opposed to my view that the Eponym Chronicle is a sober chronographic source and more reliable in its chronological details than the royal annals, which are essentially a literary work composed for the greater glory of the king.

כתבי האקדמיה הלאומית הישראלית למדעים

החטיבה למדעי הרוח

כתובות מלכי אשור

כתובות מלכי אשור

היסטוריה, היסטוריוגרפיה ואידאולוגיה

יום עיון לכבוד

חיים תדמור

בהגיעו לגבורות

כ״ה במרחשוון תשס״ד

בעריכת

ישראל אפעל ונדב נאמן

ירושלים תש״ע

האקדמיה הלאומית הישראלית למדעים

אנו מודים ליחידים ולמוסדות שבאדיבותם הרשו לנו להדפיס בספר זה (עמ׳ 70–96) ציורים שהם בעלי זכויות היוצרים עליהם, ואלה הם:
סדרת OBO, פריבורג, שווייץ (ציורים 1, 7, 8, 9, 10, 12, 15, 16, 18, 19);
הוצאת אוניברסיטת פרינסטון (ציור 3); המכון הבריטי לחקר עירק (BISI), לונדון (ציור 5);
המוזאון לאמנות, בוסטון (ציור 14); פרופ׳ דייוויד הוקינס, לונדון (ציור 17);
פרופ׳ דומיניק פראר, צרפת (ציור 23); פרופ׳ אותמר קיל
ופרופ׳ כריסטוף אילינגר, שווייץ (ציורים 24, 25).

אם תימצא השמטה של בעל זכויות או תתברר טעות בציון שמו, יבוא הדבר על תיקונו במהדורה הבאה.

עריכת הלשון בעברית
אסתר גולדנברג

עריכת הלשון באנגלית
דבורה גריינימן

התקנת הספר והבאתו לדפוס
צופיה לסמן

מסת״ב 978-965-208-178-0

סודר ב׳ארט פלוס׳, ירושלים
נדפס במפעלי דפוס ׳כתר׳, ירושלים

תוכן העניינים

פתח דבר

בקובץ זה מכונסים המאמרים שעובדו מההרצאות ביום העיון לכבוד פרופסור חיים תדמור בהגיעו לגבורות. כל המרצים הם תלמידיו של תדמור אשר השתלבו במוסדות אקדמיים בארץ ומחוצה לה והם מוסיפים לעסוק בהוראה ובמחקר בתחומים שפתח לפניהם.

בשיטת ההוראה באוניברסיטאות בארץ תלמיד חייב ללמוד שיעורים מגוונים מפי כמה וכמה מורים, ולכל מי שהשלים את חוק לימודיו היו אפוא מורים רבים. ואולם התלמידים שהיו לאנשי מחקר והוראה באקדמיה יודעים היטב כי לאמִתו של דבר, רק יחידים מבין מוריהם פתחו לפניהם את שערי המחקר, עיצבו את דרכם והשפיעו על מגמת התפתחותם. תדיר יש רק אחד, יחיד ומיוחד, שכל אחד מהם מכנהו 'המורה שלי'. הדוברים ביום העיון הם חוקרים שתדמור השפיע באופן מכריע על התפתחותם האקדמית ועל דרכם במחקר והם רואים בו את מורם המובהק. בהרצאותיהם היו הבעת תודה והכרת טובה מרובה למי שהדריכם אל עולם המזרח הקדום, לימד אותם כיצד משלבים דיסציפלינות בתחומים מתחומים שונים כדי להבהיר סוגיות מדעיות, הקנה להם כלים לחקר ההיסטוריה, ההיסטוריוגרפיה והאידאולוגיה והדביקם בהתלהבותו ובמסירותו ללימודי המזרח הקדום לענפיהם.

ב'קיצור תולדות הזמן' נזכיר רק כמה תחנות בדרכו של חיים תדמור: חרבין שבמנצ'וריה אשר בצפון סין, בית הספר בהרצליה בימים שעדיין הייתה מושבה קטנה, הגימנסיה העברית בירושלים, האוניברסיטה העברית בירושלים, המכון ללימודי אסיה ואפריקה בלונדון, המכון המזרחני של אוניברסיטת שיקגו, שנות הוראה ומחקר רבות ופורות באוניברסיטה העברית בירושלים, ובשנים 1985–2003 – פעילות ברוכה באקדמיה הלאומית הישראלית למדעים.

מכל התחנות האלה התחנה ששהה בה תדמור שנים רבות יותר מבכל תחנה אחרת היא 'כתובות תגלת־פלאסר השלישי', ולצדו חנו בה גם תלמידיו, שכתובות תגלת־פלאסר שימשו להם מעין אולפנה שראוי ללמוד בה מה הוא מחקר. הדיון השיטתי בסוגת כתובות המלכים ובכללן כתובות תגלת־פלאסר השלישי, בירור כל פרט ופרט בטקסטים שרק מעטים מהם שרדו בשלמותם, הצורך להרין את השלם מתוך עיון בחלקיו הקטועים, הדיון הטקסטואלי הממצה ולבסוף ההתלהבות המתדבקת מכל גילוי קטן או גדול שהוסיף עוד נדבך לכתב החידה הגדול – כל אלה היו בימים ההם בית ספר מושלם לפרחי החוג לאשורולוגיה. עם פרסום המהדורה המדעית של 'כתובות תגלת־פלאסר השלישי מלך אשור' בשנת 1994 למדו קוראיו לדעת מה שידעו תלמידיו של תדמור זה מכבר: החיבור הוא מופת לפרסום מדעי של טקסטים קדומים מן המזרח הקרוב.

תדמור העמיד אמות מידה חדשות ומכריעות לחקר סוגיות עקרוניות רבות בתולדות המזרח הקרוב הקדום: אידאולוגיות מלכותיות והיסטוריוגרפיה עתיקה, דרכי התעמולה של השליטים והשימוש המיוחד במילה הכתובה

כדי להעביר מסרים לקוראים וכן סוגיות חברתיות ופולחניות והשינויים שחלו במבנה החברה האשורית במרוצת הדורות. לעניין זה קבע תדמור את המונח ׳הארמאיזציה של אשור׳ – מושג שנועד להמחיש את ההשפעה המכרעת שנודעה לארמים ולשפה הארמית על אשור במאתיים השנים האחרונות לקיומה. בייחוד הדגיש את המגעים שבין ממלכות אשור, בבל ופרס ובין המערב ובכללו ארץ ישראל, וכן בירר סוגיות חברתיות, היסטוריוגרפיות וכרונולוגיות בדברי ימי המלוכה בישראל וביהודה ובתולדות שיבת ציון. בין היתר פרסם מאמרים רבים על מסעות מלכי אשור אל ארץ ישראל ואף כתובות בכתב היתדות שנתגלו בחפירות בארץ, חיבר (עם פרופסור מרדכי כוגן יחד) פירוש פילולוגי והיסטוריוגרפי לספר מלכים ב וכתב את פרק הסיכום לתולדות תקופת שיבת ציון בסדרה ׳ההיסטוריה של ארץ־ישראל׳. העיסוק באשורולוגיה ובלימודי מסופוטמיה ותרבותה לעצמם לא מנע את תדמור מלעסוק גם בפרקים חשובים בתולדות ארץ ישראל, וכל אחד משני התחומים האלה הפרה את מחקר התחום האחר.

ההרצאות ביום העיון דנו בסוגיות שבדומות להן עסק תדמור שנים רבות. האפשרויות והמגבלות שבסוגת כתובות המלכים, היסטוריה ואידאולוגיה בכתובות המלכים, מקורות ודרכי עיבודם, כתיבתן ועריכתן של כתובות מלכים למהדורותיהן, עיצוב דמות השליט בהיסטוריוגרפיה האשורית, עיצוב דמות האל באיקונוגרפיה של המזרח הקדום ומסעות מלכי אשור למערב – נושאים אלו הם חלק ממורשתו של פרופסור תדמור.

עיבוד החומר ממתכונת הרצאות למאמרים כתובים הערוכים ומוגהים בקפדנות ארך שנים אחדות, ולדאבון הלב חיים תדמור הלך לעולמו ולא זכה לברך על המוגמר. ההרצאות שנועדו לחגיגת הגיעו לגבורות היו למנחות זיכרון למורה והחוקר שעליו ייאמר ׳חבל על דאבדין ולא משתכחין׳.

ישראל אפעל
נדב נאמן

רשימת הקיצורים הביבליוגרפיים

AfO = *Archiv für Orientforschung*

AHw = W. von Soden, *Akkadisches Handwörterbuch*, Wiesbaden 1959–1981

AoF = *Altorientalische Forschungen*

ASJ = *Acta Sumerologica, Japan*

BaM = *Baghdader Mitteilungen*

BASOR = *Bulletin of the American Schools of Oriental Research*

CAD = *The Assyrian Dictionary of the Oriental Institute University of Chicago*, Chicago 1956 →

CT = Cuneiform Texts from Babylonian Tablets in the British Museum

DDD = *Dictionary of Deities and Demons in the Bible*, Leiden 1999

HUCA = *Hebrew Union College Annual*

IEJ = *Israel Exploration Journal*

IOS = *Israel Oriental Studies*

JAOS = *Journal of the American Oriental Society*

JBL = *Journal of Biblical Literature*

JCS = *Journal of Cuneiform Studies*

JNES = *Journal of Near Eastern Studies*

JSS = *Journal of Semitic Studies*

MARI = *Mari, Annales des recherches interdisciplinaires*

N.A.B.U. = *Nouvelles Assyriologiques Brèves et Utilitaires*

PSD = *The Sumerian Dictionary of the University Museum of the University of Pennsylvania*, Vol. 2, B, by Åke W. Sjöberg

RA = *Revue d'Assyriologie et Archéologie Orientale*

RAI = *Rencontre Assyriologique Internationale*

RIMA = The Royal Inscriptions of Mesopotamia, Assyrian Period

RIMA 2 = A.K. Grayson, *Assyrian Rulers of the Early First Millennium BC, I (1114–859 BC), Assyrian Periods*, Toronto– Buffalu–London 1991

RIMA 3 = A.K. Grayson, *Assyrian Rulers of the Early First Millennium BC, II (858–745 BC)*, Toronto 1996

RIMB = The Royal Inscriptions of Mesopotamia, Babylinian Period

RIMB 2 = G. Frame, *Rulers of Babylonia from the Second Dynasty of Isin to the End of Assyrian Domination (1157–612 BC)*, Toronto 1995

RLA = E. Ebeling et al. (eds.), *Reallexikon der Assyriologie*, 1 →, Berlin–Leipzig 1932 →

SAA = State Archives of Assyria

SAA I = S. Parpola, *The Correspondence of Sargon II, Part I: Letters from Assyria and the West*, Helsinki 1987

SAA II = S. Parpola & K. Watanabe, *Neo-Assyrian Treaties and Loyalty Oaths*, Helsinki 1988

SAA IV = I. Starr, *Queries to the Sungod: Divination and Politics in Sargonid Assyria*, Helsinki 1990

SAA IX = S. Parpola, *Assyrian Prophecies*, Helsinki 1997

SAA X = S. Parpola, *Letters from Assyrian and Babylonian Scholars*, Helsinki 1993

SAA XI = F. M. Fales & J. N. Postgate, *Imperial Administrative Records, Part II: Provincial and Military Administration*, Helsinki 1995

SAA XII = L. Kataja & R. Whiting, *Grants, Decrees and Gifts of the Neo-Assyrian Period*, Helsinki 1995

SAA XVI = M. Luuko & G. Van Buylaere, *The Political Correspondence of Esarhaddon*, Helsinki 2002

SAA XVII = M. Dietrich, *The Babylonian Correspondence of Sargon and Sennacherib*, Helsinki 2003

SAAB = State Archives of Assyria Bulletin

TCL = Textes Cunéiformes du Louvre

ZA = Zeitschrift für Assyriologie und Vorderasiatische Archäologie

ארץ־ישראל = ארץ־ישראל, מחקרים בידיעת הארץ ועתיקותיה

גא"ע = גנזך האוניברסיטה העברית

חיבור ועריכה, העתקה ומסירה בכתובות אשורבניפל
למלאכת הסופר המלכותי

מאת

מרדכי כוגן

התלים הרבים המתרוממים מעל למישורים הנרחבים בין הפרת ובין החידקל מקנים לנוף המסופוטמי את ייחודו הפיזי. בכל אותם תלים מצויה העדות לייחודו של הנוף התרבותי המסופוטמי, הלוא היא הממצא האפיגרפי העצום שמאפיין את התרבות המסופוטמית כתרבות הכְּתב. סיפור גילויה של תרבות זו באמצע המאה התשע־עשרה ידוע היטב, וערי אשור על תבליטיהן המרשימים ואוספי הלוחות הגדולים הן דווקא שקרעו בפעם הראשונה את החלונות אל העולם הישן־חדש הזה. הנה התברר שהנביא נחום לא הגזים בהשוותו את הסופרים האשוריים למכת ארבה: 'וְטַפְסְרַיִךְ כְּגוֹב גּוֹבָי' (ג:יז) – תעודות רבות כל כך השאירו לנו לבלרים מאומנים אלו בכל מקום שהגיעו אליו. שמותיהם של אחדים מן הסופרים מוכרים מחתימותיהם על לוחות מִנהל ומשפט. סופרים שהיו להם משרות באגף הרישום של הצבא האשורי הונצחו במעין צילום דיוקן. בתבליטי ארמון מופיעים שני סופרים – תמיד בזוגות – רושמים פרטי שלל ומונים את הרוגי הקרבות.[1] חיים תדמור נדרש לתמונה זו כשחקר את תפקידו של הסופר הארמי ואת תהליך הארמאיזציה של אשור, וכמו שאִבחן – סופר אחד מבין השניים, זה האוחז בלוח, היה טַפסר אכדי, והאחר, המחזיק במגילה, היה *ṭupšarru Aramāyu*, 'סופר ארמי'.[2]

דיוני יתרכז בחוג סופרים אחר, הרחוק מהמולת היום־יום של השוק ושל מחנה הצבא. נהוג לכנות חברים בחוג הזה 'סופרים מלכותיים', והכוונה לאחראים לחיבור הכתובות המלכותיות.[3] במקרים אחדים בלבד אפשר להוציא סופר מלכותי כזה מאלמוניתו ולקרוא לו בשמו דוגמת נַבּוּ־שַׁלַּמְשֵׁן,

1 ראה לדוגמה R.D. Barnett & M. Falkner, *The Sculptures of Tiglath-pileser III (745–727 B.C.)*, London 1962, Pls. 5–6

2 H. Tadmor, 'The Aramaization of Assyria: Aspects of Western Impact', in H.-J. Nissen & J. Renger (eds.), *Mesopotamien und seine Nachbaren: Politische und kulturelle Wechselbeziehungen im Alten Vorderasien vom 4. bis 1. Jahrtausend v. Chr., RAI XXV*, Berlin 1982, p. 452

3 עוד סופרים רבים הועסקו במנגנון הממלכתי בניהול השוטף של חיי האימפריה, ולפי תעודת המִנהל ADD 1036 (=SAA XI 36) נראה שסופרים (אישיים?) הוצמדו לבעלי תפקידים בכירים.

מחבר המכתב לאל אשור של סרגון השני.[4] בדרך כלל ידוע מעט מאוד על זהותם ועל אופן עבודתם, אבל דומני שהמונח 'סופר מלכותי' מקפל בתוכו לפחות שתי קבוצות של סופרים, ולכל אחת מהן תחום אחריות משלה בתהליך ייצור הכתובות.[5] בקבוצה הראשונה, והיא החשובה מבחינה יצירתית, היו הסופרים־המחברים. סופרים אלו הונחו בחיבור הכתובות על־ידי שני עקרונות: העיקרון הראשון, החובה להנציח בצורה הנאותה ביותר את מעשי המלך, והעיקרון השני, הצורך לעצב את היצירות לפי המסורת הספרותית. מיזוג שני עקרונות אלו בטמפרמנט האישי של כל סופר־מחבר הביא לידי התהוות הטקסט. אך כמובן, בסופו של היום היה הסופר אנוס להשביע את רצונו של 'המלך הגדול' מזמין הכתובות.[6] בקבוצת הסופרים השנייה היו הסופרים־המעתיקים. תפקידו של סופר בקבוצה זו היה לשכפל את הטקסט שנועד להטמנה בקיר או ביסודות בניין וכן להצגה בארמון או להפצה במרכזי הממלכה.[7] רוב הטקסטים שבידינו מייצגים את פרי עבודתם של המעתיקים האלה. מבין עותקי הטקסטים הרבים שנתגלו אי אפשר להצביע על הולוגרפים, הם כתבי־היד הראשונים שיצאו מתחת ידיהם של הסופרים־המחברים. אמנם קיימים הולוגרפים אחדים דוגמת המכתב לאל אשור, שמעצם סוגתו הועתק רק פעם אחת, והטקסט ששרד הוא הוא כתב־היד המקורי של מחברו.[8] לעומתו כתובות המלכים העומדות במוקד הדיון כאן הן סוגה שונה. כתובות מלכים אלו שוכפלו פעמים רבות – וההולוגרפים שלהן מי ישורם?

לא כסופרים השומריים והאכדיים מסוף האלף השלישי לפסה"נ הסופרים האשוריים. תורת לימודיהם של הראשונים בבתי הספר ל'סופרות' (*ṭupšarrūtu*) מוכרת לנו מחיבורים הסוקרים את הימים שבהם חבשו את ספסל הלימודים,[9] אך מסלול הכשרתם של האחרונים אינו ידוע. גם נעלם

4 ראה TCL 3 428

5 אינני דן כאן בחורת באבן שהעביר את הטקסט אל הקיר או אל המצבה. תפקידו של אומן זה ראוי לדיון נפרד.

6 פאלס דן ב'מיומנות הכללית' של הסופר ודירג את הקשרים בין הצדדים האידאולוגיים והטכניים; ראה F.M. Fales, 'Assyrian Royal Inscriptions: Newer Horizons', *SAAB*, 13 (1999–2001), pp. 133–136

7 עדות להפצת כתובות לכל מיני מרכזים נמצאת, למשל, בעותקי מהדורה C של האנאלים של אשורבניפל שנתגלו בנינוה ובכלח. הסעיפים הלא־היסטוריים באנאלים, שדנו בבנייה, הותאמו לכל עיר. וראה גם את דבריה של ברברה פורטר לעניין פיזור כתובותיו של אסרחדון בערי הממלכה שלא נעשתה בהן התאמה: B.N. Porter, *Images, Power, and Politics: Figurative Aspects of Esarhaddon's Babylonian Policy*, Philadelphia 1993, pp. 109–112

8 שאלות כבדות משקל הועלו בנוגע לסיווג החיבור הזה ושל דומיו כ'מכתבים לאל', והעניין צריך עיון. לעת עתה ראה L.D. Levine, 'Observations on "Sargon's Letter to the Gods"', *Eretz-Israel*, 27 (2003), pp. 111*–119*

9 S.N. Kramer, 'Schooldays: A Sumerian Composition Relating to the Education of a Scribe', *JAOS*, 69 (1949), pp. 199–215; A.W. Sjöberg, 'The Old Babylonian Eduba', in S.J. Lieberman (ed.), *Sumerological Studies in Honor of Thorkild Jacobsen on His Seventieth Birthday June 7, 1974*, Chicago 1976, pp. 159–179

מעינינו אילו כישרונות נדרשו מפֵּרח סופרים אשורי כדי שיתקבל לחוג המחברים או לחוג המעתיקים. קשרי משפחה בוודאי לא הזיקו לסופר מתחיל כשביקש לו משרה טובה.[10] בכל זאת אפשר ללמוד על מקצת תורת החיבור ודרכי ההעתקה שנלמדו בבית הספר הממלכתי לסופרים מתוך ניתוח והשוואה של עותקי הכתובות, שהרי הם מייצגים את יישומו בפועל של המקצוע הנרכש.

מקבץ הכתובות שבחרתי לבדוק הוא האנאלים של המלך אשורבניפל[11] שנערכו בכמה מהדורות שמונה פעמים לפחות במהלך כשלושים שנה.[12] מתוכָן אייחד את הדיון למהדורות B, F ו־A שהעותקים שלהן רבים למדיי ולעתים אף כמה עשרות.[13] שפע זה של כתבי־יד מאפשר בדיקה יסודית של טיב עבודת המעתיקים וחשיפת השיטות שבהן ערכו המחברים את יצירותיהם. בדיקה מן הסוג הנעשה כאן נעזרת הרבה במחקרו החשוב של ריקלה בורגר שאסף, שחזר וההדיר את רוב כתובות אשורבניפל.[14] בעשרים השנים האחרונות נחקרו גם סוגיות היסטוריות רבות מימי אשורבניפל (דוגמת פרשת גוג מלך לוד,[15] פרשת הערבים,[16] פרשת עילם[17] ופרשת

10 פרפולה הצביע על המשפחות המכובדות שבניהן 'המלומדים' איישו משרות בחוג הפנימי של אסרחדון והיו מיועציו הקרובים; וראה S. Parpola, *Letters from Assyrian Scholars to the Kings Esarhaddon and Ashurbanipal*, II, Neukirchen-Vluyn 1983, pp. xvii–xix

11 אינני נכנס כאן לדיון במינוח העדיף לסוגה זו. וראה את דבריו הנכוחים של מריו פאלס ([לעיל, הערה 6], עמ' 130–131) ואת הצעתו שם לאמץ את המונח הלטיני *res gestae*.

12 לא מכבר הציע ריקלה בורגר תיקון בחלוקת הטקסטים המוכרים לנו ובייחוד ביטול המהדורה המכונה K והגדרת מהדורה 'חדשה' G; ראה בורגר (להלן, הערה 14), עמ' 125–126, 130–132.

13 השתמרותן של מהדורות אחרות טובה פחות, אך דוגמאות מהן יובאו בעת הצורך כדי להשלים השוואות אחדות. לדעתו של ריד, ריבוי העותקים הוא אשליה, ומקום גילוים של הטקסטים הרבים היה בור אשפה. לשם נזרקו עותקי המהדורה הקודמת עם הוצאתה לאור של מהדורה חדשה וכן עותקים שנתגלו בהם שגיאות כתיב. על דעה ייחודית זו של ריד, שלא נמצאו לה תומכים, ראה J. Reade, 'Archaeology and the Kuyunjik Archives', in K.R. Veenhof (ed.), *Cuneiform Archives and Libraries*, Leiden 1983, p. 216

14 R. Borger, *Beiträge zum Inschriftenwerk Assurbanipals: Die Prismenklassen A, B, C=K, D, E, F, G, H, J und T sowie andere Inschriften*, Wiesbaden 1996. בכמה מקומות אני חולק על קריאתו של בורגר, והקריאה הנכונה הוכרעה על־ידי בדיקת הלוח (collation) הנדון.

15 M. Cogan & H. Tadmor, 'Gyges and Ashurbanipal: A Study in Literary Transmission', *Orientalia*, 46 (1976), pp. 65–85

16 I. Eph'al, *The Ancient Arabs*, Jerusalem 1982; השווה גם אל P. Gerardi, 'The Arab Campaigns of Assurbanipal: Scribal Reconstruction of the Past', *SAAB*, 6 (1992), pp. 67–103

17 P. Gerardi, 'Assurbanipal's Elamite Campaigns: A Literary and Political Study', Ph.D. Dissertation, University of Pennsylvania 1987

מצרים[18]), והדגש בכל העבודות האלה הושם בהבדלי התיאורים ובסידור אפיזודות במהדורות השונות כדי לעמוד על מהלך האירועים. יסוד מוסד בבדיקות אלו הוא ההיבט הספרותי ('הקוד הספרותי' כלשונו הקולעת של מריו פאלס[19]), ואף שבעיקרון זה הכירו כל החוקרים, נעשו הבדיקות בדרך שונה ובעומק שונה בכל עבודה. בכל זאת היבט אחד במכלול השאלות הקשורות לכתובות המלך עדיין לא נחקר, והוא היבט ההעתקה והמסירה לאחר שלב החיבור. את השאלה הזאת בחרתי להעמיד במרכז הדיון: באיזו נאמנות ניגשו המעתיקים לעבודתם? האומנם הועתקו הכתובות ככתבן וכלשונן?

אפתח בעיון הבסיסי ביותר: האִיות (האורתוגרפיה). יש להדגיש שכל הנתונים מתבססים על בדיקות שנעשו בעותקים של מהדורה אחת ולא בהשוואת עותקים של מהדורות אחדות. באופן כללי ייאמר שעותקי הטקסטים כופלים זה את זה כעולה מבחינתם ברמה המילולית, אבל ברמת האיות יש שוני רב בין העותקים ואין עותק אחד דומה למשנהו. סיבת הדבר טמונה באופי ההברתי של כתב היתדות. הדברים ידועים, ואין צורך להיכנס כאן לפרטים. בכל אופן כבר בשלב זה יש מקום להציב שאלות מספר הנוגעות לדרך ההעתקה שעליה מעידים החילופים האלה. איך קרה שמעתיק אחד פירק סימן הברתי מורכב cvc ל־cv ו־vc או להפך, צירף שני סימנים פשוטים לסימן מורכב אחד? מדוע מילה אחת פעם כתובה לפי הברות ופעם בסימן הלוגוגרם שלה? העניין תמוה אם אמנם נכונה ההנחה שהסופר רצה לשכפל את הטקסט במדויק. תמיהה זו מצטרפת לאי־תקינות אחרת שבעבודת המעתיקים, ומיד אבדוק אותה.

מעֵבר להבדלים באיות מילות הטקסט נמצא שיש הבדלים בתמליל הטקסט בעותקים של אותה מהדורה, כלומר בשכפולה. בטבלה 1 שלהלן מוצג מבחר דוגמאות לשינויים במילות הטקסט המופיעים בתוך מהדורה אחת. חילקתי את כתבי־היד לפי רוב ומיעוט, ואין בחלוקה זו קביעה מה הוא הנוסח המקורי שיצא מתחת ידי המחבר.[20]

18 H.-U. Onasch, *Die assyrischen Eroberungen Ägyptens*, Wiesbaden 1994; וראה גם את מחקרו של פאלס (להלן, הערה 19).

19 F.M. Fales, 'A Literary Code in Assyrian Royal Inscriptions: The Case of Ashurbanipal's Egyptian Campaigns', in idem (ed.), *Assyrian Royal Inscriptions: New Horizons in Literary, Ideological and Historical Analysis*, Rome 1981, pp. 169–202

20 הטקסטים מצוטטים לפי מהדורת בורגר (לעיל, הערה 14) שעל פי רוב תואמת את מספור השורות בפרסומים הראשונים של הטקסטים. יודגש שאין כוונתי לכוללניות בדוגמאות המוצגות בשתי הטבלאות שלהלן, ועליהן אפשר להוסיף רבות.

טבלה 1. שינויי טקסט בתוך מהדורה אחת

רוב כתבי־היד	מיעוט כתבי־היד
שינוי מקום הרכיבים במשפט	
שלל ארץ עילם	
*šunu **nišēšunu alpēšunu** ṣēnišunu* אותם, אנשיהם, בקרם, צאנם (F iii 43)	*šunu **alpēšunu nišēšunu** ṣēnišunu* אותם, בקרם, אנשיהם, צאנם (A 8053)
שינוי בזמן הפועל	
דבר מנחתו של בעל מלך צור	
ušēbila העביר אליי (F i 66)	***ūbila*** הביא אליי (F2, F31, BM 134433)
גורלו של אַחְשֶׁרִ מלך מני	
*ina sūq ālišu šalamtašu **iddû*** ברחוב עירו השליכו את פגרו (A iii 9)	*ina sūq ālišu šalamtašu **ittaddû*** ברחוב עירו השליכו את פגרו (A5)
החלפת הפועל בפועל אחר	
התאבדות נַבּוּ־בֵּל־שֻׁמָּתִ ונערו	
***uptatteḫū** aḫāmeš* דקרו זה את זה (A vii 37)	***urassibū** aḫāmeš* הרגו זה את זה (A5)
*puluḫti šarrūtija **isḫupšunūti*** הוד מלכותי הממם (F iii 42)	*puluḫti šarrūtija **iktumšunuti*** הוד מלכותי כיסה אותם (BM 127963)
תוספת מילה או החלפתה	
iṣbatū šēpēja אחזו ברגליי (B iv 96)	*iṣbatu šepe **šarrutija*** אחזו ברגליי המלכותיות (B16)
LÚ *nakria* אויבַי (B vii 8)	***bēl** nakria* איש (מילולית: אדון) אויבַי (B/D 20, B/D 31, A 7992)
arki PN אחרי PN (A viii 93)	***ṣér*** PN לקראת PN (A2)

המשך בעמוד 16

טבלה 1 (המשך)

רוב כתבי־היד	מיעוט כתבי־היד
קיצור או דילוג	
מתוך שלל העיר שושן *narkabāte ša šadādi ṣumbi* *ša iḫzušunu ṣāriru zaḫalû* *sisê parê rabûti ša tallultašunu* *ḫurāṣu kaspu ašlula ana māt Aššur* מרכבות קרב, מרכבה מלכותית, עגלות ששיבוצן זהב אדמדם (ו)כסף, סוסים, פרדים רבים שקישוטיהם זהב (ו)כסף – הוצאתי כשלל אל ארץ אשור (F v 15–18)	(הקטע חסר בשישה כתבי־יד של F)
יַוּת׳ע מלך הערבים הובא כשבוי *ultu mātišu alqāšu ana māt Aššur* מתוך ארצו לקחתי אותו אל ארץ אשור (A x 23)	(הפִסקה חסרה בארבעה כתבי־יד של A)
אשורבניפל נקרא למלוך על אשור *šī u ilāni abbêša tabbû šumi* היא [האלה נַנַּ] והאלים אבותיה קראו בשמי (F vi 1)	(הפִסקה חסרה בשישה כתבי־יד של F)

נוסף על הדוגמאות בטבלה 1 במקרה אחד קיצור הטקסט מכניסנו היישר לחדר עבודתו של הסופר־המעתיק. נמסר במהדורת F שבמסע נגד אֻמַנַלְדַּס העילמי נלכדו ארבעה־עשר מבצרים ועוד ערים בדרך לשושן הבירה. שתי ערים מתוכן הוזכרו בשמן ברוב כתבי־היד של F: בַּנֻנֻ ובַּשִׁמֻ, וב־F iv 55–64 תואר כיבושה של כל עיר בנפרד בעשר שורות. בשני כתבי־יד סיפור זה נתקצר לארבע שורות, ושתי הערים מופיעות יחד כיחידה אחת (F 42 [Ec. Bib. B]; F 47 [Ec. Bib. C]). ראוי לציין שהסופר־המעתיק של כ״י Ec. Bib. B, לאחר שנקט דרך קיצור, שכח לרגע את התיאור המתומצת שעתה זה רשם וחזר לכתוב בשנית את הקטע על כיבוש בַּשִׁמֻ, שש שורות מיותרות לגמרי![21]

21 ייתכן שיש כאן עדות ששני כתבי־יד שונים זה מזה נמצאו ׳על שולחנו׳ של המעתיק. דומה שהגרסה המורחבת היא ראשונית וסיבות של טעם או שטח פנוי לכתיבה השפיעו על בחירת הגרסה המקוצרת; וראה: M. Cogan, 'Ashurbanipal Prism F: Notes on Scribal Techniques and Editorial Procedures', *JCS*, 29 (1977), pp. 99–102. לדעה אחרת ראה בורגר (לעיל, הערה 14), עמ׳ 51–52.

יש להטעים שכל ההבדלים שציינתי הם בין עותקים שונים זה מזה של אותה הכתובת באותה המהדורה, ואין מדובר בהבדלים בין גרסאות ערוכות של מהדורות שונות זו מזו. מי אחראי לחילופים או להשמטות אלו – המעתיק או המחבר? נוכל לחדד את השאלה אם נשווה תופעות אלו לדומותיהן בקטעי טקסטים שהועברו ממהדורה למהדורה. כזכור, בפרקי זמן לא־קצובים יצאה לאור מהדורה חדשה של האנאלים ובה עדכון הפעולות הצבאיות. עדכון היסטורי זה נכרך במסגרת ספרותית הפותחת בקילוסי המלך ומסיימת בתיאור בנייה ממלכתית או ציבורית חדשה. בדרך כלל חזרו הסופרים־המחברים על קטעים שלמים ממהדורות קודמות אך לא לפני שערכו אותם. בטבלה 2 אביא דוגמאות אחדות לשינויי עריכה בין המהדורות.

טבלה 2. שינויי טקסט בין מהדורות

מהדורה קודמת	מהדורה מאוחרת
החלפת שם במקבילו	
תיאור אויבי המלך	
ittakil ana ***ṭēm*** *ramanišu* סמך על הבנתו (A i 57; C ii 22)	*ittakil ana* ***emūq*** *ramanišu* סמך על כוחו (B i 56)
מלכי מצרים תכננו מעשי איבה	
ana ***marê*** *māt Aššur* נגד בני ארץ אשור (B ii 5)	*ana* ***ummanāt*** *māt Aššur* נגד חיילי ארץ אשור (A ii 6)
וַתַ׳ע הערבי	
uṣallâ ***šarrūti*** התחנן אל מלכותי (B vii 96)	*uṣallâ* ***bēluti*** התחנן אל אדנותי (C ix 93)
החלפת פועל במקבילו	
לאור כיבוש מצרים נאמר על מלכי מצרים	
ina maškanišun ***ulzissunūti*** הצבתי אותם במשרותיהם (B i 91)	*ina maškanišun* ***apqidšunūti*** מיניתי אותם במשרותיהם (A i 113)
לאות כניעה בעל מלך צור את בנו	
iššâ *ana epeš ardūtija* הביא אליי להשתעבד לי (B ii 56)	***ušēbila*** [*ūbila*] *ana epeš ardūtija* העביר אליי להשתעבד לי (F i 66 [F2, F 31, BM 134433]; A ii 59)

המשך בעמוד 18

טבלה 2 (המשך)

מהדורה קודמת	מהדורה מאוחרת
החלפת פועל במקבילו (המשך)	
תיאור ההרס שנזרע בארץ מני	
mālak 10 ūmê 5 ūmê ***ušaḫrirma*** מהלך עשרה ימים, חמישה ימים השמתי (את המחוז ההוא) (B iii 51)	*mālak 10 ūmê 5 ūmê* ***ušaḫribma*** מהלך עשרה ימים, חמישה ימים החרבתי (את המחוז ההוא) (C iv 63; F ii 37; A iii 2–3)
את אוהלי הערבים	
išātu ušaḫizū ***ipqidu*** *ana girra* הציתו באש, העלו באש (B viii 11; C x 16)	*išātu ušaḫizū* ***iqmû*** *ana girri* הציתו באש, שרפו באש (A x 16)
החלפת שם ארץ	
העדפת הצורה הספרותית על הצורה השגרתית למצרים וכוש	
ana ***māt Makan u māt Meluḫḫa*** למַגן ומֶלוּחָה (F i 36)	*ana* ***māt Muṣur u māt Kūsi*** למצרים וכוש (B ii 18; A ii 28)
ענייני סגנון	
הרחבה	
הפסקת תשלומי מנחה של וַתֶ׳ע הערבי	
iklâ tāmarti מנע (את) מתנות(יו ממני) (B viii 3; C x 6)	*iklâ tāmarti* ***mandattašu kabittu*** מנע (את) מתנות(יו ממני), מנחתו הכבדה (A vii 90)
הרחבה סיפורית	
כניעת מלכי החוף הפיניקי	
Yakinlu šar māt Aruada- *Mugallu šar māt Tabala* *Sandišarme šar māt Hilakka ...* *iknušū ana šēpēja* יַכִּנְלֻ מלך אַרְוַד, מֻגַּלֻ מלך תַּבַּל, סַנְדִסַרְמֶ מלך חֵילֶךְ ... נכנעו לרגליי (B ii 71ff.; C iii 102ff.; F i 70ff.)	היחידה נתפצלה, ולכל מלך סיפור כניעה נפרד (A ii 63–76)

המשך בעמוד 19

טבלה 2 (המשך)

מהדורה קודמת	מהדורה מאוחרת
תקבולת	
קבלת התפילה שהתפלל אשורבניפל לפני הקרב עם תַּמָּרִתֻ העילמי על־ידי האֵלים מתוארת בתקבולת ספרותית או במשפט פשוט	
tanēḫija imḫurū ***ismû zikir šaptīja*** הם [האלים] קיבלו את אנחתי; הם שמעו את דבר שפתיי (B vii 53)	***ismû unnīnija*** הם שמעו את תחינתי (F iii 18)
	unnīnija *ilqû* ***išmû zikir šaptīja*** הם קיבלו את תחינתי; הם שמעו את דבר שפתיי (C viii 43; A iv 10)
תוספת מידע או החלפתו	
בשמעו על פרוץ המרד במצרים	
ēgugma iṣṣaruḫ kabatti *adkêma emūqija ṣirāti* כעסתי ונתרתחו קרביי גייסתי את כוחותיי הנעלים (B i 65; C ii 34)	*ēgugma iṣṣaruḫ kabatti* ***assî qātēja uṣalli Aššur u Ištar Aššuritu*** *adkêma emūqija ṣirāti* כעסתי ונתרתחו קרביי נשאתי את ידיי והתפללתי אל אשור ואשתר האשורית גייסתי את כוחותיי הנעלים (A i 65)
תַּנְת־אַמֹן מופיע כ־	
בן אחותו (*mār aḫātišu*) של תרהקה (B ii 11; C iii 29)	בן שַׁבַּכּ (A ii 22)

נוסף על הדוגמאות בטבלה 2 ראוי לציין כמה דוגמאות למידע שבמהדורה מאוחרת נתוסף על המידע שניתן במהדורות קודמות ושאפשר לכנותו 'השלמת פרטים חסרים'.

(א) במהדורה C מופיעה במלואה רשימת המלכים הווסאלים שהצטרפו למסע למצרים. היא חסרה בכל המהדורות שלפניה ולא הועתקה למהדורה A שלאחריה.

(ב) במהדורה A מופיעה רשימה שמית מלאה של עשרים מלכי מצרים שמרדו באשור. חמישה מהם מופיעים במהדורה C, ובמהדורה B הרשימה חסרה לגמרי.

(ג) במהלך הקרבות בעילם נלכדה עיר המבצר בית־אִמְבִּ ואנשיה נענשו קשה (F iv 46–61). במהדורה A נוספה ההערה ההיסטורית שבית־אִמְבִּ הראשונה נהרסה בידי סנחריב, סבו של אשורבניפל, ושסנחריב בנה בית־אִמְבִּ אחרת במקומה. זו העיר שכבש אשורבניפל (A iv 126–132).

כעת נוכל לנסח את השאלה המרכזית שלנו ביתר חדות: האם העתיקו הסופרים את המקור (Vorlage) שלהם בנאמנות? זאת אומרת, האם הם ראו במקור טקסט חתום שאין לשנותו וחובה שכל מילה בו תופיע בעותק החדש?

לדעתי, הממצא שנסקר מביא לידי המסקנות שלהלן, ואציג אותן מן הקלה אל הכבדה.

א. מתקבל הרושם שהסופרים־המעתיקים ביקשו להעתיק את הטקסט שקיבלו כמות שהוא, ולא התכוונו לשנותו או לתקנו אף שבאיות ניכרים הבדלים בכל העותקים ובכל המהדורות. הבדלי איות אלו יכלו להיווצר בכמה מצבים. המצב הראשון: המעתיקים ישבו באולם ורשמו לפי הכתבה את דברי הקריין (האם הסופר־המחבר הוא שהכתיב?). השוני בין הטקסטים משקף את הביצוע האישי של כל סופר־מעתיק, שרשם את ההקראה לפי הכרתו והשכלתו. ייתכן גם מצב אחר: המעתיקים ישבו להם כל אחד בפינת העבודה שלו, ולפניהם מונח המקור שהיו אמורים להעתיק. כל סופר קרא לעצמו שורה או שתיים, ואז פנה ללוח החלק לכתוב מן הזיכרון את השורות[22] בלי שחש חובה להעתקה מדויקת של כל הברה והברה לפי סימניה. בשני המצבים שדמיינתי הטקסט לא נתפס כחתום, והמעתיקים לא חויבו לאיית את מילות הטקסט בצורה אחידה.[23]

בתמליל היה המצב שונה. המעתיקים לא תמיד הקפידו הקפדה יתרה בהעתקת המקור. השינויים שהרשו לעצמם לעשות בתמליל דומים לשינויים שהכניסו סופרים־מחברים כאשר ערכו מהדורה חדשה, אבל אין להמעיט בשוני בין השניים. מצד המעתיק לא הייתה כל כוונה לגעת בתמליל, וכל שינוי נעשה בהיסח הדעת ובלא תשומת לב. בקיאותו בנוסחאות השכיחות בכתובות, שרכש מתוך ניסיון רב בהעתקה, אפשרה לו להחליף שֵׁם או פועל במקביליהם. הדבר נעשה מתוך שגרת הכתיבה. הוא הדין לשינוי מהותי יותר כגון קיצור רשימת ערים או רשימת שלל. אם הוזכרה כל עיר בנפרד או כולן ביחידה ספרותית אחת, כנראה לא היה מי שיִפקח על התוצאה

22 על סמך העדות שבכתיבה מכווצת כגון *šat-ra-na* בשביל *šat-ra a-na* ו־*la-ma-ri* בשביל *la a-ma-ri* תיאר גרייסון מצב שבו הסופר 'כתב מה ששיננו שפתותיו במקום מה שראו עיניו' וכינה את התהליך 'הכתבה עצמית' (auto-dictation); וראה A.K. Grayson, 'Old and Middle Assyrian Royal Inscriptions-Marginalia', in M. Cogan & I. Ephʿal (eds.), *Ah, Assyria...: Studies in Assyrian History and Ancient Near Eastern Historiography Presented to Hayim Tadmor*, Jerusalem 1991, pp. 265–266

23 במקומות אחדים אפשר להבחין בכתב ידם המיוחד של סופרים אחדים, בין סופר שכתב בכתב אנכי ובאות זעירה ובין סופר שכתב במלוכסן ואף באותיות גדולות יחסית.

הסופית וידרוש ממנו תיקון והתאמה למקור.[24] ממילא טעמה של הכתובת לא נסתר על־ידי השינויים שהכניס המעתיק.[25]

ב. הסופרים־המחברים, שלא כמעתיקים, לא היססו לערוך את הטקסטים שעמדו לרשותם. בחברו כתובת חדשה נשען המחבר על כל המהדורות הקודמות ולא רק על המהדורה האחרונה. אפילו כתובות בנות עשרות שנים, מימי ראשית שלטונו של המלך, יכלו לשרתו. וכשהעתיק קטע ממהדורה קודמת לא היה כפוף לניסוחה. כיוון שהתחנך המחבר על ברכי 'הקוד הספרותי' – אותו מאגר ביטויים ומליצות מקובלים שהיו לקלישאות אצל הסופרים – הוא ידע להרכיב את הכתובת המבוקשת לפי טעמו. אמנם במקרים רבים העביר סעיפים שלמים בלי לשנותם, אבל באחרים החליף מילים במקבילותיהן. נדמה שיש כאן ביטוי לרצונו של המחבר לשוות לכתובת גוון אישי על־ידי שימוש בניסוחים שהיו חביבים עליו.[26]

במהדורות אחדות בולט השימוש ביומני מסע, ברשימות מִנהל ובחומר משרדי אחר המשווים לכתובת פן אותנטי. מחברה של מהדורה A, למשל, גדש את כתובתו בפרטים שנדלו מסוגות אלה, ונגלית כאן אפוא התעניינותו בנושאי ראליה. ובכל זאת בדיקה רחבה של מהדורה A, הכוללת השוואה למהדורה B הקודמת לה, מגלה שמחבר מהדורה A החסיר דיווחים ראליים אחדים שנרשמו במהדורה B, כגון רשימת ערים כבושות בארצות מני ומדי.[27] חידה היא מדוע העדיף עליה רשימה מפורטת של אתרים במדבר הסורי

24 בקולופונים לכתובות המלכותיות נרשם תאריך ההעתקה (כלומר סיום הכתיבה) בלבד, שלא כלוחות מסוגות אחרות שעליהם צוין 'נכתב, נבדק והוהדר'. לעניין זה עיין בדבריו הנכוחים של ליברמן במאמרו S.J. Lieberman, 'Canonical and Official Cuneiform Texts: Towards an Understanding of Assurbanipal's Personal Tablet Collection', in T. Abusch, J. Huehnergard & P. Steinkeller (eds.), *Lingering over Words*, Atlanta 1990, p. 332

25 עלו הצעות לייחס שינויים מן הסוג הנדון כאן ל'סופרים פרובינציאליים' (באואר) או לסופרים שעבדו במקומות מחוץ לנינוה, כגון העיר אשור (ויידנר); ראה T. Bauer, *Das Inschriftenwerk Assurbanipals*, Leipzig 1933, p. 8; E. Weidner, 'Assurbanipal in Assur', *AfO*, 13 (1939), pp. 207, 210. והשווה אל דעתה של פנינה לינג־ישראל בקשר לתופעות דומות בכתובות אחדות של סנחריב. את ההבדלים היא זוקפת לחיוורח של הסופרים במרכז שונה מן המרכז שלמדו בו סופרי המלך בנינוה; וראה P. Ling-Israel, 'The Sennacherib Prism in The Israel Museum – Jerusalem', in J. Klein & A. Skaist (eds.), *Bar-Ilan Studies in Assyriology dedicated to Pinhas Artzi*, Ramat Gan 1990, pp. 217, 220. כל אלה הן ספקולציות שאין להן בסיס.

26 לבדיקות ספרותיות בכתובות סרגון השני ראה J. Renger, 'Neuassyrische Königsinschriften als Genre der Keilschriftliteratur: Zum Stil und zur Kompositionstechnik der Inschriften Sargons II. von Assyrien', in K. Hecker & W. Sommerfeld (eds.), *Keilschriftliche Literaturen*, Berlin 1986, pp. 109–128; לעניין כתובות סנחריב ראה E. Frahm, *Einleitung in die Sanherib-Inschriften*, Wien 1997, pp. 245–266

27 השווה את B iii 1–36 אל A iii 126–129.

שנכבשו במסעות נגד השבטים הערביים.[28] האם הביא בחשבון את המגבלות של כלל אורך הכתובת? למהדורה A כ־1200 שורות המשתרעות על עשרה טורים ומובן שהיה צריך להחליט אם לקבל כל דיווח או לדחותו.[29] כנראה, שיקולים אחרים מעבר למשיכה לאותנטי הנחו אותו בעריכת כתובתו. מי יודע אם לא היה כאן גיוון לשם גיוון, עוד עדות לרצונו של הסופר־המחבר להשאיר סימן אישי בטקסט בשעה שכללי החיבור היו מקובעים כל כך.

הרחבות התיאורים במהדורות מסוימות בדרך כלל נועדו להוסיף לשבחו של המלך – לגבורתו, לאדיבותו ואף לאדיקותו דוגמת הפנייה בתפילה לאל לפני היציאה לקרב וקבלת תשובה באמצעות חלום או נבואה. מבחינת הסופר־המחבר תוספות כאלה אפשרו לו להפגין את בקיאותו בסוגות ספרותיות מגוונות מלבד הכתיבה האנאליסטית השגרתית, והעניין טעון בדיקה יסודית.

לקראת סיום ראוי לעיין בהצעתו של בעל היובל שלנו בסוגיית זיהוים של הסופרים־המחברים. חיים תדמור מזהה את מחבר הכתובות המלכותיות במונח *ummanû*, וכך הוא מסביר: 'literally, "master," designates the highest rank of a scholar of the scribal art... the *ummanû* were responsible for drafting the royal inscriptions'.[30] אכן, *ummanû* מציין מומחה, אך מונח זה שימש בשביל מומחים מלומדים, בעלי מקצוע בכל תחום שבו נדרשו שנים רבות של לימוד וניסיון עד שישיגו דרגת רב־אמן. *ummanû* נמצאו בין מגידי העתידות למיניהם – האצטגנינים והמנחשים – וכן בקרב צורפי הכסף והזהב,[31] וכולם הוכתרו בתואר 'רב־סופר'. ה־*ummanû* הרשומים בגרסה אחת של 'רשימת המלכים הסינכרוניסטית' היו, כנראה, היועצים הבכירים ביותר בממלכה.[32] במקצועות אחדים נעשתה העבודה

28 ראה A viii 96–113, 120–121; ix 9–32. המידע 'החדש' של מהדורה A לא הובא במהדורות האנאלים הקודמים אלא ב'מכתב לאל'. כך ברור שלסופר הייתה גישה לחיבורים מגוונים ('מאגרי מידע') וגם לחיבורים שלא שרדו ואינם ידועים לנו.

29 במבט ראשון בפרשיות שנכללו במהדורה F נראה כאילו קיצר המחבר בדיווחים הקודמים כדי לפנות מקום לדיווח החדש על מה שהתרחש בעילם. הוא תמצת גם את ענייני עילם שהופיעו במהדורה B, ומכאן שכוונתו לא הייתה להביא תמונה שלמה על אודות יחסי אשור־עילם. דומה שבחר לעצב תקציר של תולדות אשורבניפל שבמרכזו כיבוש שושן, הכול בשישה טורים. דרכו לא נתקבלה, ועל כך מעידה מהדורה A המורחבת.

30 H. Tadmor, 'Propaganda, Literature, Historiography: Cracking the Code of the Assyrian Royal Inscriptions', in S. Parpola & R.M. Whiting (eds.), *Assyria 1995*, Helsinki 1997, p. 4

31 אחיקר החכם, יועץ המלך סנחריב, מכונה *ummanû* בטקסט מן התקופה הסלווקית; וראה J.C. Greenfield, 'The Wisdom of Ahiqar', in S.M. Paul, M.E. Stone & A. Pinnick (eds.), *ʿAl Kanfei Yonah*, I, Jerusalem 2001, pp. 334–336

32 ראה A.K. Grayson, 'Königslisten und Chroniken', *RLA*, 6, 1980–1983, pp. 116–125; וראה גם את הערתו של פרפולה במאמרו S. Parpola, 'The Forlorn Scholar', in F. Rochberg-Halton (ed.), *Language, Literature, and History: Philological and Historical Studies Presented to Erica Reiner*, New Haven 1987, p. 257, note 1; וכן ליברמן (לעיל, הערה 24), עמ' 312–314.

בצוותים, וכפי שהראה אופנהיים, לראש כל צוות היה 'רב־סופר'.[33] אולי יש מקום לשחזר מִדרג (היירכיה) דומה גם לסופרים שעסקו בחיבור הכתובות. ליד הרב־סופר, בכיר היוצרים ובפיקודו, היו עוד סופרים, מחברים גם הם, שעיסוקם היום־יומי היה חיבור כתובות בסוגות למיניהן. לרשות המחברים האלה היה צוות מעתיקים שדאגו לשכפול החיבורים ולהפצתם.[34]

במהלך עשור אחד, שנות הארבעים של המאה השביעית לפסה"נ, היה בנינוה בולמוס של כתיבה. מהדורות רבות של אנאלים נתחברו, ולכל אחת דיוקן משלה. אין סיבה לחשוב שהצוות בלשכת הסופרים נתחלף בתוך פרק זמן קצר זה. ככל הנראה, כך היו אותם סופרים־מחברים אחראים למהדורות השונות והמגוונות. ברי שנסיבות פוליטיות ומדיניות השפיעו על דמות הכתובות ורכיביהן, ויותר מכול הן מילאו את רצונו של בעל־הבית – המלך, שפיקח על אופן הצגת דמותו. אשורבניפל השתבח שהיה בר־אוריין בחכמת הסופרים,[35] ואולי לא מופרז לדמיין אותו מדריך את הסופרים בכל הנוגע לתוכן הכתובות. והנה בלוח אחד שרשום עליו אוסף כתוביות שנועדו ללוות תיאורי קרב על תבליטי קיר בארמון[36] אנו מוצאים שהוכנו כמה גרסאות לאירוע אחד, והן היו שונות זו מזו באורך התיאור ואף בסיפור שגוללו. כמובן, רק אחת הגרסאות עלתה על הקיר. ואיך נבחרה? הסופר רשם בקצה הלוח: 'עותק של לוח כתיבה [מעץ] שהוקרא לפני המלך'.[37] מתקבל על הדעת שהסופר־המחבר הכין כמה נרטיבים והמלך הצביע על הנוסח שיילווה אליו בהיסטוריה.[38]

33 A.L. Oppenheim, 'Divination and Celestial Observation in the Last Assyrian Empire', *Centaurus*, 14 (1969), pp. 117–118

34 בדיונו בהתפתחות ספרות המקרא הציע שמריהו טלמון ש'המחברים והמעתיקים לא היו קבוצות נפרדות ברורות', אלא המחבר היה 'אישיות אחת' (*unio personalis*) שיכלה למלא את כל המשימות הכרוכות בכתיבה ובמסירה (S. Talmon, 'The Textual Study of the Bible: A New Outlook', in F.M. Cross & S. Talmon [eds.], *Qumran and the History of the Biblical Text*, Cambridge, Mass. 1975, p. 336). הסוגות שדן בהן טלמון ופרקי הזמן הארוכים בין חיבור היצירה ובין עותקיה שונים בהרבה מאלה של הכתובות שאנו עוסקים בהן, ולכן המודל שלו אינו מועיל לנו.

35 M. Streck, *Assurbanipal und die letzten assyrischen Könige bis zum Untergange Nineveh's*, II, Leipzig 1916, pp. 254–257, lines 11–19

36 E.F. Weidner, 'Assyrische Beschreibungen der Kriegs-Reliefs Assurbanaplis', *AfO*, 8 (1932–1933), pp. 176–203; P. Gerardi, 'Epigraphs and Assyrian Palace Reliefs: The Development of the Epigraphic Text', *JCS*, 40 (1988), pp. 1–35; M. Cogan, 'A Plaidoyer on behalf of the Royal Scribes', in *Ah, Assyria*... (above, note 22), pp. 121–128

37 *gabarî lēʾi ša ina pān šarri šašmûni* (ויידנר, שם, עמ' 186); גם בורגר (לעיל, הערה 14), עמ' 306 (יש לתקן שם את ההפניה לעבודתו של הונגר, מס' 545).

38 ואין זה המקרה היחיד שבו נתבקש מלך אשור להכריע בשאלת הנוסח הסופי של כתובת. במכתב שנשלח אל אסרחדון מאת נַבּוּ־רַאִם־נִשֵׁשׁ: 'נכתוב שם את שם המלך על אבן היסוד שהנחנו ביסודות חומת העיר תַּרְבִּצ. יכתוב נא אדוני המלך מה נכתוב [עליו] ולפי זה נכתוב' (SAA XVI 143, obv. 6–11). ברברה פורטר התמודדה עם שאלה זו, והיא נוטה לראות בסופרי אסרחדון יועצים בכירים אשר בכתיבתם עזרו לנסח את המדיניות הממלכתית הרשמית; וראה פורטר (לעיל, הערה 7), עמ' 109, הערה 236.

לימים הייתה היסטוריה זו למושא מחקריו של חיים תדמור, רב־אמן בפיענוח הסודות של כתובות המלכים. זה יובל שנים הוא מלמדנו להקשיב קשב רב לדבר המלך ויועציו. במעמד חגיגי זה לכבוד מורנו אין מתאימה יותר מברכת ה־*ummanû* המופיעה בנוסחים שונים במכתבים שכתבו למלך: 'יִזכה אותך האל הטוב באריכות ימים, בבריאות הגוף ובריאות הנפש' כדי שיוסיף ללמד אותנו 'איך עושים היסטוריה'.

מצודת־סרגון (דוּר־שַׁרֻּכִּין)

דיוקנו של המלך הבונה

מאת

אביגדור ויקטור הורוויץ

בשנת 1977 זכיתי ללמוד אצל פרופסור חיים תדמור את האנאלים של סנחריב, טקסט שכל תלמיד לאכדית מתנסה בו. קראנו את תוארי המלך והלכנו בכל מסעותיו לארצות שהגיע אליהן ואף לירושלים הגענו. והנה בתום המסע השמיני אמר המורה 'עד כאן!' והציע שנעבור לכתובת של אשורבניפל. הפצרתי בו שנמשיך הלאה ושנקרא גם את סוף הכתובת, הלוא הוא תיאור הבנייה (Baubericht). לי נראה כאילו לפרופסור תדמור אין עוד עניין בטקסט כי מוצה כביכול תוכנו ההיסטורי. אך כיוון ששקדתי בימים ההם על עבודת דוקטור שנושאה היה סיפורי הבנייה המסופוטמיים והמקראיים, בשבילי רק התחיל העניין האמִתי.

במאמר זה, שנכתב לכבוד מורנו בהגיעו לגבורות, אנתח תיאור בנייה רב־עניין ומיוחד שפרופסור תדמור עצמו כבר הזכיר והאיר בכמה ממחקריו. אשתדל להראות על־ידי עיון ספרותי מה אפשר ללמוד מן התיאור מעבר לפרטים הטכניים של הבנייה ושיש בו אף לקבוע את המשמעות האידאולוגית שהייתה לבניין החדש בעיצוב דיוקנו של המלך. כלומר, הבניין שבנייתו מתוארת היה סמל אילם הניתן לכמה פירושים, ובא תיאור הבנייה ומסביר למתבונן בבניין איך יפענח אותו ואיך יחשוף בו את דיוקנו של המלך הבונה.

כידוע, תיאור בנייה היה רכיב שגרתי ברבות מן הכתובות המלכותיות ממסופוטמיה למן האלף השלישי לפסה״נ ואילך, ולמען האמת היה זה הרכיב החשוב ביותר.[1] כתובות אלו חוברו כדי לפאר את הבניינים ואת בוניהם, להסביר את סיבות הבנייה ולזַכּות את המלך הבונה בשם עולם, בתהילת הדורות ובברכת האלים. תיאור הבנייה אינו תוספת לכתובת המלכותית או נספח לסיפורי המלחמות והכיבושים. נהפוך הוא! תיאור הבנייה הוא עיקר

1 על הכתובות המלכותיות המסופוטמיות לסוגיהן ראה בין השאר D.O. Edzard, 'Königsinschriften. A. Sumerisch', *RLA*, 6, 1980–1983, pp. 59–65; J. Renger, 'Königsinschriften. B. Akkadisch', *ibid.*, pp. 65–77 (ושם ספרות); ח' תדמור, אשור, בבל ויהודה: מחקרים בתולדות המזרח הקדום, ירושלים תשס״ו, עמ' 1–49. על פי רוב כתובות הבנייה נחשבות לסוג משנה של כתובות ההקדשה.

הכתובת ואף טעם קיומה, ועליו נוספו שאר המעשים כספיח. גם במרוצת השנים, בימי האימפריה האשורית, כשנהייתה כתובת הבנייה למסגרת ספרותית דקה לקורות המלכים היא לא יצאה מחזקתה הראשונה – כתובת שאת שם המלך הבונה היא מנציחה על מעשי ידיו.

תיאורי הבנייה המסופוטמיים נכתבו בדרך כלל בנוסחאות סטראוטיפיות ולפי תבנית ספרותית קבועה. התיאורים ומשמעותם בעיצוב דמותו של המלך נחקרו באופן חלקי בספרי על בניית בתי מקדש במקרא ובמזרח הקדום[2] וביתר פירוט בספרה של סילבי לקנבכר על תיאורי הבנייה של מלכי אשור עד לתגלת־פלאסר השלישי.[3] לצד הסקירות המקיפות הללו יש להזכיר ספר אחר של לקנבכר על בניית ארמונו של סנחריב בנינוה, 'הארמון שאין לו מתחרה',[4] ומאמר קצר של סימו פרפולה על בניית דור־שַׁרֻּכִּין (Dūr-Šarru-ukīn), 'מצודת־סרגון', כיום חורסאבאד.[5] מחקר זה התבסס על חליפת המכתבים המלכותית, אך נדרש גם לעדותן של הכתובות המלכותיות.

בין התיאורים השגרתיים והנוסחאות הנדושות מצאנו תכופות תיאורים החורגים מן הדפוס המקובל והמסורתי כדי להדגיש פן מיוחד בדמות המלך והבניין. אשורנצרפל השני ב'כתובת המשתה' המפורסמת מתאר בפירוט רב את חנוכת ארמונו החדש בעיר כלח ואף רושם את תפריט האוכל לכל סוגיו וגווניו ואת הכמויות האדירות שהוגשו במרוצת עשרה ימים ל־69,574 חוגגים שבאו מכל כנפות תבל.[6] הוא גם מפרט את ארבעים ושניים זני העץ האקזוטיים שהביא מכל הארצות שכבש ואשר נטע בגן סביב ארמונו. במזכרות האלה שהביא ממסעותיו רמז שבירתו היא בבואה של אימפריה

2 ראה V. (A.) Hurowitz, *I Have Built You an Exalted House: Temple Building in the Bible in Light of Mesopotamian and Northwest Semitic Writings*, Sheffield 1992

3 ראה S. Lackenbacher, *Le Roi bâtisseur: Les récits de construction assyriens des origines à Teglatphalasar III*, Paris 1982

4 ראה S. Lackenbacher, *Le palais sans rival: Le récit de construction en Assyrie*, Paris 1990. תיאור הבנייה של נינוה עמד במרכז הרצאתה של מרתה ריוורולי על הנושא 'נינוה: מאידאולוגיה לטופוגרפיה'; ראה M. Rivaroli, 'Nineveh: From Ideology to Topography', *Iraq*, 66 (= D. Collon & A. George [eds.], *Nineveh, RAI XLIX*, I, London 2005), pp. 199–205. ראה גם J.M. Russell, *Sennacherib's Palace Without a Rival at Nineveh*, Chicago 1991. הספר דן בבניית ארמון סנחריב בנינוה ובמשמעותו האידאולוגית באמצעות תבליטי הקיר מן הארמון וכתובות המלוות את התבליטים.

5 ראה S. Parpola, 'The Construction of Dur-Šarrukin in the Assyrian Royal Correspondance', in A. Coubet (ed.), *Khorsabad, le palais de Sargon roi d'Assyrie – Actes du colloque organisé par le service culturel du musée du Louvre les 21 et 22 janvier 1994*, Paris 1995, pp. 47–77

6 ראה D.J. Wiseman, 'A New Stela of Aššur-naṣir-pal II', *Iraq*, 14 (1952), pp. 23–39 (= RIMA 2, pp. 288–293)

רחבה החובקת תבל ומלואה. כתובות סנחריב על בניית ׳הארמון שאין לו מתחרה׳ מדגישות את אוצרות הטבע שנגלו בימיו ושימשו חומרי בנייה ואת הטכנולוגיה הנחותה בימי קודמיו והחידושים הטכנולוגיים, ההנדסיים והאמנותיים שחידש המלך עצמו בחכמתו המופלגת. תיאור הבנייה פותח בפיוט יוצא דופן המהלל את נינוה המרכזת בתוכה את כל טקסי הפולחן והמלאכות המתוחכמות והנסתרות. צורות העיר וטקסיה כתובים מעולם בכתב השמים, ומכאן שהעיר מגלמת את כל הטכנולוגיה החדשה ואת הפולחן המושלם, ואף אפשר ללמוד אותם שם.[7] עם כל המעלות הטובות האלה ה׳ארמון שאין לו מתחרה׳ נהיה לתצוגה ראוותנית של גילוי, המצאה וקדמה, ואפשר להשוותו לארמון הבדולח ב׳תערוכה הגדולה׳ (The Great Exhibition) המפורסמת, שערך הנסיך אלברט בשנת 1851.

והנה גם סרגון השני, שסיפר באנאלים ובשאר כתובות ארמונו על בניין דור־שַרֻּכִּין, בירתו החדשה,[8] השאיר כתובת אחת החורגת מן השגרה באופן מפתיע, והיא ראויה לעיון נפרד.[9] הכתובת נחרתה על עשרות רבות של גלילי

7 לכתובות סנחריב ראה עתה E. Frahm, *Einleitung in die Sanherib-Inschriften*, Wien 1997, esp. pp. 71–86. התיאור הארוך ביותר בא בעותק E. ראה D. Luckenbill, *The Annals of Sennacherib*, Chicago 1924, pp. 103–116. בתחילת תיאור הבנייה כתוב:

Ina ūmēšuma
Ninua māḫazu ṣīru // ālum narâm Ištar
ša napḫar kidudê ilāni u ištarāti bašû qerebšu
temennu darû // duruš ṣâte
ša ultu ullā itti ṣiṭir burummê eṣrassu eṣretma // šūpû ṣindūšu
ašru naklu // šubat pirište
ša mimma šumšu šipir nikilti // gimir pelludê niṣirti Lalgar šutābulu qerebšu

ביום ההוא
נינוה העיר הקדושה הַנִּשָּׂאָה, העיר האהובה של אשתר,
שכל טקסי האלים והאלות בתוכה,
מפלס הבנייה הנצחי, היסוד הקדמוני,
שמקדמת דנא בכתב השמים צוירה צורתה ובלטו תקנותיה,
המקום המחוכם, מושב הסודות,
שכל סוג של מלאכה מתוחכמת, כללות הטקסים, סוד ה־*Lalgar* (מים תחתונים) נלמדים בתוכה.

8 העיר הזאת איננה מוזכרת בפירוש בתנ״ך, אך יש לקשור אותה לעיר רסן המוזכרת בפרשת נמרוד בבראשית י:יב; ראה V. A. Hurowitz, ‘In Search of Resen (Genesis 10:12): Dūr-Šarrukīn’, in Ch. Cohen et al. (eds.), *Birkat Shalom: Studies in the Bible, Ancient Near Eastern Literature and Post-Biblical Judaism Presented to Shalom M. Paul on the Occasion of his Seventieth Birthday*, Winona Lake, Ind. 2008, pp. 513–526

9 ראה A. Fuchs, *Die Inschriften Sargons II. aus Khorsabad*, Göttingen 1994. לתעתיק הטקסט ותרגומו לעברית ראה להלן בנספח א, עמ׳ 42. לארמון החדש ראה P. Albenda, *The Palace of Sargon King of Assyria*, Paris 1986

חומר זעירים.[10] פרסם אותה ד"ג ליונס בשנת 1883,[11] תרגם אותה לאנגלית דניאל לקנביל בשנת 1927,[12] וההדירה מחדש אנדראס פוקס בשנת 1993.[13]

10 עשרה עותקים שנתגלו בחפירות הצרפתים אבדו כשטבעה ספינת המשלוח בחידקל בשנת 1855. כתובות מעין אלה היו אמורות להיטמן ביסודות הבניינים ובקירותיהם, וכצפוי, פוקס ([לעיל, הערה 9], עמ' 9) משייך את כתובות הגליל אל ה־verborgene Inschriften ('הכתובות המוטמנות'). מבין כתובות הגליל שחשפו ויקטור פלאס והמשלחת הצרפתית נגלו שתיים טמונות בקיר בין חדר 18 לחדר 20, וארבע־עשרה אחרות נמצאו טמונות בקירות P ו־P1 (V. Place, *Nineveh et l'Assyrie, avec essais de restauration par Félix Thomas*, I, Paris 1867, pp. 62, 111–112). לפי גרנט פריים (G. Frame, התכתבות אישית), בחפירות מטעם אוניברסיטת שיקגו נמצאו 55 או 49 גלילים בכמה אתרים ובכללם הקירות בבניינים שונים. כל זה צפוי. אולם הכינוי 'כתובות מוטמנות' איננו מתאים במדויק לכל העותקים. לפי דו"ח החפירות של אוניברסיטת שיקגו, לפחות עשרה עותקים נמצאו בארמון F (ראה G. Loud & C.B.A. Altman, *Khorsabad*, Part II: *The Citadel and the Town*, Chicago 1938, pp. 77, 98, 105). שמונה מהם היו על רצפת חדר 17, אחד בחדר 16 באותו הבניין, אחד בחדר 28 ואחד בטרסה מחוץ לארמון F, קרוב לפני האדמה (פריים הודיע לי שבמוזאון עירק שבבגדד יש עוד כאחד־עשר עותקים ובכללם ארבעה מארמון F, חדרים 16, 17, אחד מחוץ לבית K ואחד בקיר של הארמון. אחד מהם מופיע בתצלום *Minerva*, 14 (2003)). זאת אומרת, לא מעט כתובות גליל נמצאו יחד חשופות, ולא השתמשו בהן כצפוי ככתובות בנייה. אם אין כאן טעות החופרים בתיאור הממצא (אפשרות שהעלה פריים), יש לשאול למה שימשו העותקים שלא נטמנו? העותקים נמצאו בבניין שהיה בולט החוצה מן הקיר בפינה הדרום־מערבית של העיר, ויש להניח שהיה שייך לאדם אמיד וחשוב ממשפחת המלך או מאנשי החצר. לפי החופרים, החדרים בבניין היו גדולים, ובהם היה בעל הארמון מבלה את שעותיו הפרטיות ומארח את אורחיו. קשה להניח שבעל הבית וחבריו בילו את זמנם בקריאת כתובותיו של המלך. בארמון F נמצאו רק עשרה חפצים קטנים ובהם (המספרים על־פי לאוד, חורסאבאד, עמ' 97–99) שרידי שנהבים מגולפים (מס' 71, 72); חותם־טביעה מאבן (מס' 107); שתי טביעות חותם (מס' 115, 118); שתי משקולות דמויות ברווז (מס' 180, 185); כלי ברזל (מס' 223); שבר כלי מחרס בצורת חיה (מס' 246); גרזן־אבן (מס' 261). החותם, טביעות החותם והמשקולות עשויים ללמד על פעילות סופרים כלשהי או על פעילות מִנהלית בארמון, אלא שממצאים אלו לא נמצאו בחדרים שבהם נמצאו הכתובות. ועוד זאת: לא נמצאו בחדרים אלו חומר כתוב אחר או חומרי כתיבה, ולכן קשה להניח שהיו בבניין בית ספר, ארכיון, ספרייה או אולפן לסופרים שתפקידם היה להעתיק ולהנפיק כתובות בכמויות גדולות. מפתח לחידה אולי יימצא בעובדה שגליל אחד השמור במוזאון הבריטי בא מנינוה, וגליל אחר הנמצא במוזאון אוניברסיטת פנסילווניה בפילדלפיה בא מצ'נצ'י (Chenchi). אם כן, מתברר שעותקים של הכתובת הופצו ונשלחו למקומות אחרים לצורך כלשהו. הייתכן שבעל הבית של ארמון F היה פקיד שאחראי להפצת הכתובת ושנשמרו עותקים בביתו לאכסון לפני ייצואם? אנדראס פוקס (בהתכתבות אישית) הציע שריבוי הכתובות מעיד על רצונו של סרגון להגדיל את הסיכוי שמלך עתיד ימצא את הכתובת. כנראה, הוא גם רצה שבני דורו ידעו על המעשה, ולכן הכין עותקים למשלוח.

11 ראה D.G. Lyons, *Keilschrifttexte Sargon Königs von Assyrien (722–705 v. Chr.)*, Leipzig 1883, pp. 1–12, 31–39, 58–79

12 ראה D.D. Luckenbill, *Ancient Records of Assyria and Babylonia*, II, Chicago 1927, pp. 60–66

13 ראה פוקס (לעיל, הערה 9), עמ' 29–44, 289–296. בכתובות סרגון ובהן כתובת הגליל דן גם רנגר במחקר שלא פורסם ולא עמד לרשותי (J. Renger, The Inscriptions of

עותקי הכתובת נחלקים לשתי מהדורות – האחת מלאה והאחת מקוצרת (?), שחסר בה קטע של עשר שורות מתיאור הבנייה (שורות 44–53).[14] להלן אדון במהדורה המלאה. הגלילים יועדו להיטמן ביסודות הבניינים ובקירותיהם כדי שאת הכתובת החרותה בהם יקראו האלים והמלכים העתידים לשקם את הבניין, וכיוון שהכתובת נכתבה לפני תום הבנייה, לא הוזכרה בה חנוכת העיר, שלא כהזכרתה בכתובות החקוקות על קירות הארמון ועל הפסילים. עם זה, מוזכר בה אכלוס העיר.[15]

בכתובת כשבעים ושבע שורות ארוכות. היא מתחילה בשם המלך, ואל השם נלווית באיחוי בלתי מקושר רשימה ארוכה של תוארי מלכות. התארים מתרחבים על־ידי משפטים משועבדים המתחילים במילת היחס *ša*, 'אשר', והכוללים פעלים בהטיית סוביונקטיב. התארים הראשונים עניינם בחירת המלך בידי האלים (שורות 1–3) והחסדים שעשה לכמה ערים קדושות (שורות 4–6). שאר התארים קשורים לכוחו הצבאי, והרחבות התארים נהיות למעשיות קצרות על אודות מסעותיו לארצות מארצות שונות (שורות 7–33). כל אלה כדרך 'כתובות הראווה' (Display Inscriptions) או Prunkinschriften), ובלשון פרופסור חיים תדמור – 'כתובות הסיכום' (Summary Inscriptions).

תיאור הבנייה מתחיל קרוב לאמצע הטקסט, בשורה 34. הוא איננו פותח בנוסחה השגרתית *ina umēšuma* 'ביום ההוא'.[16] הפעילות החברתית והצבאית אינה מתוארת כנרטיב רצוף אלא היא מתבהרת מתוך רשימת התארים הנלווים לשם המלך *Šarru-ukīn*,[17] ואף תיאור הבנייה פותח בחזרה על הציון *šarru*, שבו התחילה הכתובת כולה. מבחינת התחביר ולאור מה שכתוב לפני התואר *šarru* יש המשך לשורת התארים, אך מבחינת התוכן

(Sargon II of Assyria, Introduction [Ms. 1978]). רנגר מזכיר את מחקרו במאמרו על הכתובות המלכותיות האכדיות (לעיל, הערה 1), מאמר שהיה לפני פוקס.

14 לפי פריים, גם הגלילים שלא פורסמו שייכים לשתי הקטגוריות הללו.

15 תיאור הבנייה בגליל דומה במיוחד לתיאור שנחקק על רצפת הארמון באולם 14, ואילו תיאורי הבנייה הרשומים באנאלים, על קירות הארמון ובמקומות אחרים קצרים ופשוטים יותר. חלק מתיאור הבנייה הנוגע לרכישת הקרקע מצוטט בשינויים מסוימים בתעודה של סרגון שבה הוא מחדש מענק קרקעות שהעניק המלך אדד־נררי החמישי. ראה L. Kataja & R. Whiting, *Grants, Decrees and Gifts of the Neo-Assyrian Period*, Helsinki 1995, pp. 20–22, No. 19. לדיון בתעודה ובהקבלות בין הכתובות ראה J.N. Postgate, *Neo-Assyrian Royal Grants and Decrees*, Rome 1969, pp. 62–69, No. 32; pp. 117–118

16 תיאורי בנייה המתחילים בנוסחה השגרתית באים בכתובות באולם XIV (פוקס [לעיל, הערה 9], עמ' 78, שורה 27), באנאלים (שם, עמ' 181, סעיף 424), ב'כתובות הראווה' (שם, עמ' 236, סעיף 153) וב'כתובות הרצפה' (שם, עמ' 252, שורה 18; עמ' 257, שורה 23; עמ' 267, שורה 90; עמ' 274, שורה 28).

17 קריאת השם איננה חד־משמעית. הכתיב הלוגוגרפי הנפוץ הוא LUGAL.GI.NA או XX.GI.NA, אבל הכתיבים המפורשים יותר הם LUGAL/XX-*ú-kin* שפירושו 'המלך הכין/כונן' או LUGAL-*ke-e-nu* 'המלך היציב'. ראה פוקס (לעיל, הערה 9), עמ' 414–415.

ולאור מה שכתוב אחריו זו התחלה חדשה. ואולם שלא כתארים הקודמים, ההרחבה כאן כתובה במשפטים עצמאיים שלמים עם פעלים אינדיקטיביים וסיפור רצוף מתפתח. מתקבל שמבחינה דקדוקית, תחבירית וכמותית תיאור הבנייה הוא עיקר הכתובת.

תוכנו הבסיסי של התיאור פשוט למדיי.[18] המלך מחליט להקים עיר חדשה במקום שומם[19] כדי להביא שפע לארצו ולעמו. הוא מצווה לבנות את העיר ורוכש קרקעות, ולשם כך הוא משלם מחיר הוגן או מציע קרקע חלופית למי שמעדיף קרקע. הוא מתפלל לאלים ומקווה לקבל את הסכמתם, והם מצווים עליו לבנות את העיר. במועדים המתאימים והמיועדים לכך הוא לובן לבנים, מניח את היסודות ובונה את העיר. בעיר יש מקדשים וארמונות, והיא מוקפת חומה כפולה ובה שמונה שערים הנפתחים לשמונה הרוחות.[20] המלך מושיב בעיר אנשים מכל מיני ארצות ומעסיק מומחים לעשותם 'פה אחד' וללמדם את יראת האל והמלך. בתמורה למעשיו האלים מברכים אותו.[21] הכתובת נחתמת בקללות לפוגע במעשי המלך. התיאור כתוב לפי

18 ראה הורוויץ (לעיל, הערה 2), עמ' 72–74. פוקס ([לעיל, הערה 9], עמ' 374–378) מציג ניתוח סינופטי של כל כתובות סרגון עם רישום כל הרכיבים העניינים המופיעים בהן.

19 מכל מלכי אשור שפיתחו ערי בירה חדשות רק סרגון בנה עיר חדשה לחלוטין. לדעת ון דה מירופ, סרגון השווה כאן את עצמו לאַדַפַּ כדי להדגיש שמעשהו בבניית עיר חדשה היה מעשה קמאי של ימי בראשית. ראה M. Van De Mieroop, *The Ancient Mesopotamian City*, Oxford 1997, p. 61. פינקל וריד משווים את המעשה החדשני למעשי גילגמש שבנה את חומות ארך בשחר ההיסטוריה וסרגון הגדול שבנה את אבד, וראה I.I. Finkel & J.E. Reade, ‘Assyrian Heiroglyphs’, *ZA*, 86 (1996), pp. 244–268, esp. p. 262

20 אם נוסיף על שמונת השערים ואֵליהם את שתי החומות והאֵלים הקשורים בהן, נמצא עשרה אלים ובהם שבעה אלים ושלוש אלות, וכל זה לפי מספרי השלמות 3, 7, 10. על־ידי הקדשת השערים והחומות לאלים וקריאת הביצורים על שם הברכות שהאלים מעניקים לעיר ולמלך סרגון הוא מוסיף הגנה אלוהית להגנה הפיזית שנתנו השערים והחומות כאילו הוא מקיף את העיר באלים הגדולים עצמם. לפי משפט המבוא לתיאור (שורה 66), שמונת השערים המוקדשים לשמונה אלים גדולים פונים (*miḫret*) ל'שמונה רוחות'. ואולם תיאור החומה עצמו מחולק לארבעה משפטים (שורות 67–70), וכל משפט מזכיר שני שערים ורוח אחד – מזרח, צפון, מערב ודרום. בחפירות נתגלו רק שבעה שערים, כי בצד המערבי של העיר, שבו שוכן ארמון המלך, שער אחד בלבד. האוריינטציה של העיר איננה מתאימה בדיוק לתיאור, כי העיר מוסבת באופן שהחומות אינן עוברות בקו מזרח-מערב וצפון-דרום. שמונת האלים ושתי החומות מחולקים לחמישה זוגות (שמש ואדד, אלי הנחש; אנליל ובת זוגו מֻלִּסֻ; אַנֻ ובתו אשתר, אלי השמים; אֶאַ ובֵּלֶת־אִלִי שפעלו יחד ביצירת האדם במיתוס אתרחסיס; אשור ונִנֻרְתַ, הנחשבים לאלים הראשיים בפנתאון האשורי). המכנה המשותף לכל אל ובן או בת זוגו אינו משתקף בתואר האלוהות המצורף לשם האל המשקף את התפקיד העצמאי של האל או של האלה. שמש ואדד מזֻוָּגים בגלל תפקידם בנַחַש, אך שמש נקרא 'הנותן לי להציג את רינת ניצחוני' כי הוא אל גיבור, ואילו אדד נקרא 'מחזיק בשבילו שפע', כי גשמיו מפרים את האדמה; אֶאַ ובֵּלֶת־אִלִי מזווָגים בגלל שיתוף הפעולה שלהם ביצירת האדם, אך תוארו של אֶאַ משקף את תפקידו כאל של מי התהום דווקא וכן הלאה.

21 בשורה 75 נכתב *ilāni āšibūte šamê erṣetim u āli šâšu qibītī imgurūma // epēš āli u šulbur qerbīšu išrukūnni ana dārīš*, 'האלים יושבי השמים, הארץ ו(יושבי) העיר

הדפוס המסורתי של סיפורי בנייה, וכשהכתובת מתארת את סרגון דבק בדגם התנהגות מסורתי היא מראה בהבלטה שהמלך הגשים את ייעודו כדת וכדין והוא ראוי למלוך.

ואולם עיון חוזר בכתובת מראה שהסיפור איננו שגרתי כלל וכלל ומידת החידוש שבו אינה פחותה ממידת הישן והמסורתי שבו. אכן, הסיפור מלא תכונות מיוחדות ומעשים יוצאי דופן שאין כמותם בתיאורי בנייה אחרים. הדברים האלה דורשים הסבר, ובהם נחשפות פנים חשובות באידאולוגיה המלכותית בכלל ובדיוקן המיוחד שביקש סרגון לשוות לעצמו בפרט.

עם היסודות התוכניים המיוחדים ראוי למנות את היסודות האלה: התיאור הארוך והמיוחד של הסיבה לבניית העיר ומטרותיה, רכישת הקרקעות, פירוט התאריכים ללבינת הלבנים וייסוד העיר, קביעת אורך החומה כשווה לערך המספרי של שם המלך וכן אכלוס העיר. התאריכים מתוארים בפסקאות הלקוחות מאסטרולב B לחודשי סיוון ואב,[22] ומצאנו גם מובאות מאנומה אֶלִשׁ[23] ורמז למבוא ולחוקים 36-41 אשר בקודקס חמורבי. גם רכישת הקרקעות מנוסחת בשפה דומה בשטרות רכישה שהשתמרו מימי סרגון. כל אלה הם סימנים מובהקים לבקיאות המחבר ביצירות מופת ובכללן יצירות בבליות, והם מוסיפים לרטוריקה של החיבור ממד אינטר־טקסטואלי חשוב שעוד ניתן עליו את הדעת. אחרון אחרון, לשון התיאור הן מבחינת האגרון

ההיא קיבלו את דבריי והעניקו לי לעולם את עשיית העיר ואת ההזדקנות בקרבה׳. יש בברכה זו חזרה ותמצית הדברים (מתוך הפיכת הסדר) שביקש המלך בתפילתו לפני בניית העיר בשורות 53-54 ובייחוד בשורה 54: *aḫrataš umē ina ṭub libbi u bu'āri qerbuššu erēbi*, ׳להיכנס בתוכה לאחרית הימים בטוב לב ובריאות׳, ובשורה 55: *epēš āli // ḫerê nāri iqbûni* ׳ציווני לבנות את העיר ולכרות את התעלה׳.

22 בתיאורי הבנייה מקובל שפעולות חשובות בעבודה מתחילות בנוסחה השגרתית *ina arḫi šēmi ūmi mitgari*, ׳בחודש גורלי וביום מתאים׳, ואולם בכתובת שלנו המועדים נקבעים על־ידי מובאה מן האסטרולב. על הפסקה בכתובת ראה R.S. Ellis, *Foundation Deposits in Ancient Mesopotamia*, New Haven–London 1968, p. 175, No. 14; M.E. Cohen, *The Cultic Calendars of the Ancient Near East*, Bethesda, Md. 1993, p. 314. לאסטרולב B (KAV 218), חלק א ראה E. Reiner & D. Pingree, *Babylonian Planetary Omens*, II: *Enūma Anu Enlil, Tablets 50–51*, Malibu 1981, p. 151. לדיון כללי באסטרולבים ראה W. Horowitz, *Mesopotamian Cosmic Geography*, Winona Lake, Ind. 1998, pp. 154–166 (הורוביץ מכין מהדורה חדשה של האסטרולבים עם פירוש מקיף). הכתוב בשורות 34-37 באסטרולב על חודש סיוון (*araḫ nalban šarri šarru nalbana ilabbin mātāti bītātīšina ippušū araḫ Kulla ša mātim*, ׳חודש מלבן המלך. המלך במלבן ילבן; הארצות את בתיהן יבנו; חודש האל כֻּלַּ של הארץ׳) מקביל לכתוב בכתובת הגליל על חודש *Sītaš* (סיוון) בשורה 58 (*ana labān libnāti epēš āli u bīti araḫ Kulla nabû šumšu*, ׳ללבינת לבנים ובניית עיר ובית ״חודש כֻּלַּ״ נקרא שמו׳). שורה 10 באסטרולב הנוגעת לחודש אב (*Girra ištu šamê urradamma*, ׳האל גִּרַּ יֵרֵד מהשמים׳) מקבילה לשורה 61 בכתובת הגליל המכנה את חודש אב *araḫ arād Gibil* (׳חודש ירידת גִּבִּל׳).

23 על תיאור החומה בשורה 66 ותיאור העולם באנומה אֶלִשׁ, לוח ה, שורה 10 ראה להלן (עמ׳ 32). על *sunnunu rāṭīšun* בשורה 39 ובאנומה אֶלִשׁ, לוח ג, שורה 135 ראה להלן בנספח ב: השפה המיוחדת (עמ׳ 50). מתעוררת השאלה, כמובן, אם הכירו הסופרים של סרגון את אנומה אֶלִשׁ במהדורה בבלית או אשורית.

הן מבחינת התחביר מסולסלת ונשגבה, ואף שהיא נעימה לאוזן היא קשה להבנה.

אדון עכשיו בחמישה דברים מיוחדים בתיאור הבנייה, ואשתדל להראות שהם מצטרפים למסר אחיד על דמות העיר והמלך שבנה אותה.

א. תיאור העיר על מקדשיה, ארמונותיה, שעריה וחומותיה כתוב בשפה פשוטה ואף דומה לתיאורי ארמונות וערים של מלכים אחרים ובהם תגלת־פלאסר השלישי[24] וסנחריב.[25] מספר השערים משתנה ממקום למקום וכן השמות הראוותניים הניתנים לשערים בכל עיר, אך השמות הם מאותו הסוג בבטאם ברכה שאֵל מסוים מברך בה את העיר, העם או המלך.[26] פרפולה כבר ציין שהמשפט המתחיל את תיאור החומה זהה בלשונו לאנומה אֶלִש המתאר את בריאת העולם. בכתובת כתוב (שורה 66):

ina rēše u arkāti *ina* ***ṣēlī kilallān*** *miḫret 8 šārī 8* ***abullāti aptēma*** -
(1) **מלפנים ומאחור**, (2) **בשני הצדדים** נגד שמונה הרוחות שמונה
(3) **שערי עיר** (4) **פתחתי**

אין ספק שיש כאן רמיזה על־ידי ציטוט והפיכת סדר הרכיבים לנאמר על מרדוך והיקום בסיפור הבריאה אנומה אֶלִש (לוח ה, שורה 10):

iptēma abullē ṣēlī kilallān // *šigāru udannina* ***šumēla u imna***
(4') **הוא פתח** (3') **שערי עיר** (2') **בשתי הצלעות** // את הבריח חיזק
(1') **שמאלה וימינה.**[27]

בהשוואת בירתו החדשה לעולם כולו סרגון מכריז שהבירה היא בבואה של היקום או מיקרוקוסמוס, ומה שנעשה בתוכה אמור לשקף את הנעשה בעולם כולו.

יתר על כן, בעשותו מעשה בריאה סרגון ממילא מצייר את עצמו כבורא, ובמקום אחר (שורה 38) הוא מתאר את עצמו כ־*apkallu*, החכם הקדמון, ואת לידתו הוא מתאר במונחים הדומים לתיאור הבא באנומה אֶלִש של לידת

24 ראה H. Tadmor, *The Inscriptions of Tiglath-pileser III King of Assyria*, Jerusalem 1994, pp. 174–175, Summary Inscription 7: 35'–36'

25 ראה פרהם (לעיל, הערה 7), עמ' 77–78, שורות 162–199, שמדובר בהן בארבעה־עשר שערים.

26 ראה לקנבכר (לעיל, הערה 3), עמ' 107–109.

27 משפט כמעט זהה מופיע אצל סנחריב (פרהם [לעיל, הערה 7], עמ' 77, שורות 162–165): *Ana erbetti šārī 14 abullāti pānu u arka ina ṣēlī kilallān ana erēbi u aṣê ušaptâ qerebšu*, 'לארבע הרוחות ארבעה־עשר שערים לפנים ומאחור בשתי הצלעות לכניסה וליציאה פתחתי בתוכו'. בהפיכת איברי הטקסט המצוטט במובאה נהג המחבר לפי כלל רטורי הידוע מן התנ"ך שזכה לכינוי 'חוק זיידל'. ראה מ' זיידל, חקרי מקרא, ירושלים 1978. על נוהג זה בכתבים מסופוטמיים הערתי בספרי V.A. Hurowitz, *Divine Service and Its Rewards: Ideology and Poetics in the Hinke Kudurru*, Beer Sheva 1997, p. 101. בהבדל 'מלפנים ומאחור' בכתובתנו לעומת 'ימינה ושמאלה' בסיפור הבריאה יש לראות החלפה של ביטויים נרדפים.

האלים בכלל ולידת מרדוך בפרט.[28] כמו כן עצם התיאור של אתר הבנייה (שורות 37–35) כמקום שמעולם לא הוצמח בו ירק, לא נחרש במחרשה ולא היו בו מעיינות מזכיר לנו את תיאורי העולם בטרם נברא, המאפיינים את הפתיחות לכמה סיפורי בריאה מסופוטמיים.[29] מכל אלה אנו למדים שבניית העיר היא בחזקת בריאה חדשה והמלך הוא הבורא.

ב. צורת העיר היא בבואה של היקום, ולא זו בלבד אלא היא יושבה באוכלוסין שהובאו מארבע כנפות הארץ (שורה 72). האנשים האלה מוזכרים פעמיים, ויש קשר מילולי בין הזכרותיהם, קשר המושך את תשומת הלב לאחת מתכונותיהם התרבותיות.

(1) בתחילת התיאור וקביעת ייעודה של העיר קרא סרגון לאנשים שלמענם נבנתה העיר *atmû rēšēti* (שורה 40). מונח זה, המתהדהד בסוף התיאור בלשון *atmê la mitḫurti* (שורה 72), מופיע רק ברשימה לקסיקלית כנגד הביטוי הנפוץ לאנושות *napḫar ṣalmāt qaqqadim*, 'כל שחורי הראש'.[30] משום־מה לא התייחסו המילונים למשמעות המילולית של *atmû rēšēti*.[31] ואולם ברור שפְּשט המונח קשור בדיבור. והנה בהמשך הכתובת ובטקסטים אחרים *atmû* מופיע עם *lišānu* יחד. כמו כן מצאנו במכתבי סרגון ואסרחדון אל האל אשור את המשפט ***lišān rēšēti*** PN *ana Aššur bēlīya ultēbila*, שיש לפרשו 'הנני שולח את הדובר הטוב ביותר, פלוני, לאשור אדוני'.[32] סביר להניח

28 בשורה 38 מופיע צמד המילים *rabû*//*šiāḫu* (גדל // צמח). צמד זה מופיע פעמיים במיתוס אֶתַנַ ופעם באנומה אֶלִשׁ (לוח א, שורה 11) בנוגע לגדילת האלים הראשונים. כמו כן יש להשוות את *lēʾi inî kalama šinnat apkalli* שבאותה השורה אל תיאור מרדוך הַנֶּהֱרֶה באנומה אֶלִשׁ (לוח א, שורה 88) *leʾû leʾûti apkal ilī Bēl*. לפי פוקס ([לעיל, הערה 9], עמ' 292, הערה 61), *apkallu* המוזכר כאן הוא אַדַפַּ, אך בבואו בהקשר שיש בו רמיזות אחרות ללידת האלים באנומה אֶלִשׁ ייתכן שהוא מרדוך או אשור דווקא. ראה גם CAD, A/2, s.v. *apkallu*, p. 172b; ון דה מירופ (לעיל, הערה 19), עמ' 61.

29 ראה P. Michalowski, 'Negation as Description: The Metaphor of Everyday Life in Early Mesopotamian Literature', *Aula Orientalis*, 9 (1991) [*Festschrift M. Civil*], pp. 131–136

30 שימו לב שבהמשך הכתובת (שורות 41–40) סרגון מזכיר את *akû* (הנכה / העני), *marṣu* (החולה) ואת *amēlūtu* (האנושות). רביעייה זו מסודרת בסדר כיאסטי (א–ב // ב'–א'), ונמצא ש־*atmû rēšēti* מקביל ל־*amēlūtu*, והנהנים מחסדי המלך בבניין העיר החדשה הם הנכים החולים באנושות כולה. הדעות חלוקות בהוראת המילה *akû*: פוקס, בעקבות מילונו של פון זודן (*AHw*, p. 30), מפרש 'נכה'; מילון שיקגו (CAD, A/1, p. 283b) מפרש אותה 'עני' ('destitute'). הפירוש 'נכה' יכול להסתמך על התקבולת עם *marṣu* הנוצרת על־ידי הכיאסמוס שצוין כאן. הפירוש של מילון שיקגו יכול להתבסס על ההקשר המידי כי מתוארת הצלת אנשים מרעב. אף ייתכן שהמחבר מתכוון לשתי ההוראות ולא הבחין בין מילים הומונימיות שלא כמו שהבחין מילון שיקגו.

31 לקנביל ([לעיל, הערה 12], עמ' 63) תרגם 'the choicest things', אך אין לזה משמעות בהקשר הנוכחי, ויש להניח שלקנביל לא הבין את משמעות המונח. פוקס ([לעיל, הערה 9], עמ' 292) הלך בעקבות המילונים ותרגם 'Menschheit' מתוך התעלמות מן המשמעות המילולית של המונח. יש לתמוה ולשאול איך הקורא בעולם העתיק, שלא הזדקק למילון, הבין את המונח בהיתקלו בו בפעם הראשונה בקריאת הטקסט.

32 'herewith I am sending *the best orator*, so-and-so, to Aššur my lord'

ש־*atmû rēšēti* נרדף בהוראתו הבסיסית ל־*lišān rēšēti* וגם פירושו 'הדובר הטוב ביותר'. ביטוי זה הולם את האנושות, כי מבין בעלי החיים דרי העולם ומשמיעי הקול רק לאדם יכולת הדיבור, ואולי יש מקום להזכיר את אונקלוס לבראשית ב:ז המתרגם את 'ויהי האדם לנפש חיה' במילים 'והות באדם לרוח ממללא'. אם כן, דור־שַׂרְכִּין נבנתה לטובתם ולרווחתם של המעולים במדברים, ועוד נראה שהייתה מיושבת בני אדם שדיברו שפות רבות.

(2) המילה *atmû*, המופיעה בכינוי הנדיר לאנושות, חוזרת גם בהמשך הכתובת וגם שם בקטע שהקשרו הוא ציון האנושות. לקראת סופו של תיאור הבנייה מסופר על אכלוס העיר, ושם נאמר (שורות 72–74):

baʾūlāt arbaʾi / *lišānu aḫītu* // *atmê la mitḫurti* / ***āšibūte šadê u māti***
mala irteʾu nūr ilāni bēl gimri
ša ina zikir Aššur bēlīya ina mēzez šibirrīya ašlula
pâ ištēn ušaškinma // *ušarmâ qerebšu.*
mārī māt Aššur / *mūdûte inî kalama*
ana šūḫuz ṣibitte / *palāḫ ili u šarri*   *aklī šāpirī umaʾʾiršunūti.*

תושבי ארבע (**כנפות הארץ**), (דוברי) לשון זרה, דוברי (שפה ש)אין לה שווה (=בלתי ניתנת לתרגום), **יושבי ההר והארץ**,
כל שרעה אותם אור האלים (שַׁמַש), אדון הכול,
ששָׁביתי בעוז מַטִי בדבר אשור אדוני,
שמתי להם 'פה אחד' והושבתי (אותם) בתוכה.
בני ארץ אשור, יודעי חכמות כולן,
(כדי) ללמד התנהגות טובה של יראת האל והמלך
שלחתים (להיות) מפקחים ושולטים (מדריכים).[33]

סרגון הושיב בבירתו אנשים מכל העולם, ולא זו בלבד אלא שאפיינו את התושבים לשונם הזרה ואי־יכולתם להבין זה את זה ולהתקשר איש עם

(CAD, R, s. v. *rēšu*, p. 273a). ואולם בכרך קודם של המילון המשפט תורגם כך: 'I am sending herewith the first report by PN to my lord Aššur' (CAD, L, s. v. *lišānu*, p. 212b), וברור שהתרגום החדש עדיף. את המונח *lišān rēšēti* פון זודן (*AHw*, p. 556) מתרגם 'Hofberichterstatter', 'כתב החצר', בלי להידרש למשמעות המילולית של המונח. בורגר מתרגם את המונח 'Rehtor' במרכאות כפולות. כאמור, שני הטקסטים המשתמשים במונח הם מכתבים לאל, האחד של סרגון (ה'מסע השמיני' הנודע) והאחד של אסרחדון (R. Borger, *Die Inschriften Asarhaddons, Königs von Assyrien*, Graz 1956, pp. 102–107). בשני הטקסטים המונח מופיע בהקשרים זהים: בסוף המכתב לפני ציון מספר האנשים הזעום שנהרגו במסע הצבאי המתואר בגוף המכתב. ייתכן שנושא התואר הזה הוא השליח שנשלח לאל כדי לקרוא אותו לפניו, והרי מכתב כזה שראוי שיקרא אותו נואם מעולה ראוי גם שייכתב בשפה נעלה.

33 לדיון מעמיק בפסקה זו ראה C. Uehlinger, *Weltreich und 'eine Rede': Eine neue Deutung der sogenannten Turmbauerzählung (Gen 11, 1–9)*, Fribourg 1990, pp. 470–474. אילינגר סבור שראשיתו של סיפור מגדל בבל נעוצה בבניית דור־שַׁרְכִּין ובעזיבתו הפתאומית עם מותו של סרגון. רק בשלב מאוחר יותר שוכתב הסיפור בהשפעתה של בניית בבל בידי נבוכדנאצר.

רעהו. אך כדי לתקן את המצב המלך 'שם להם פה אחד'. *pâ ištēn/eda šakānu* הוא ביטוי שכיח ופירושו 'לשתף פעולה',[34] ואילו *pâ ištēn šuškunu* פירושו 'לגרום לשיתוף פעולה'. אולם אין מקרא יוצא מידי פשוטו, ובמקרה זה הכוונה בוודאי שסרגון גרם שהתושבים החדשים גברו על קשיי השפה שהפרידו ביניהם, שהרי ראשית הפִסקה מאפיינת את אנשי הארצות כדוברי שפות זרות שאינם מבינים זה את זה,[35] והרי מטבע הדברים מדובר כאן בריבוי שפות דווקא ולא באי שיתוף פעולה סתם.

כמו כן ביצירת הבנה בין דוברי שפות השונות זו מזו בעיר הבירה ביטא סרגון את שליטתו בעולם רב־הלשונות ואף שיקף רצון או ניסיון של ממש להשליט שפה אחת בכל האימפריה. אם הכוונה גם להבנה הדדית ולשיתוף פעולה דווקא, נמצא שסרגון שאף להביא לידי הרמוניה בעיר ובעולם.[36]

ועוד זאת. בדומה לסיפור המקראי על מגדל בבל גם אנשי מסופוטמיה ייחסו את ריבוי השפות לקללה אלוהית ובייחוד בפרשה מפורסמת מאגדת 'אֶנְמֶרְכַּר ואדון ארץ אַרַטַּ', הידועה בשם 'הלחש של נֻדִמֻד'.[37] מה במקרא אף בתפיסה המסופוטמית בעולם האידאלי בימי בראשית דיברו שפה אחת עד שבא אל וקלקל. אם כן, בדור־שַׁרֻּכִּין ניסה סרגון להשיב לאחור את גלגל ההיסטוריה ולהחזיר את העולם לימי הזוהר והאחדות שקדמו לבלבול השפות. בדור־שַׁרֻּכִּין מתקיימת נבואת צפניה (ג:ט) 'כי אז אהפך אל עמים שפה ברורה לקרא כלם בשם ה' לעבדו שכם אחד'.[38]

34 פון זודן מתרגם 'eines Sinnes machen' (*AHw*, s.v. *pû* I D, pp. 872b–873a). מילון שיקגו מתרגם 'to make act in unison' (CAD, Š/1, s.v. *šakānu*, p. 141a). ניתן להשוות את הביטוי לביטוי האנגלי 'speak the same language', שפירושו להבין זה את זה ולשתף פעולה.

35 ראה אילינגר (לעיל, הערה 33), עמ' 472.

36 שאיפה זו סותרת, כמובן, את המציאות בימי סרגון, שהיו מלאי מלחמות כפי שמעידים האנאלים שלו ואף החלק הראשון של כתובת הגליל הנידונה כאן.

37 ראה אילינגר (לעיל, הערה 33), עמ' 409–429; י' קליין, 'למוצאן והתפתחותן של לשונות הארץ – ההשקפה השומרית והמקראית', בתוך M. Cogan et al. (eds.), *Tehilla le-Moshe: Biblical and Judaic Studies in Honor of Moshe Greenberg*, Winona Lake, Ind. 1997, pp. 77*–92*; J. Klein, 'The so-Called "Spell of Nudimud" (ELA 134–155): A Re-examination', in S. Graziani, M.C. Casaburi & G. Lacerenza (eds.), *Studi sul Vicino Oriente Antico dedicati alla memoria di Luigi Cagni*, Napoli 2000, pp. 563–584

38 את הפסוק הזה יש לפרש לפי יונתן שתרגם 'ארי בכן אשני על עממיא ממלל חד בהיר', וראה מה שכתב מרדכי יו"ט מרגלית בפירושו לצפניה על אתר: 'והנה על פי הספור בבראשית י"א היתה כל הארץ שפה אחת ודברים אחדים, ולפי שמרדו בהקב"ה בלל את שפתם עד אשר לא שמעו איש שפת רעהו. וכנגד בלבול הלשונות ופרוד הדעות בראשית הימים יבוא באחרית הימים יחוד הלשון והלב, כי מתוך הענין אנו למדין שהשפה הנהפכת אחת תהיה' (תורה נביאים וכתובים עם פירוש מדעי בעריכת א' כהנא, תל־אביב תר"צ). פירוש 'ברורה' כ'אחת' מתחזק על סמך התקבולת אחת // ברה בשיר השירים ו:ט, ואף בפסוק שבספר צפניה המילה 'ברורה' מקבילה ל'אחד'. להקבלה בין פסוק זה ובין 'הלחש של נֻדִמֻד' ראה קליין (לעיל, הערה 37). סרגון מעוניין שתושבי העיר החדשה יִרְאו את האל ואת המלך והמומחים מלמדים

העניין בשפת הדיבור של תושבי הבירה עשוי להסביר את אחת התכונות הבולטות ביותר בכתובת. בכתובת יותר מארבעים מילים וביטויים יחידאיים, צורות יחידאיות של מילים נפוצות, מילים המופיעות רק ברשימות לקסיקליות, מילים נדירות ומילים מרקע שומרי, עילמי או בלתי מזוהה. גם אלים נקראים בשמות פיוטיים ונדירים.[39] אנדראס פוקס העיר שחלק מן הטקסט כמעט בלתי ניתן לתרגום כי יש בו אוצר מילים עם מראית עין מלומדת (pseudogelehrten Wortschatzes).[40] אולם השפה המיוחדת והמוזרה איננה דבר של מה בכך, וקשה לחשוב שהמחבר רק משתעשע ומתרברב בהצגת יכולתו הלשונית.[41] אם כן, למה לו שפה משונה כל כך?

לדעתי, העניין בדיבור כאפיון האנושות מצד אחד ושימת פה אחד לתושבי העיר מצד אחר קשורים זה לזה, והצירוף מסביר את השפה המיוחדת של הטקסט. סרגון מבקש להדגים ולהשמיע מעין שפה שנשמעה בעיר החדשה על־ידי שימוש בשפה מסולסלת ומלומדת. העיר נבנתה בשביל 'הנואמים הטובים ביותר', והמלך ציפה שידברו מן הסתם 'אכדית של המלך' ואם תרצו, 'אכדית של שבת'.[42] תושבי העיר הם הדוברים הנעלים, ולפיכך אף לשון הכתובת יפה ונעלה.

אותם גם את זה. לעניין הבאת מומחים ללמד אוכלוסייה חדשה את דרכי ארצם החדשה ראה את המסופר בספר מלכים ב יז:כה-כח. על ההקבלה המעניינת כבר עמד חיים תדמור במאמרו 'עיר־מלך ועיר־קודש באשור ובבל', בתוך העיר והקהילה: קובץ הרצאות שהושמעו בכנס השנים־עשר לעיון בהיסטוריה [כ"ח-ל' בכסלו תשכ"ז], ירושלים 1968, עמ' 200–201; וראה גם S. Paul, 'Sargon's Administration Diction in II Kings 17 27', *JBL*, 88 (1969), pp. 73–74

39 ראה להלן בנספח ב: השפה המיוחדת (עמ' 50).

40 ראה פוקס (לעיל, הערה 9), עמ' 289.

41 רנגר ([לעיל, הערה 1], עמ' 76) רושם את הסגולות האלה כמאפיינות את הכתובות המלכותיות האשוריות בכללותן, אך נראה לי שכתובת הגליל הזאת יוצאת דופן בריבוי השימוש בהן.

42 מתעוררת השאלה איזו שפה למדו התושבים. שלוש האפשרויות העולות על הדעת הן ארמית, אכדית או שתיהן, אך קלושה האפשרות שמדובר בארמית, שכן אין בכתובת מילים שרקען ארמי, והארמית התפשטה תחילה בחלק המערבי של האימפריה האשורית. יש להזכיר את דברי פרפולה (S. Parpola, SAA I, pp. xv–xvi) שעל אף השתרשות הארמית במִנהל האשורי עד לסוף המאה השמינית לפסה"נ התקשרו הפקידים ביניהם בעיקר באשורית. הוא מצטט מכתב (CT 54 10) שממנו משתמע שסרגון התעקש שפקידיו יכתבו אליו באכדית וישיבו לו כלשון מכתביו הוא. האכדית הייתה שפת המושלים, ואילו הארמית הייתה שפת הנשלטים. לדעתו, סרגון התנגד לקבלת מכתבים בארמית בין מטעמי גאווה בין מטעמי ביטחון. על מכתב זה ושאלת השפה בימי סרגון ראה גם M. Dietrich, SAA XVII, p. xv, p. 5 No. 2. דיטריך סבור שהפקידים לא שמרו את הפקודה ומכל מקום כתבו בארמית, אך המכתבים לא שרדו בגלל מפגעי הטבע. עדות איקונוגרפית לשימוש בכתב ארמי או בשפה הארמית בימי סרגון יש בתבליט מדור־שַׁרֻּכִּין המראה את המצור על עיר בארץ מני ובו אדם קורא ממגילה. לפי חיים תדמור, המגילה כתובה ארמית, ומתוך קריאה האדם מתרגם אותה לשפה המקומית, שהיא מנאית. ראה ח' תדמור, 'על מקומה של הארמית בממלכת אשור: שלוש הערות על תבליט של סרגון', ארץ־ישראל, כ (תשמ"ט), עמ' 249–252; H. Tadmor, 'The Aramaization of Assyria: Aspects of Western Impact', in

ג. עניינו של המחבר בלשון מתבטא גם בשני מדרשי שם. בין החלטת המלך לבנות עיר חדשה ובין בקשתו מן האלים לאשר את התכנית עומד קטע שאין כיוצא בו בתיאורי בנייה אחרים (שורות 50–52):

kīma zikir šūmīya
ša ana ***naṣār kitti u mīšari*** */* ***šūtešur*** *la le'î / la* ***ḫabāl enši***
imbûni ilāni rabûti-
kasap eqlēt āli šâšu kī pî ṭuppāte šāyyāmānūte kaspu u siparru
ana bēlīšunu utīrma //
aššu riggāte lā šubšî
ša kasap eqli lā ṣebû
eqlu miḫir eqli ašar pānûšunu šaknu addinšunūti.

לפי קריאת שמי,
אשר לשם **שמירת צדק ויושר** ו(אשר) **לעשיית צדק** עם חוסר היכולת ו(אשר) **לאי־עושק החלש**
קראוני האלים הגדולים –
(את) כסף שדות העיר ההיא כפי לוחות המכירה, כסף ונחושת,
החזרתי לבעליהם;
וכדי שלא לגרום לרעה,
למי שלא חפצו בכסף השדה נתתי שדה תמורת שדה במקום ששמו את פניהם (במקום שרצו).

מעשה זה מזכיר את הצעת אחאב לנבות היזרעאלי (מל"א כא:ב), אך שלא כדעת אליהו, סרגון מצטייר פה כעושה צדק במיטבו. ומה לקניית שדות בדרכי צדק ולשמו של המלך, שנתנו לו האלים? חיים תדמור כבר ציין שיש כאן מדרש מורחב על השם *Šarru-ukīn* או *Šarru-kīnu*.[43] המשמעות הראשונית של השם היא, ככל הנראה, 'המלך הלגיטימי' או 'המלך היציב'. ואולם למדרש אין עניין בפירוש המקורי, האטימולוגי. אדרבה! הוא דורש אותו 'המלך צודק', 'המלך עשה צדק' או 'מלך הצדק' כאילו היה *Šar-kitti*.[44]

H.-J. Nissen & J. Renger (eds.), *Mesopotamien und seine Nachbarn: Politische und kulturelle Wechselbeziehungen im Alten Vorderasien vom 4. bis 1. Jahrtausend v. Chr., RAI XXV*, Berlin 1982, pp. 449–470; P. Garelli, 'Importance et rôle des Araméens dans l'administration de l'empire assyrien', in *ibid.*, pp. 437–447

43 ראה H. Tadmor, 'Monarchy and the Elite in Assyria and Babylonia: The Question of Royal Accountability', in S.N. Eisenstadt (ed.), *The Origins and Diversity of Axial Age Civilizations*, Albany, N.Y. 1986, pp. 203–225, esp. p. 215; אילינגר (לעיל, הערה 33), עמ' 473–474. אחרי שהשלמתי את כתיבת מאמרי זה הופיע מחקר מפורט על שמו של סרגון, אופן קריאתו, פירושו ושימושיו המדרשיים, וראה E. Frahm, 'Observations on the Name and Age of Sargon II and Some Patterns of Assyrian Royal Onomastics', *N.A.B.U.* 2005, No. 44

44 בתעודת המענק SAA XII No. 19, המצטטת את כתובת הגליל שלנו, בשורה 5 מצאנו כתוב *ša ana la ḫabāl enše šūšur la le'î* [...] LUGAL *kīnu*, וברור שהטקסט משקף

יתרה מזו, הטקסט מסביר את הצדק שנהג בו סרגון ברכשו את הקרקעות, ואם נדייק בלשון של מדרש השם, נשמע הד לנאמר במבוא המפורסם לחוקי חמורבי. ייעודו של חמורבי היה

mīšaram *ina mātim ana šūpîm*
raggam *u ṣēnam* ***ana ḫulliqim***
dannum ***enšam ana la ḫabālim***
לגרום להופעת **יושר בארץ**,
לאבד את הרעה ואת הרשע
כדי שהחזק לא **יעשוק את החלש**

ומעשה חמורבי בקיום ייעודו היה

Ana ***šutēšur*** *nišī mātim…*
Kittam u mīšaram *ina pī mātim aškun*
להביא **יושר** לאנשי הארץ
שמתי **צדק ויושר** בפי (אנשי) הארץ

גם בעצם המעשה של סרגון נשמע הד לחוקי חמורבי. אמנם אין לטעון שמלך אשור מתפאר בקיום מדויק של חוק מסוים של מלך בבל הנערץ. אולם חוקים 36–41 של חמורבי עוסקים ברכישת שדות והחלפתם (חוק 41 *upīḫ*), ומצאנו בהם לסירוגין את המילים *eqlum*, *kaspum*, *ṭuppu* ומילים גזורות מן הפועל *šâmu* ובכללן *šāyimānum*. דבר חשוב במיוחד מצאנו בחוק 37 *eqlum… ana bēlīšu itâr*, מילים וצורות שנמצאות בכתובת הגליל של סרגון. כלומר, מעשה סרגון הוא בתחום עניינם של חוקי חמורבי, ובתיאור המעשה אף מהדהדת לשון החוקים. גם אם סרגון איננו מקיים את חוקי חמורבי במלואם, הוא עושה דבר הדומה לקיומם.[45]

את ההבנה המדרשית של שם המלך. המהדירים קטיה (Kataja) ווייטינג (Whiting) תרגמו שם 'The true king […] whose lordship the goddess Ninmenanna has magnified, that he might not oppress the weak, and may cause the feeble to prosper', אבל על סמך מדרש השם ברור שמוטב לתרגם 'The just king […] whose lordship the goddess Ninmenanna has magnified, that he might not oppress the weak, and may do justice with the feeble'. ראוי לציין ששם המלך *Šarru-ukīn* מופיע, כנראה, גם בכתב תמונתי כדיוקן של מלך אשור המחזיק בידו מטה או קנה (GI, *qanu*), והוצע שתמונה זו מייצגת את המילה 'מלך' ואת הסימן של משפט וצדק. ראה L.D. Morenz, 'Bild-poetische Umsetzungen von Personnamen: Sargon II. und Aššur-šarrat', *AoF*, 30 (2003), pp. 18–27, esp. p. 22. אם כך הדבר, נמצא שמדרש שם המלך כמלך צדק היה נפוץ בקרב הסופרים האשוריים ולא היה מוגבל לכתובת הגליל הזאת בלבד, והשווה אל פינקל וריד (לעיל, הערה 19).

45 על שימוש מדרשי בחוקי חמורבי ביצירה ספרותית מן התקופה הבבלית החדשה (המכונה 'נבוכדנאצר, מלך המשפט') עמדתי במאמרי V.A. Hurowitz, 'Hammurabi in Mesopotamian Tradition', in Y. Sefati et al. (eds.), *'An Experienced Scribe Who Neglects Nothing': Ancient Near Eastern Studies in Honor of Jacob Klein*, Bethesda, Md. 2005, pp. 497–532

נמצא שברכישת הקרקעות כדת וכדין קיים סרגון את שליחותו וייעודו המגולמים בשמו שנתנו לו האלים, והשדות שעליהם הוקמה העיר עדים שהמלך נהג ביושר ועשה צדק לפי מסורת חמורבי זכור לטוב.

ד. מדרש שם אחר מסוג מיוחד מופיע בתחילת תיאור החומה, ושם כתוב (שורה 65):

šár šár šár šár géš+u géš+u géš+u 1 UŠ 3 *qanî 2 ammāti nibīt šumīya*
mišiḫti dūrīšu aškunma

16280 אמות, (כ)קריאת / (כ)מניין שמי, שמתי את מידת (האורך של) חומתו

מדרש השם הראשון פתח במילים *kīma zikir šumīya*, 'כקריאת שמי'. כאן מוזכר *nibīt šumīya*, שפירושו 'קריאת שמי' או 'מניין שמי', אך אין הבדל ממשי בין שני המונחים. צמדי מילים הגזורות מן הפעלים *nabû // zakāru* נפוצים מאוד בספרות האכדית, וכאשר בכתובת אחת מופיעות שתי המילים בהקשרים דומים יש מקום לקשור ביניהן. והנה בהמשך תיאור השערים והחומות (שורות 67–70) מצאנו בערבוביה את המונחים *zikra, šūma zakāru* *nabû, nibīta šakānu* ו־*šūma qabû*, וברור שהמונחים נרדפים ומתחלפים. ואולם מדרש שם זה שונה מקודמו. במקום לפרש את השם הוא מתרגם אותו למספר, ואת המספר הוא קושר בקשר כלשהו עם חומת העיר. האופי הקריפטוגרפי של המספר ידוע היטב, אך הכוונה המדויקת של המדרש הזה עדיין לוטה בערפל והוצעו לו הסברים מהסברים שונים ובכללם פירוש בדרך הגימטריה.[46] מכל מקום, ברור שאורך החומה מבטא את שם המלך וזהה לו בדרך כל שהיא. יש כתובות בנייה אחרות המוסרות את מידות הבניין, אך רק כאן מצאנו קשר בין אורך החומה ובין שם מלך, והדבר דורש הסבר. מתברר שאפשר לצרף את שני מדרשי השם ולפרשם יחד.[47] מצד אחד, אורך החומה שווה לשמו של סרגון, ומצד אחר שם המלך מבטא את מעשיו הצודקים. והנה, לפי העיקרון שאם א' שווה לשם ב' וב' שווה לג' אזי א' שווה לג' נמצא: אורך החומה = סרגון = מדרש השם של סרגון, שהוא המלך עושה

46 ראה J. Oppert, 'Sechshundert drei und fünfzig: Eine babylonische magische Quadrattafel', *ZA*, 17 (1903), pp. 60–74, esp. pp. 67–69; E.F. Weidner, 'Šilkan(ḫe)ni. König von Muṣri, ein Zeitgenosse Sargon II', *AfO*, 14 (1941–1944), pp. 40–53, esp. p. 49; E. Leichty, 'The Colophon', in R.D. Biggs & J.A. Brinkman, *Studies Presented to A. Leo Oppenheim, June 7, 1964*, Chicago 1964, pp. 147–154, esp. p. 152, note 18; S. Lieberman, 'A Mesopotamian Background for the So-Called *Aggadic* "Measures" of Biblical Hermeneutics?', *HUCA*, 58 (1987), pp. 157–225, esp. p. 192; W. von Soden, *Aus Sprache, Geschichte und Religion Babyloniens*, Neapel 1989, p. 334, note 33; M. Powell, 'Masse und Gewichte', *RLA*, 7, 1987–1990, pp. 457–517, esp. pp. 474–475

47 ראוי לציין שבכתובת הגליל אין מוזכר כלל שם העיר דור־שַׁרֻּכִּין על אף העניין בשמות שבכתובת זו. לא כך הדבר בשאר כתובות הבנייה הנוקבות בשם העיר סמוך לתחילת תיאור הבנייה (למראי מקום ראה פוקס [לעיל, הערה 9] עמ' 375, מס' 13).

צדק, וממילא אורך החומה = מעשי הצדק של המלך. הווה אומר, העיר שנבנתה בצדק מגלמת את הצדק של המלך ששמו נקרא עליה, והרואה את החומה נזכר בשם המלך ואף זוכר את הצדק שלו.[48] במילים אחרות, החומה עצמה היא מעין תמונה של צדק המלך ודיוקן של המלך העושה צדק. גם המלך וגם הצדק שהוא עושה מוּבְנִים בתוך העיר.

ה. העיר כדיוקן המלך. יש להודות שהצעתי שהעיר היא מעין דיוקן של המלך מוזרה לכאורה, אך אפשר להביא לה ראיה מפורשת מן הטקסט. בקללות המסיימות את הכתובת נאמר (שורה 76):

> אשר ישנה את מעשי ידיי ויעשה את קלסתר פניי לבלתי מוכר (*bunnānīya usaḫḫû*),
> (ואשר) יבטל (את) הצורות (*uṣurātu*) שיצרתי וימחק את סימני ההיכר שלי (*simātēya*),
> אשור, שַׁמַש, אֲדַד, והאלים היושב(ים) בקרבו
> ילקטו את שמו וזרעו מהארץ, ויושיבוהו בכריעה תחת אויביו.

מה הוא 'קלסתר פניי'? הקללות המסיימות את הכתובות המלכותיות מתייחסות על פי רוב לפגיעה בכתובת, בחפץ או בבניין שעשייתם תוארה בגוף הכתובת. לפי המנהג הזה, פוקס הציע שהמילים 'אשר ... ויעשה את קלסתר פני לבלתי מוכר (*bunnānīya usaḫḫû*)', מכוונות למי שיטשטש את תמונות המלך המקשטות את הארמונות.[49] אולם לתמונות כאלה אין זכר בגוף הכתובת, וכתובות אחרות של סרגון המזכירות תבליטים אינן מכנות אותם במילה זו. כמו כן יש כתובות של סרגון המזכירות את ה־*bunnannû* של האלים, שהם פסליהם אך לא של המלך.[50] אם כן, מה כוונת 'קלסתר הפנים שלי'?[51] לדעתי, כוונת הכתוב למראה העיר כולה, כי מראה העיר

48 עיין בדברי פינקל וריד ([לעיל, הערה 19], עמ' 263): 'Sargon II, with his new city, was conforming to the pattern of Mesopotamian rulers set on creating a new world-order, and the name he chose for it, Dūr-Šarrukīn, confirmed the nature of his aspirations. They even had physical expression in the city-wall of Ḫorsābād, whose length was described as the mathematical equivalent of the royal name.'

49 פוקס (לעיל, הערה 9), עמ' 296, הערה 99. מה שנאמר כאן על ה־*bunnannû* יפה גם לשאר הדברים, לצורות (*uṣurātu*) ול'סימני ההיכר' של המלך (*simātu*) וכנראה, אין הכוונה לחפצים ממש אלא לחוקים ולתכונות המתאימות למלך שאפיינו את העיר.

50 פוקס (לעיל, הערה 9), עמ' 49, שורות 16–18; עמ' 51, שורות 17–21.

51 לאות הכרה בקושי תרגם מילון שיקגו 'Whoever alters my handiwork, [and] makes its [text: my] features unrecognizable' (CAD, B, p. 318b). התרגום 'its features' למילה *bunnānīya* הוא תרגום מתקן אך בלא הצדקה ושלא לצורך. על המונח *bunnannû* ראה גם I. Winter, 'Art in Empire: The Royal Image and the Visual Dimensions of Assyrian Ideology', in S. Parpola & R.M. Whiting (eds.), *Assyria 1995*, Helsinki 1997, pp. 359–381. בעמ' 368 וינטר מסבירה בלא תיקון את הצירוף הנדון: 'Sargon II...pronounces a curse against anyone who

בקלסתר פניו של המלך. מובן מאליו שהעיר איננה הצורה הפיזית של המלך, אך כבר ראינו שהיא משקפת דברים מופשטים כגון מעשיו ומידותיו: הרואה את העיר רואה את המלך במידותיו הרצויות, והפוגע בתכונות המיוחדות של העיר ששיווה לה המלך, היינו במשפט, כאילו פוגע בקלסתר פניו של סרגון עצמו, ונגד פגיעות כאלה הכתובת מתריעה.

לסיכום, מה היא דמותו של סרגון העולה מתיאור הבנייה כאשר קוראים אותו כפירוש לעיר עצמה?

קודם כול, העיר היא בבואה של העולם,[52] ואם כך, המלך הבונה את העיר ממלא את תפקיד האל הבורא המעצב את צורת היקום, וכך נרמז בטקסט עצמו.[53]

שנית, העיר עצמה היא דיוקן מופשט של המלך המזכיר את מידותיו ובייחוד את היותו מלך הצדק.[54]

שלישית, העולם מלא בני אדם המדברים שפות רבות, וגם את העיר החדשה מאכלסים אנשי כל הארצות המדברים שפות רבות. סרגון גרם שכל תושבי העיר מבינים זה את זה, ואף הנחיל לכולם את יראת האל. זה הביטוי לנעשה באימפריה שלו או זו משאלת לבו ותכניתו המדינית להשכין הרמוניה ולתת שפה אחת בתבל כולו. בהנחלת פה אחד לאנושות המלך מחזיר את העולם לימי בראשית.

רביעית, העיר נבנתה על אדמות שקנה באורחות צדק מלך צדק, ואורך חומת העיר מזכיר לרואה אותה את מלך הצדק ואף את צדק המלך הבונה.

הרואה את העיר דור־שַׁרֻּכִּין באספקלריה של כתובת הגליל יראה אפוא עולם חדש ואידאלי ומלך אידאלי. העולם הזה מיוסד על צדק ומלא אנשים בני כמה ארצות שכולם מבינים זה את זה ויראים את האל, והכול בזכות המלך הבונה, המלך שהעיר היא דיוקנו – סרגון.

---

would alter or damage his features'. אפשר לומר שהעיר דור־שַׁרֻּכִּין היא *ṣalam bannunnî* של המלך, ואסור לשנות דבר כל שהוא בעיר, כי המשנה דבר בעיר פוגע בקלסתר המלך עצמו.

52 פרפולה ([לעיל, הערה 5], עמ' 49, 69 הערה 1) משווה את צורת העיר (ריבוע) אל Mandala, שהוא סמל בודהיסטי ליקום, ומציין שערים מסופוטמיות אחרות ובהן כלח, בבל ובורסיפה בנויות אף הן באותה הצורה. על סמך השימוש בסמלים המתבטא בכתובתנו ראוי לציין שלפי רואף וזגול (M. Roaf & A. Zgoll, 'Assyrian Astroglyphs: Lord Aberdeen's Black Stone and the Prisms of Esarhaddon', *ZA*, 91 [2001], p. 287), גם בכתב האסטרוגליפי המונח *kibrāt erbetti*, 'ארבע כנפות תבל', ציורו הוא ריבוע, וצורה זו מבטאת את התפיסה המסופוטמית שלעולם ארבעה צדדים וארבע פינות.

53 זיהוי המלך עם האל הבורא, בין שזה מרדוך בין שזה אשור, מתחזק על סמך הרמיזות לאנומה אֶלִש (לוח א, שורות 11, 88) בתיאור המלך בשורה 38, כפי שהוזכר לעיל, הערה 17.

54 גילום המלך בעיר שבנה מתאים במקצת להמצאת כתב תמונתי חדש בימי סרגון ולשימוש בכתב חדש זה לקישוט ארמונו. לא נגזים אם נאמר שדור־שַׁרֻּכִּין הוא ההיירוגליף האולטימטיבי. על הכתב החדש ראה פינקל וריד (לעיל, הערה 19); רואף וזגול (לעיל, הערה 52), עמ' 264–295.

נספח א

תיאור הבנייה בכתובת הגליל של סרגון השני מלך אשור

(על־פי פוקס [לעיל, הערה 9], עמ' 29–44, 289–296, שורות 34–77)[55]

מטרות העיר וההחלטה לבנותה (שורות 34–49)

šarru itpēšu // muštābil amat damiqtim
<ša> ana šūšub namê nadûte // u petê kišubbê zaqāp ṣippāte
iškunu uzunšu
uḫummī zaqrūti ša ultu ullâ ina qerbīšun urqitu lā šūṣāt / biltu šuššê
ṣurruš uštābilma //
kigallum šuḫrubtu ša ina šarrāni maḫrūte epinnu la īdû šer'i šuzuzimma /
šulsê alāla
libbašu ublamma
īnî tamerti lā kuppi karattu petêma // kī gipiš edî mê nuḫši šušqî eliš u šapliš

šarru pēt ḫasīsi / le'i inî kalama / šinnat apkalli
ša ina milki nēmeqi irbûma // ina tašīmti išēḫu
māt Aššur rapaštum
ti'ûtu nešbê u bulluṭ libbi // tillenû simat šarrūti sunnunu rāṭīšun
atmû rēšēte ša ina sunqi ḫušaḫḫi eṭērimma
ina zabāl karāni akû la naḫaršuše // u bibil libbi marṣi baṭilta lā rašê
aššu šamnī balti amēlūti mupaššiḫ šer'āni ina mātīya lā aqārimma //
šamaššammī kī Nissabi ina maḫīri šâmi
šurruḫ naptani simat paššūri ili u šarri
ḫatê unnāte // gimir ŠÁM-ga-ni itatêšu šuzuzzi
urru u mūšu ana epēš āli šâšu akpud

simak Šamaš dikugal ilāni rabûti mušakšid ernittīya qerbuššu šubnû aqbīma
Magganubba
ša ina šēpī Muṣri šadê ina muḫḫi namba'i u rēbit Ninâ kīma dimti nadû

55 התעתיק המקושר המובא להלן מחולק למשפטים ולחלקי משפטים וצוינו בו קווים נטויים כדי להראות את המבנה הפיוטי של היצירה. התרגום לעברית איננו משקף את תחביר האכדית ונועד לאפשר לקורא להבין את משמעות הכתוב ולא את צורתו. בסוגריים העגולים שבתרגום מובאים השלמות או הסברים לצורך הבנת הכתוב.

תרגום

מטרות העיר וההחלטה לבנותה (שורות 34-49)

המלך המומחה, המהרהר בדברים טובים,
ששם את אוזנו (הפנה את לבו) ליישוב המדברות המוזנחים
ולפתיחת השדות השוממים ולנטיעת המטעים –
הרהר בקרבו (החליט) ל(גרום) שהצוקים הגבוהים שמימי קדם לא הוצמח בהם ירק יישאו יבול;
ולבו הביאו (החליט) שהאדמה הקשה החרבה שב(ימי) המלכים הקודמים לא ידעה מחרשה
תעמיד תלמים (תיחרש) ותביא לידי זמירת הילולים (שירי עבודה),
ו(אף החליט) לפתוח כאסם(?) עינות מדשאות בלי בארות,
(כדי) להשקות למעלה ולמטה במי שפע כמו גאות נחשול.

המלך פקוח האוזן (החכם), בעל היכולת בחכמות כולן, השני לאַפְּכַּלֻ (הווזיר החכם הקדמון),
שגדל בעצת חכמה ושצמח בתבונה –
(כדי לאפשר שב)ארץ אשור הרחבה
מזון שׂובע ומְחַיית הלב, *tillenû* (=בירה?) המתאים למלכות יזרמו בגרונם (של אנשיה),
(וכדי) להציל את כל הדוברים הראשונים במעלה (האנושות) ה(נתונים) ברעב ובמחסור,
ו(כדי ש)הנכה לא יגהק בנשיאת יין(?),
ו(כדי שב)משאת נפשו של החולה לא תהיה בטלה (=שלא יתאכזבו מחפצם),
(ו)כדי ששמנים, גאוות האנושות המרגיעה את הגידים, לא יהיו יקרים בארצי,
ו(כדי ש)בשוק (יהיה אפשר) לקנות שומשומין כמו דגן,
(וכדי) לפאר את הארוחה המתאימה לשולחן האל והמלך,
(וכדי) לחתות/לגרד(?) את השדות(?),
(כדי) כל ??? בגבולו להעמיד –
(כדי להביא לידי כל זאת) תכננתי יומם ולילה לעשות את העיר ההיא.

את מקדש שַׁמַשׁ, השופט העליון של האלים הגדולים, הנותן לי להשיג את רינת ניצחונותיי בקרבו
ציוויתי לבנות;
ו(העיר) מַגַּנֻבַּ,
המוצבת כמו מגדל לרגלי הר מוצרי, בראש המבועים ורחובות נינוה,

ša 3 ME 50 ÀM *malkē labirūte ša ellamuʾa bēlūt māt Aššur ēpušūma iltanapparū baʾūlāt Enlil,*
ayyuma ina libbīšunu ašaršu ul umaššīma / šūšubšu ul īdēma / ḫerê nārīšu ul izkur.
ina mērešīya palkî
ša ina qibīt Lugal-abzu bēl nēmeqi tašīmta sunnunūma malû niklāti //
u ḫissat uznīya palkāte
ša eli šarrāni abbīya Ninmenanna bānīt ilāni ušāteru ḫasīsi
ana šūšub āli šâšu / zuqqur paramāḫi atmān ilāni rabûti u ekallāti šubat bēlūtīya
urra u mūša akpud / aṣrimma / epēssu aqbi.

רכישת קרקעות (שורות 50–52)

kīma zikir šūmīya
ša ana naṣār kitti u mīšari / šūtešur la leʾî / la ḫabāl enši imbûni ilāni rabûti-
kasap eqlēt āli šâšu kī pî ṭuppāte šāyyāmānūte kaspu u siparru ana bēlīšunu utīrma, //
aššu riggāte lā šubšî
ša kasap eqli lā ṣebû eqlu miḫir eqli ašar pānûšunu šaknū addinšunūti.

תפילת המלך והמצווה האלוהית לבנות את העיר (שורות 53–55)

*al-*ŠU *banîšu miḫret* UG ŠU UL
ana Šigga u Lugal-dingirra dayyinūte tēnišēte talimāni ina tēmēqi ušaqqīma //
aḫrataš umē ina ṭub libbi u buʾāri qerbuššu erēbi
ina SUG *Dimgalkalamma ana Šaʾuška rāšibat Ninâ attaši qātī.*
zikri pîya kēnum kī ulu šamni eli nābī ṣīrūti bēlīya maʾdiš iṭībma
epēš āli // ḫerê nāri iqbûni.

הכנות לבנייה (גיוס עובדים, עשיית לבנים וייסוד העיר; שורות 56–61)

nannûššun lā mušpēlu attakilma
baḫūlātēya gapšāte adkēma // allu tupšikku ušašši.

ina Ṣītaš araḫ bīn Daragal
pāris purussê // mušaklim ṣaddi
Nanna šamê erṣetim // qarrad ilāni Sîn

אשר 350 מלכים עתיקים שעשו לפני אדנות ארץ אשור

ו(אשר) הנהיגו שוב ושוב את אנשי אנליל,

אף (לא) אחד מתוכם לא מדד את מקומו ולא ידע ליישבו ולא ציווה לחפור את נהרו

בחכמתי הרחבה,

שבמצוות לֻגַל־אַבְזוּ (אֶאַ) אדון החכמות (היא) מוצפת תבונה ו(היא) מלאה תחכומים,

ו(ב)חכמת אוזניי הרחבות (חכמתי המופלגת),

שנִנְמֶאַנֵ, בונַת האלים, הותירה את אוזניי (הרבתה את חכמתי) על המלכים אבותיי,

ליישוב העיר ההיא, להגבהת המקדש דביר האלים הגדולים והארמונות מושב אדנותי

יומם ולילה תכננתי, יזמתי וציוויתי לעשותו.

רכישת קרקעות (שורות 50-52)

לפי קריאת שמי,

אשר לשם שמירת צדק ויושר ו(אשר) לעשיית צדק עם חוסר היכולת ו(אשר) לאי־עושק החלש

קראוני האלים הגדולים –

(את) כסף שדות העיר ההיא כפי לוחות המכירה, כסף ונחושת, החזרתי לבעליהם;

וכדי שלא לגרום לרעה,

לאלה שלא חפצו בכסף השדה נתתי שדה תמורת שדה במקום ששמו את פניהם (במקום שרצו).

תפילת המלך והמצווה האלוהית לבנות את העיר (שורות 53-55)

את העיר ... לבנות אותה לפני ...

לאל שַׁגַּ (דַמְקֻ) ולֻגַל־דִנְגִר (אַדַּה, שר־אלי), דייני האנושות, הרימותי את שתי ידיי בתפילה נרגשת;

ו(כדי) להיכנס בתוכה לאחרית הימים בטוב לב ובריאות,

במקדש(?) דִמְגַלְכַלַּמַ נשאתי את ידי לאלה שַׁאֶשְׁכַּ, מפחידת נינוה.

דבר פי הנכון היטיב מאוד כמו שמן טוב על האלים הנישאים אדוני,

ו(הם) ציווני לבנות את העיר ולכרות את התעלה.

הכנות לבנייה (גיוס עובדים, עשיית לבנים וייסוד העיר; שורות 56-61)

בטחתי במצוותם שאיננה משתנית,

ואת אנשיי האדירים גייסתי, וגרמתי (להם) לשאת מעדר וסל לבנים.

ב(חודש) Ṣītaš (=סיוון), החודש של בן־דַּרַגַּל (אנליל),

המחליט החלטות, המגלה אותות,

(שהוא) נַנַּ(ר) של השמים והארץ, גיבור האלים סין,

ša ina šimat Anim Enlil u Ea Niššiku ana labān libnāti epēš āli u bīti
araḫ Kulla nabû šumšu
ina eššēši ša mār Bēl igigalli palkê Nabû ṭupšar gimri mumair kullat ilāni
ušalbina libnassu.

ana Kulla bēl uššē libitte // u Mušda šitimgallum ša Enlil
nīqû aqqi / serqu asruqma / attaši šuillakku.
ina Abi araḫ arād Gibil mubbil qarbāte raṭubte[56] *// mukīn temēn āli u bīti*
uššēšu addīma // ukīn libnassu.

תיאור הבניינים (שורות 62–71)

parakkī rašdūti ša kīma kiṣir genni šuršudū
ana Ea Sîn u Ningal Adad Šamaš Ninurta ēpuša qerbuššu.
ekal šinnipīri ušî taskarinni musukkanni erēni šurmēni daprāni u buṭni
ina qibītīšunu ṣīrte ana mūšab šarrūtīya abnīma
bīt ḫilāni tanšil ekal māt Ḫatti miḫret bābīšin aptiqma
gušūrī erēni šurmēni ukīn ṣeruššin.

šár šár šár šár géš+u géš+u géš+u 1 UŠ 3 *qanî 2 ammāti nibīt šūmīya*
mišiḫti dūrīšu aškunma //
eli aban šadê zaqri ušaršida temēnšu.

ina rēše u arkāti ina ṣēlī kilallān miḫret 8 šārī 8 abullāti aptēma -

Šamaš-mušakšid-ernittīya
šūmī abul Šamaš

Adad-mukīl-ḫegallīšu
u abul Adad ša miḫret šadî azkur;

Enlil-mukīn-išdī-ālīya
zikrī abul Enlil

Mullissu-mudeššat-ḫiṣbi
u Mullissu ša miḫret iltāni ambi;

Anum-mušallim-epšēt-qātīya
nibīt abul Anim

Ištar-mušameḫḫat-nišīšu;
u Ištar ša miḫret amurri aškun;

Ea-muštēšir-nagbīšu
šumī abul Ea

Bēlet-ilī-murappišat-talittīšu
u abul Bēlet-ilī ša miḫret šūti aqbīma;

Aššur-mulabbir-palê-šarri-ēpišīšu-nāṣir-perīšu *dūršu;*
Ninurta-mukīn-temēn-aduššī-ana-labar-ūmī-rūqūti *šalḫûšu.*

56 קריאה לפי תיקונים המוצעים במילון שיקגו (CAD, R, s.v. *raṭbu*, p. 218). הטקסט
mu-uš-pil am-ba-te ra-ṭu-ub-te

אשר בגורל (שקבעו) אַנֻ, אנליל, ואֶאַ־נִשְׁכּוּ ללבינת לבנים ובניית עיר ובית
'חודש כֻּלַּ' (אל הלבנים) נקרא שמו,
בחג של בן־בֵּל, החכם המופלג, (שהוא) נבו, סופר הכול, מנהיג כל האלים –
גרמתי שילבנו את לבנותיה.

ל(אל) כֻּלַּ, האדון של יסודות הלבנה, ו(ל)אל מֻשְׁדַ הארדיכל של אנליל,
הקרבתי קרבנות, פיזרתי מנחת קמח, ונשאתי לחש.
ב(חודש) אב, החודש של ירידת גִּבִּל (אל האש) המייבש את השדה הרטוב והמכונן מפלס היסוד של העיר והבית,
הנחתי את יסודותיה וכוננתי את לבנתה.

תיאור הבניינים (שורות 62–71)

דבירים מיוסדים, המיוסדים כמו קשר ההרים
בניתי בקרבה בשביל (האלים) אֶאַ, סין ונִנְגַל, אַדַד, שַׁמַש, (ו)נִנֻרְתַּ.
ארמון שנהב, הבנים, אשכרוע, מסוכן, ארז, שורמנו, ברוש ואלה
במצוותם הנישאת למושב מלכותי בניתי,
ובֵּת־חִלַּנִ, דומה לארמון של ארץ חתי, לפני שעריהם יצרתי,
וקורות ארז ו(עץ) שורמנו כוננתי מעליהם.

16280 אמות, (כ)קריאת / (כ)מניין שמי, שמתי את מידת (האורך של) חומתו,
ועל האבן של הר גבוה ייסדתי את מפלס יסודותיו.

מלפנים ומאחור, בשני הצדדים, נגד שמונה הרוחות שמונה שערי עיר פתחתי,

'שמש־נותן־לי־להשיג־את־רינת־ניצחוני',
את שמות שער שמש
(ו)'אדד־מחזיק־(בשביל העיר)־שִׁפְעוֹ'
ושער אדד אשר כלפי מזרח קראתי;

'אנליל־מכונן־יסודות־עירי'
את שם שער אנליל
(ו)'מֻלִּסֻ־מדשיאת־שגשוג'
ומֻלִּסֻ אשר כלפי צפון קראתי;

'אַנֻ־משלים־את־מעשי־ידיי',
את קריאת שער אַנֻ
(ו)'אשתר־מפרה־את־אנשיה (של העיר)'
ואשתר אשר כלפי מערב קראתי;

'אֶאַ־מזרים־נבכיו'
את שמות שער אֶאַ
(ו)'בֵּלֶת־אִל־מרחיבה־ולדיו'
ושער בֵּלֶת־אִל אשר כלפי דרום קראתי;

'אשור־מאריך־בימים־את־תור־השלטון־של־המלך־בונהו־(ו)שומר־פריו (של המלך)'
(שם) חומתו;
'נִנֻרְתַּ־מכונן־מפלס־היסוד־של־החומה־לאורך־ימים־רחוקים' (שם) חומתו החיצונה.

אבלוס העיר (שורות 72-74)

ba'ūlāt arba'i / lišānu aḫītu // atmê la mitḫurti / āšibūte šadê u māti
mala irte'u nūr ilāni bēl gimri
ša ina zikir Aššur bēlīya ina mēzez šibirrīya ašlula
pâ ištēn ušaškinma // ušarmâ qerebšu.
mārī māt Aššur / mūdûte inî kalama
ana šūḫuz ṣibitte / palāḫ ili u šarri *aklī šāpirī uma''iršunūti.*

ברכת המלך (שורה 75)

ilāni āšibūte šamê erṣetim u āli šâšu qibītī imgurūma //
epēš āli u šulbur qerbīšu išrukūnni ana dārīš

קללה לפוגע במעשי המלך ובדיוקנו (שורות 76-77)

ša epšet qātīya unakkarūma / bunnanīya usaḫḫû
uṣurāt eṣṣiru ušamsaku / simatēya upaššaṭu
Aššur Šamaš Adad u ilāni āšib libbīšu
šumšu zērāšu ina māti lilqutūma / ina šaplān nakrīšu ušēšibūšu kamis

אכלוס העיר (שורות 72-74)

תושבי ארבע (כנפות הארץ), (דוברי) לשון זרה, דוברי (שפה ש)אין לה שווה (=בלתי ניתנת לתרגום), יושבי ההר והארץ,
כל שרעה אותם אור האלים (שַמַש), אדון הכול,
ששָביתי בעוז מַטֵי בדבר אשור אדוני,
שמתי להם 'פה אחד' והושבתי (אותם) בתוכה.
בני ארץ אשור, יודעי חכמות כולן,
(כדי) ללמד התנהגות טובה של יראת האל והמלך
שלחתים (להיות) מפקחים ושולטים (מדריכים).

ברכת המלך (שורה 75)

האלים יושבי השמים והארץ ו(יושבי) העיר ההיא קיבלו את דבריי,
והעניקו לי לעולם את עשיית העיר ואת ההזדקנות בקרבה.

קללה לפוגע במעשי המלך ובדיוקנו (שורות 76-77)

אשר ישנה את מעשי ידיי ויעשה את קלסתר פניי לבלתי מוכר,
(ואשר) יבטל (את) הצורות שיצרתי וימחק את סימני ההיכר שלי,
אשור, שַמַש, אַדַד והאלים היושב(ים) בקרבו
ילקטו את שמו וזרעו מהארץ, ויושיבוהו בכריעה תחת אויביו.

נספח ב

השפה המיוחדת

אלה המילים והביטויים הנדירים והמיוחדים המופיעים בתיאור הבנייה:

שורה 35: *uḫummī zaqrūti*

צורת תואר הפועל *uḫummiš*, 'כמו הר', מתועדת היטב כמטפורה ליציבות כיסא המלכות, אך הצורה השמנית העצמאית מופיעה רק ברשימות לקסיקליות, פעמיים אצל סרגון ועוד במקום אחד.

שורה 36: *kigallum šuḫrubtu*

kigallum מלשון *kikallû* במשמעות 'אדמה מוזנחת'. זו מילה טכנית שאולה משומרית ומופיעה רק בתעודות כלכליות.

šuḫrubtu צורת שפעל הגזורה מן הפועל הנפוץ *ḫarābu*. צורה זו מופיעה רק כאן ובטקסט אחד אחר.

שורה 37: *īnî tamerti lā kuppi karattu petêma*

karattu היא מילה יחידאית.

שורה 38: *le'i inî kalama*

inû במשמעות 'ידע טכני' באה רק בכתובות סרגון ופעם אחת אצל אשורבניפל.

שורה 39: *tillenû simat šarrūti sunnunu rāṭīšun*

tillenû היא מילה יחידאית ופירושה איננו ידוע. על סמך הקבלה בין הצירוף שבכתובת ובין אנומה אֶלִש (לוח ג, שורה 135) ייתכן שהיא מילה ליין או למשקה.

sunnunu היא צורת בניין D של *sanānu*, המופיעה רק ברשימות לקסיקליות. צורת בניין D מופיעה רק כאן ובאנומה אֶלִש (לוח ג, שורה 135) בצירוף זהה, וייתכן שכתובתנו נסמכת על הכתוב שם. לפי פוקס ([לעיל, הערה 9] על אתר), המילה מופיעה עוד פעם אחת בכתובתנו (שורה 47) במקום שרגילים לקרוא *zunnunu*.

שורה 40: *atmû rēšēte* – ביטוי יחידאי המופיע ברשימה לקסיקלית *Malku: šarru* עם *napḫar ṣalmāt qaqqadim*. הופעת המילה *atmû* בטור ה־*malku* דווקא יכולה לשמש סימן שהיא שאולה.

שם: *ina zabāl karāni akû la naḫaršuše*

naḫaršušu מופיעה רק כאן ובטקסט אחד אחר. ייתכן שפירושה נוחר או מגהק.

שורה 42: *ḫatê unnāte*

ḫatû היא מילה נדירה וקשה לפירוש. מילון שיקגו (CAD, Ḫ, s. v. *ḫatû* B, p. 152a) משאיר את הביטוי בלא תרגום, אך פון זודן (*AHw*, p. 336b) רושם את הצירוף הזה בערך *ḫatû* II, שהוא מקשר עם השורש העברי חת"ו (והכוונה בוודאי לחת"ה). הוא רושם עוד שתי היקרויות של המילה.

unnātu, שהוא ציון לסוג של אדמה או קרקע, מופיע רק ברשימות לקסיקליות ובכתובות של סרגון. רקעו הלשוני איננו ידוע.

שורה 43: *Šamaš dikugal ilāni*

dikugal היא מילה פיוטית השאולה משומרית.

שורה 47: *ša ina qibīt Lugal-abzu bēl nēmeqi tašimta sunnunūma malû niklāti*

Lugal-abzu הוא כינוי פיוטי לאֶאָ.

שורה 48: *Ninmenanna bānīt ilāni*

השם *Ninmenanna* הוא צורה מורחבת של *Ninmenna* והוא כינוי לאלה נינגל.

שורה 51: *šāyyāmanūtu* – 'קנייה', צורה יחידאית הגזורה מן הפועל *šâmu* 'לקנות'.

שורה 52: *aššu riggāte lā šubšî*

riggatu היא צורה יחידאית של *raggu*.

שורה 53: *ana Šigga u Lugal-dingirra dayyinūte tēnišēte talimāni ina tēmēqi ušaqqīma*

Lugal-dingirra הוא כינוי פיוטי לאדד.

talimānu במשמעות 'שתי ידיים' היא צורה מקוצרת ויחידאית של המילה הנדירה *atulimānu*, המופיעה רק ברשימות לקסיקליות ובכתובת אחת של אשורבניפל.

שורה 54: SUG *Dimgalkalamma* – בית מקדש בלתי ידוע לאלה *Šaʾuška*, אלת נינוה.

על המקדש בדֵר ל(אל) אִשְׁתָּרָן בשם É.dim.gal.kalam.ma ראה A. R. George, *House Most High: The Temples of Ancient Mesopotamia*, Winona Lake, Ind. 1993, p. 76, No. 166

שורה 55: *nābī ṣīrūti bēlīya*

nābu במשמעות 'אל' היא מילה נדירה המופיעה רק כאן, ברשימות לקסיקליות וכרכיב בשמות פרטיים, והיא מילה עילמית.

שורה 56: *nannûššun lā mušpēlu attakilma*

nannû במשמעות 'מצווה' מופיעה רק כאן ועוד בשני מקומות. אחד מהם הוא תפילה לאלה *Nanâ*, וייתכן שהיא מופיעה שם כלשון נופל על לשון המשחק עם שם האלה נַנַּ. בהמשך הפסקה מוזכר אל הירח (*Nanna(r)*), ייתכן אפוא שגם כאן יש משחק מילים בבחירת המילה הנדירה.

שורה 57: *ina Ṣītaš araḫ bīn Daragal*

Ṣītaš הוא כינוי לחודש סיוון, ומחוץ לטקסט לקסיקלי הוא מופיע רק פה. עצם השימוש בשם חודש בכתב הברתי מפורש ולא בלוגוגרם הוא נדיר.

Daragal הוא כינוי לאנליל.

bīn Daragal הוא כינוי לסין. *bīnu* היא מילה פיוטית ל'בן' במקום *māru*.

שורה 62: *parakkī rašdūti*

המילה *rašādu* והצורה *šuršudu* במשמעות 'ייסוד' הן מילים נפוצות, אך צורת שם התואר *rašdu* מופיעה רק פה ובטקסט מקביל של סרגון ואולי באפוס של תֻּכֻּלְתִּ־נִנֻרְתַּ.

שורה 71: *adušsu* – 'חומה'. מילה המופיעה רק פה וברשימה לקסיקלית.

שורה 74: *inu* – 'חכמת מעשה', חכמה מיוחדת לבעלי מלאכה מסוימת. היא מופיעה פעמים מספר בכתובות סרגון ופעם אחת בכתובת של אשורבניפל. על המיוחדות שבמילה זו עמד חיים תדמור במאמרו 'עיר־מלך ועיר־קודש באשור ובבל' (לעיל, הערה 38), עמ' 201.

שם: *ana šūḫuz ṣibitte*

ṣibittu היא מילה שכיחה, אך בהוראת 'התנהגות נכונה' היא מופיעה רק בכתובות סרגון ואולי עוד בשני מקומות.

גם החלק הראשון של הכתובת (שורות 1–33) איננו נקי מלשונות מיוחדות ונדירות אך במידה פחותה, ואלה הן:

שורה 1: *baʾʾit Aššur* – מבוקש על־ידי האל אשור. תואר מלכות יחידאי.

שורה 21: *sandâniš* – כמו לוכד ציפורים. שם תואר גזור מ־*ušandû*. מופיע רק כאן ועוד בכתובת אחת של סרגון.

שורה 22: *armaḫu* – ׳סבך׳. המילה מופיעה רק ברשימות לקסיקליות. כנראה, מילה זרה.

שם: *gišginiš* – כמו מטה המשמש נשק. המילה *gišginû* שאולה משומרית ושוב מופיעה רק בשתי כתובות של תגלת־פלאסר הראשון. כאן היא שם תואר.

שורה 24: *pulungēšun* – ׳גבולם׳. צורה פיוטית נדירה ל־*pulukku*. מתוך ארבע היקרויות רק כאן מופיע אנפוף ל־/gg/ < /ng/.

שורה 25: *nabāsiš* – כמו צמר אדום. המילה *nabāsu*, ׳צמר אדום׳, מופיעה תמיד בהשוואות אחרי *kīma*, ורק סרגון בכתובתנו ועוד במקום אחד משתמש בה כבתואר פועל.

שורה 26: *nābiʾu* – ׳מנהיג׳. לפי פון זודן (*AHw*, p. 779), בינוני פועל מ־*nepû*. הצורה מופיעה רק כאן וברשימה לקסיקלית.

שורה 28: *napādiš* – מילה לא מובנת המופיעה רק כאן ועוד בכתובת אחת של סרגון.

שורה 30: *maʾû* – ׳שליט׳. מילה יחידאית. לפי מילון שיקגו (CAD, M/1, p. 435b), ייתכן שהיא קשורה בפועל *muʾû*, ׳להלל׳.

שורה 32: *bārānû* – ׳מורד׳. המילה גזורה מ־*bārtu*, ׳מרד׳, והיא מופיעה שלוש פעמים אצל מלכי אשור האחרונים – סנחריב, אסרחדון ואשורבניפל – אך הופעתה הראשונה היא כאן, ואולי היא המצאה של סופרי סרגון.

שורה 33: *pāru* – ׳עור׳. מילה שאולה משומרית. היקרויותיה רק כאן וברשימות לקסיקליות.

שם: *illuriš* – כמו צמח ה־*illuru*. שם הצמח שכיח, אך בצורת תואר הפועל הוא בא רק כאן ועוד בכתובת אחת של סרגון.

שם: *usīmūma* – צבע בצבע אדום. פועל בבניין D גזור מ־*siāmu*. המילה שכיחה בבניין G, אך בבניין D היא מופיעה רק כאן ועוד בשני טקסטים שאחד מהם איננו ברור.

אסרחדון, מצרים ושוּבְּרִיָה[*]

פוליטיקה ותעמולה

מאת

ישראל אפעל

פתיחה

בחורף 673 לפסה״נ, בסוף שנת שבע לאסרחדון, יצא צבא אשור לכבוש את מצרים. המסע הסתיים בתבוסה שאל נכון הייתה מן הקשות שנחלה אשור מעולם.[1] כמה חודשים אחר כך יצא אסרחדון נגד שובריה, ממלכה קטנה

* מראי המקום לכתובות אסרחדון רשומים לפי מהדורת בורגר (R. Borger, *Die Inschriften Asarhaddons, Königs von Assyrien*, Graz 1956), כתובות אשורבניפל רשומות לפי מהדורת שטרק (M. Streck, *Assurbanipal und die letzten assyrischen Könige bis zum Untergange Ninivehs*, Leipzig 1916) והכרוניקות לפי מהדורת גרייסון (A.K. Grayson, *Assyrian and Babylonian Chronicles*, Locust Valley, N.Y. 1975) אלא אם כן צוין אחרת.

1 העדות הוודאית היחידה על כישלון המסע הראשון למצרים באה בכרוניקה הבבלית שבה כתוב ׳שנת 7 (לאסרחדון), ה׳ באדר. חיל אשור הוכה במצרים׳ (Chron. 1 iv 16). בכרוניקת אסרחדון על אותה שנה נאמר ׳שנת 7, ח׳ באדר. צבא אשור [...] אל ^{uru}*Šá-amîlê*^{meš}׳ (Chron. 14:20). להשקפה כי ^{uru}*Šá-amîlê*^{meš} אינו אלא גלגול של Silê ראה G. Fecht, 'Zu den Namen ägyptischer Fürsten und Städte in den Annalen des Assurbanipal und der Chronik des Asarhaddon', *Mitteilungen des deutschen archäologischen Instituts, Abteilung Kairo*, 16 (1958), pp. 116–119. ניסיון הרמוניזציה בין שני הכתובים כרוך בקשיים אפיגרפיים ופונטיים (ראה A. Spalinger, 'Esarhaddon and Egypt: An Analysis of the First Invasion of Egypt', *Orientalia*, 43 [1974], pp. 300–301). אף ראוי לשים לב שבכרוניקת אסרחדון לא הוזכרה כל מפלה של צבא אשור במצרים. גישה אחרת קושרת את יעד המסע של צבא אשור, על־פי כרוניקת אסרחדון, עם העיר ^{uru}*Šá-amîlê*^{meš} אשר באזור בית־אַמֻּכַּנ שבדרום בבל (M. Dietrich, *Die Aramäer Südbabyloniens in der Sargonidenzeit (700–648)*, Neukirchen-Vluyn 1970, pp. 19, 39, 56 note 1). עיר זו הייתה מקום מושבו של מושל בית־אַמֻּכַּנ בימי אסרחדון. מהשקפה זו נובע בהכרח שצבא אשור פעל בה בעת בשני מקומות שהיו מרוחקים כאלף ק״מ זה מזה, אלא שהשקפה זו גם היא קשה. הערכת ההבדל בין הכתובים הנ״ל יש לעשות מתוך בחינה מקפת של היחס הטקסטואלי בין שתי הכרוניקות, ותוצאותיה רחוקות מהכרעה; ראה J.A. Brinkman, 'The Babylonian Chronicle Revisited', in T. Abusch, J. Huehnergard & P. Steinkeller (eds.), *Lingering over Words: Studies in Ancient Near Eastern Literature in Honor of W.L. Moran*, Atlanta 1990, esp. pp. 91–94. המסע הראשון למצרים לא היה המבצע הכושל היחיד של צבא אסרחדון. בכרוניקות

ששכנה לרגלי הרי הטאורוס, ממזרח לנהר חידקל העליון וממערב לימת ואן.[2] לפי ה׳מכתב לאל׳ של אסרחדון, עילת המלחמה בשובריה הייתה המקלט שהעניק מלכה לפליטים פוליטיים אשוריים וסירובו להסגירם לידי מלך אשור למרות דרישות חוזרות ונשנות אליו בעניין הזה.[3] ב׳מכתב לאל׳ נמסר כי משנוכח מלך שובריה שמלך אשור אינו מסתפק במגעים דיפלומטיים אלא עולה על ארצו עם צבאו מיהר להצהיר על כניעה מוחלטת ומידית. אולם אסרחדון דחה את המחוות הנוגעות ללב של מלך שובריה ומחץ את ארצו ביד קשה: צר על אֻפֻּמֻ בירתו וכבשה, הגלה רבים מתושבי הממלכה, חילק אותה לפחוות והסב את שמותיהן של עשרות מעריה.

שובריה נכבשה בחודש טבת (או באדר, ראה להלן, עמ׳ 58), בשנת 8 לאסרחדון (672 לפסה״נ). 16-14 חודשים אחר כך, בניסן שנת 10 למלכותו (671 לפסה״נ), שב אסרחדון ועלה על מצרים.[4] הפעם עלה בידו להכות את חילו של תרהקה (בן השושלת הכ״ה, הנובית), להשתלט על הדלתא של הנילוס וללכוד את מוף הבירה. עם ההצלחה הצבאית הזאת התחיל שלטונה של אשור במצרים, שלטון שנמשך כעשרים שנה. בכתובות אסרחדון נמסר

ובמכתבי שאלה לאל שַׁמַשׁ מתועד מסע שנערך בשנת 6 לאסרחדון (675/4 לפסה״נ) נגד מֻגַּלֻ שליט מֶלִד (ראה Chron. 1 iv 10; Chron. 14:15; SAA IV 3–5, 9; בכרוניקות כתוב רק על היציאה למסע אך לא נמסרו תוצאותיו). משתיקת הכתובות המלכותיות בנוגע למסע זה ומהזכרת מֻגַּלֻ במכתב אל אסרחדון משנת 671 לפסה״נ (השווה אל SAA X 351) מסתבר כי המסע לא נסתיים בהצלחה. עם זה, אפשר שהמסע למֶלִד היה מצומצם בהיקפו (מן המכתבים אפשר להבין שהיה בפיקוד הרב־סריס), ועל כן גם רישום כישלונו היה קטן יחסית, ואילו כישלון המסע למצרים לא יכול להיות קטן מחמת התנאים הגאוגרפיים שהתנהל בהם. כאמור, מצוי תיעוד לא־ספרותי על המסע נגד מֻגַּלֻ, ואולם עד כה לא נתגלו תעודות לא־ספרותיות על המסע הראשון של אסרחדון למצרים.

2 על שובריה כמדינת ספר בגבולה הצפוני של האימפריה האשורית ועל תולדותיה במאות התשיעית-השביעית לפסה״נ ראה B.J. Parker, *The Mechanics of Empire: The Northern Frontier of Assyria as a Case Study in Imperial Dynamics*, Helsinki 2001, pp. 230–246

3 Gbr. II i 16, 21–22, 29–30. לפי Gbr. I 3, הפליטים שמדובר בהם היו אישים בעלי מעמד נכבד במערכת השלטון האשורית, שהיו אופוזיציה לאסרחדון, שלא כעריקים סתם שנמלטו מאשור לשובריה מפני עבודת המס וחובת השירות בצבא (על האחרונים כתב פרקר [לעיל, הערה 2], עמ׳ 233, 242-243). ליכטי, המזהה את הפליטים הנדונים עם יריבי אסרחדון – אֶחיו ובראשם אַרְד־מֻלִּשׁ – שעמם נאבק למן ראשית מלכותו, משער שהאחים ותומכיהם נמלטו בשנת 680 לפסה״נ לאֻרַרְטֻ (לאחר שאסרחדון גבר על מתנגדיו ועלה למלוכה), ואחר כך נאלצו לברוח משם לשובריה (עם תומכיהם מאנשי אֻרַרְטֻ) מחשש ששלטונות אֻרַרְטֻ יסגירום לידי אסרחדון (E. Leichty, 'Esarhaddon's "Letter to the Gods"', in M. Cogan & I. Eph'al [eds.], *Ah, Assyria...: Studies in Assyrian History and Ancient Near Eastern Historiography Presented to Hayim Tadmor*, Jerusalem 1991, pp. 52–57). בכך הוא גם מסביר את הצורך לכתוב לאלים דין וחשבון מפורט על המסע נגד שובריה ואת פעילותו של אסרחדון, כחודשיים לאחר סיום אותו מסע, להסדרת ירושת מלכותו בין שני בניו.

4 בחישוב זמן זה הובא בחשבון ששנת 8 לאסרחדון הייתה מעוברת ונכלל בה חודש אדר שני.

כי לאחר הכיבוש נלקח במצרים שלל רב, הוגלו גולים (בהם בני משפחת המלוכה ובכללם אֶשַׁנְחֻרֻ יורש העצר) ובעלי מקצועות נחשבים (רופאים, מגידי עתידות, חרטומים, משביעי נחשים וחרשי מתכת לסוגיהם ועוד), מונו מושלים ופקידים בכירים, הוטלו מסים שנתיים והוסבו שמות ערים.

מאמר זה מבקש להציע אינטרפרטציה פוליטית לתיאורי מסעו השני של אסרחדון למצרים ולמלחמתו בשובריה מתוך תשומת לב מיוחדת לפעילות התעמולתית והספרותית שנלוותה אליהם.[5] לא יידונו כאן המהלכים האופרטיביים של המלחמות הללו ואף לא מדיניותו של אסרחדון כלפי מצרים לאחר כיבושה.[6]

בדוננו במסעות אסרחדון לכיבוש מצרים עלינו לזכור כי קודם שהוחל בניצול המנוע להנעת צבאות ולהספקת מים בזירת המזרח התיכון הייתה יכולת תנועתם של צבאות במדבר סיני מוגבלת מחמת הקושי להשקותם. קשיי המעבר הודגשו במיוחד כאשר היו קצותיהן של דרכי הרוחב שבמדבר בשליטתם של גופים מדיניים־צבאיים יריבים. בצליחת מדבר סיני שצלח צבא שהתעתד להילחם במבואות ארץ היישוב שמעבר לו היה אפוא משום סיכון גבוה. אם נכשל בקרב, לא נתאפשר לו למזער את התבוסה על־ידי ניתוק מגע ונסיגה. המדבר שבעורפו הביא לידי היכחדותו.[7] כך מן הסתם תם מסעו הראשון של אסרחדון למצרים.

מושג על התוצאות הצבאיות והפוליטיות האפשריות של כישלון כזה יתקבל מעיון במפלת נבוכדנאצר מלך בבל במסעו למצרים בשנת 601 לפסה״נ. בעטייה של מפלה זו נאלץ נבוכדנאצר לעמול שנתיים ומעלה על שיקום צבאו, וזעזועים פוליטיים חמורים פקדו חלקים של האימפריה הבבלית שנים

5 לרווחתם של סופרי אסרחדון, החלטה (שנתקבלה בתחילת מלכותו) שלא לציין בכתובותיו ההיסטוריות את מסעי המלחמה לפי מספרם הסידורי או לפי שנת המלוכה (*palû*) שבה נערכו – כפי שהיה נהוג בכתובות מלכי אשור שקדמו לאסרחדון – פטרה אותם מן הצורך להתמודד עם בעיית הדיווח על המסע שנכשל ואפשרה להם להתעלם ממנו בחיבוריהם. השווה, למשל, אל הדרך שבה התמודדו סופרי סנחריב עם אי־כיבוש ירושלים (ח׳ תדמור, ׳מלחמת סנחריב ביהודה: בחינות היסטוריוגראפיות והיסטוריות׳, ציון, נ [תשמ״ה], עמ׳ 74–78) ואל הדרך שנקטו סופרי סרגון כדי ליצור תמונה של הצלחות רצופות מדי שנה בשנה, אף שרציפות כזאת לא הייתה קיימת בפועל (H. Tadmor, 'The Campaigns of Sargon II: A Chronological-historical Study', *JCS*, 12 [1958], pp. 22–40, 77–100). חריגה בכתובות אסרחדון מן הנוהג הנדון, היינו ציון מספרם של מסעי צבא, יש במהדורת הדין וחשבון שחובר לאחר כיבוש מצרים במסע השני של אסרחדון נגדה. במהדורה זו שרדו ציוני ׳המסע השני׳ (נגד צידון; ראה Nin. S 2 [תדמור (להלן, הערה 18)] = Borger, Nin. D והבחנותיו של בורגר בעמ׳ 38, 49) ו׳המסע העשירי׳ (נגד מצרים; ראה Frt. F obv. 6).

6 על המהלכים הצבאיים והמִנהליים של אסרחדון במלחמתו נגד מצרים ועל תיאוריהם בכתובותיו ראה A. Spalinger, 'Esarhaddon and Egypt: An Analysis of the First Invasion of Egypt', *Orientalia*, 43 (1974), pp. 295–326

7 לעניין המשמעויות הלוגיסטיות והאסטרטגיות של מדבר סיני כחיץ בין ׳הסהר הפורה׳ ובין מצרים עד מלחמת העולם הראשונה עיין I. Ephʿal, *The Ancient Arabs*, Jerusalem–Leiden 1982, pp. 137–142; א׳ גלילי, מערכת רפיח 217 לפסה״נ: טקטיקה, אסטרטגיה ולוגיסטיקה בעולם ההלניסטי, ירושלים תשנ״ט, עמ׳ 194–212.

רבות.[8] אפשר להעריך כי מטבע הדברים תוצאה דומה הייתה צפונה בכישלון מסעו הראשון של אסרחדון למצרים. אולם כפי שנראה, אסרחדון – שלא כנבוכדנאצר – הגיב במהירות ובנחישות דעת ועלה בידו להתאושש ולכבוש את מצרים התחתית בתוך כשנתיים ומחצה לאחר המפלה הקשה.

אולם בתחילה היה על אסרחדון להראות כי עם כישלון המסע הראשון במבואות מצרים לא חוסלה עצמתה של אשור. פעילותו הנמרצת וחסרת הרחמים כלפי שובריה מתפרשת כמיועדת להזכיר לכול – לאויבים חיצונים ובייחוד לנתינים וליריבים־בכוח בפנים האימפריה[9] – כי כוחה של אשור עמה וכי עונש קשה נכון לכל מתמרד ומזלזל בשַליטה.[10] שובריה לא הייתה אלא ממלכה קטנה, ונראה שמיגורה לא היה אתגר חריג שמעבר ליכולתה הצבאית של אשור לאחר המפלה במצרים. ואכן, צבא אשור לא התמהמה ועלה על שובריה לאחר התארגנות מהירה. למן המפלה במצרים ועד לכיבוש שובריה חלפו 10–12 חודש.

החיבורים האשוריים המצויים בידינו מן הסוג המכונה 'מכתבים לאל' מעטים ביותר, ועל סמך זאת אפשר לקבוע כי לא לאחר כל מסע מלחמה נכתבו חיבורים כאלה אלא לעתים נדירות ולרגל אירועים צבאיים שיוחסה להם חשיבות מיוחדת. כזה הוא ה'מכתב לאל' של סרגון, שנכתב אחרי המכה שהנחית על צבא אֻרַרְטֻ, יריב שעצמתו הייתה ניכרת. כאמור, אי אפשר לראות בממלכת שובריה יריב בסדר גודל דומה. נכון יותר לקבוע כי כשם שכיבוש שובריה היה התגובה הפוליטית על כישלונו הצבאי של אסרחדון במצרים, כך היה ה'מכתב לאל' שלו תגובה ספרותית־תעמולתית הולמת על כישלון זה.[11] יצירה זו מתאפיינת בתכונות ספרותיות

8 ראה I. Eph'al, 'Nebuchadnezzar the Warrior: Remarks on his Military Achievements', *IEJ*, 53 (2003), pp. 180–183

9 לדעת א"ל אופנהיים, הממוענים האמִתיים של ה'מכתב לאל' היו תושבי העיר ההיסטורית אשור, שנהנתה ממעמד מיוחד אצל המלכות והייתה בה אופוזיציה ניכרת לאסרחדון. לפי תפיסה זו נועד התיאור הנרחב של היחס הקשוח כלפי מלך שובריה להמחיש ליסודות העוינים שבעיר אשור את נחישות דעתו של אסרחדון להגיב בחומרה על כל הפרה של שבועת נאמנות לו (A.L. Oppenheim, 'Neo-Assyrian and Neo-Babylonian Empires', in H.D. Lasswell, D. Lerner & H. Speier [eds.], *Propaganda and Communication in World History*, I: *The Symbolic Instrument in Early Times*, Honolulu 1979, esp. pp. 125ff.).

10 במכתב שאלה לשַמַש (SAA IV 18) שאל אסרחדון אם רוּסָה (השני) מלך אֻרַרְטֻ ובעלי בריתו הקימרים עתידים לתקוף את שובריה ולספח לתחום שליטתם מצודות שבגבולה (לא ידוע מתי נכתבה תעודה זו, אך ברור שקדמה לכיבוש שובריה בידי אסרחדון, שאחריו חדלה מלהיות ישות ממלכתית וחולקה לשתי פחוות). ייתכן אפוא שבכיבוש שובריה הקדים אסרחדון את מלך אֻרַרְטֻ ואף אותת לו שלא ימהר לנצל את חולשת אשור לאחר הכישלון במצרים.

11 ציון המקור הנדון כ'מכתב לאל' משמש כאן כמקובל בחקר כתובות אסרחדון. להסתייגות מהגדרתו כ'מכתב לאל' ראה L.D. Levine, 'Observations on "Sargon's Letter to the Gods"', *Eretz-Israel*, 27 (2003), p. 117*, note 6. מהסתייגות זו נגזרות מסקנות לעניין המטרות ההיסטוריוגרפיות של היצירה, ואני נוטה לקבלן. יצוין שעל אף החשיבות התעמולתית והפוליטית הניכרת שיוחסה בשעתה לכיבוש שובריה

מיוחדות.[12] בסגנונה ובפירוט הפעולות שתוארו בה שימשה דגם שהשפיע על מהדורת הדין וחשבון של המסע השני לכיבוש מצרים. בכתובים ב׳מכתב לאל׳ ובמהדורת הדין וחשבון על הפעולות נגד שובריה ומצרים ניכר דמיון בתיאורי תשועת מרדוך לצבא אשור בשלבים הגורליים של פעילותו, בפירוט קבוצות הגולים לפי מקצועותיהם, בחלוקת הארץ לאחר כיבושה למחוזות משנה ובהסבת שמות ערים. שתי היצירות הללו נכתבו בתוך שנתיים לכל היותר.

כיבוש מצרים היה הישג צבאי, כלכלי ופוליטי כביר שנשא גם פֵּרות תעמולתיים. לאחר הניצחון נטל אסרחדון לעצמו את התואר ׳מלך מלכי מצרים, פתרוס וכוש׳[13] (בווריאנט של כתובת Klch. D הוא מוכתר ׳מלך מצרים, מביס מלך מֶלוּחָה׳[14]). תואר זה, המבטא הישגיות ועצמה, מופיע לא רק בכתובותיו ההיסטוריות אלא גם נחקק על פסלי החיות (colossi) הגדולים שניצבו בארמונו אשר בכלח.[15] אין הוא משקף את המציאות הפוליטית כהווייתה: תחום שליטתו של אסרחדון לא השתרע הרחק מעבר למוף. מדרום למוף עדיין שלט תרהקה, שאמנם נפגע קשה משאיבד את השליטה על אזור הדלתא וכן את בנו יורש העצר ואת נשיו ואחרים מבני משפחתו שנתפסו ונלקחו לאשור, אך טרם הובס סופית. תחום השליטה האשורית במצרים לא הורחב אלא בימי אשורבניפל, שכבש את נוא מידי תרהקה ואף הביס את יורשו תַּנֻת־אַמֹן.

כעולה מן ה׳מכתב לאל׳ אין לאירוע זה זכר במונומנטים של אסרחדון שנתגלו במערב האימפריה (עיין עליהם להלן, עמ׳ 61–66). כיבוש מצרים (במסע השני נגדה) האפיל על ההישג שבכיבוש שובריה עד שפגה חשיבותו של ההישג הזה.

12 על תכונותיו של ה׳מכתב לאל׳ ועל דרך חיבורו עיין I. Ephʿal & H. Tadmor, 'Observations on Two Inscriptions of Esarhaddon: Prism Nineveh A and the Letter to the God', in Y. Amit et al. (eds.), *Essays on Ancient Israel in Its Near Eastern Context: A Tribute to N. Naʾaman*, Winona Lake, Ind. 2006, pp. 163–168

13 ראה Mnm. A obv. 16; Trb. B 5; Klch. D 3; Ass. H 5–7; והשווה גם אל Mnm. C 5–6

14 J.M. Russell, *The Writing on the Wall: Studies in the Architectural Context of Late Assyrian Palace Inscriptions*, Winona Lake, Ind. 1999, pp. 293–294. בכתובת AsBbA obv. 28–29 מוצג אסרחדון כ׳מלך מלכי תילמון, מַגַן ומֶלוּחָה׳. מצירוף מגן ומלוחה אל תילמון בכינויי הנדון בכתובת, שאין מצרים ושללה מוזכרים בה ונראה שנכתבה לפני כיבוש מצרים (על ההבחנה בין AsBbA-D ובין AsBbE-H ראה אצל בורגר, עמ׳ 78), מסתבר שהוא קשור לפעילותו של צבא אסרחדון באזור המפרץ הפרסי (המסע אל ארץ בַּזוּ?); להזכרת תילמון, מגן ומלוחה במקורות לא־ספרותיים מסופוטמיים מן התקופה הקדם־שושלתית עד המאה השביעית לפסה״נ בזיקה ברורה לאזור המפרץ הפרסי והאוקיינוס ההודי ראה W. Heimpel, 'Das Untere Meer', *ZA*, 77 (1987), pp. 22–91. לעומת זאת תוארו של אסרחדון המוזכר בכתובת Klch. D קשור בבירור לכיבוש מצרים (השווה גם אל Frt. F 7(?), 15; וכיוצא בו בכתובת אשורבניפל A i 52); על משמעות מגן ומלוחה (בלי תילמון) ככינויים למצרים וכוש עיין W. Heimpel, 'Magan', *RLA*, 7, 1987–1990, p. 196; idem, 'Meluḫḫa', *RLA*, 8, 1993–1997, p. 55

15 ראה ראסל (לעיל, הערה 14), עמ׳ 149–151, 293–294.

המסגרת הכרונולוגית

כדי להיטיב לחוש ולהבין את מהלך פעילותו הפוליטית, הצבאית והתעמולתית של אסרחדון למן מסעו הראשון למצרים ועד למותו חשוב לתת את הדעת לגורם הזמן בהחלטותיו ובדרך התנהלות מהלכיו. לשם כך ראוי להקדים ולהתבונן בנתונים הכרונולוגיים שבידינו על המהלכים האלה. הנתונים עולים ממקורות מכמה סוגים, שדרגת אמינותם אינה אחידה. כאשר אין התאמה בין הנתונים שבכרוניקות הבבליות (המאוחרות לימי אסרחדון) ובין אלה שבכתובותיו נראה שיש להעדיף את הנתונים בני זמנו. לנוחות הקריאה וכדי למנוע טעות בהתאמת התאריך האשורי למניין השנים המקובל לפסה"נ יצוינו האירועים לפי מניין שנות מלכותו של אסרחדון:

שנת 7	אדר	תבוסת צבא אשור במצרים. כישלון המסע הראשון לכיבושה.[א]
שנת 8	טבת(?)/אדר	כיבוש שובריה.[ב]
שנת 9	ניסן-אייר	השבעת אמונים לאשורבניפל ולשַמַש־שֻם־אֻכִּן כיורשיה העתידים של מלכות אסרחדון.[ג]
שנת 10	ניסן	יציאה לכיבוש מצרים (המסע השני).[ד]
	תמוז/תשרי	ניצחון במצרים. כיבוש מוף.[ה]
שנת 12	י' מרחשון	אסרחדון מת בדרכו למצרים.[ו]

א Chron. 1 iv 16. על בעייתיות הכתוב ב־Chron. 14:20 עיין לעיל, הערה 1.

ב השווה אל 'שנת 8 לאסרחדון. טבת, יום שבור (*ḫepi*; היינו '[הלוח שממנו הועתק הטקסט] שבור'). ארץ שובריה נלכדה ונבוזה. בכסלו שללה הובא לארץ' (Chron. 1 iv 19–21); 'אדר (שנת 8, השווה אל שורה 23), י' (בחודש). חילות אשור... שובר[יה]' (Chron. 14:24). הכתוב בשורה 21 בכרוניקה הבבלית (Chron. 1) – 'כסלו, שללה (של שובריה?) הובא לארץ' – קשה (הבאת שלל שובריה לערי אשור, כמצוין ב'מכתב לאל' [Gbr. II iii 21–22] מתקבלת על הדעת. לעומת זאת הכתוב על הבאתו לארץ שבדרום בבל מעורר תמיהה; ראה ברינקמן [לעיל, הערה 1], עמ' 94). על סמך הציון כי המקור שעמד לעיני מחבר הכרוניקה היה קטוע אפשר שהמילה 'טבת' בשורה 19 אינה מכוונת כלל לארץ ולהבאת שלל אליה כי אם לאירוע אחר, ואין ללמוד ממנה על מועד כיבושה של שובריה. על סמך בדיקת הלוח שעליו כתובה הכרוניקה הבבלית ברינקמן מעיר עוד כי קריאת מספרי השנים 7 ו־8 אינה ודאית וכי אפשר לקראם 8 ו־9 בהתאמה (שם, עמ' 95, הערה 128). לענייננו אין לקריאה חלופית זו השפעה על קביעת הזמן שחלף ממסעו הראשון של אסרחדון למצרים ועד לכיבוש שובריה. אולם קריאה מוצעת זו של המספרים החלופיים כרוכה בקושי, שכן אין היא משאירה זמן מספיק אחרי כיבוש שובריה להכנה לקראת המסע השני למצרים.

לפי ה'מכתב לאל', הקרב המכריע על אֻפֻּמֶ, בירת שובריה, התחולל לאחר שאש פגעה בחומתה בליל כ"א בכסלו (Gbr. II ii 1–9). סביר אפוא שכיבוש שובריה הושלם זמן לא רב לאחר שנפלה בירתה. בין המפלה במצרים ובין כיבוש שובריה הבדילו אפוא 10–12 חודשים. בתוך פרק זמן זה נדרש אסרחדון לשוב ממצרים לאשור (מהלך שנמשך לא פחות מחודשיים ומחצה בתנועה מְנהלית), להיערך למסע נגד שובריה, לנוע אליה (בתנועה מְנהלית של כשבועיים נוספים) ולכבשה בפעולות שמקצתן לפחות היו כרוכות בלוחמת מצור שאף היא דורשת

זמן.[16] לוח זמנים צפוף זה מעיד על הנמרצות שבפעילות אסרחדון כלפי שובריה, שנבעה ממאמציו לשקם את מעמדה הפוליטי של אשור שנפגע פגיעה אנושה במסע הראשון נגד מצרים.

ג בכרוניקות לא נאמר דבר על שנת 9 לאסרחדון. שתיקתן בעניין שנה זו לא נבעה ממחסור במקורות וסיבתה הייתה שאכן, לא נערכה פעולה צבאית באותה שנה. הדבר עולה בבירור מתוך Frt. F obv. 1–6ff.: סוף הכתוב על הפעילות נגד שובריה ותיאור המסע השני נגד מצרים מובאים ברצף אחד בלא כל חציצה ביניהם. אותה התופעה ניכרת בטור ה של מנסרה Nin. S (השווה אל Nin. S 3 col. b; Nin. S 4 col. b אצל תדמור [להלן, הערה 18]).

ממסמכים אחדים מתברר כי בשנת 9, שבה שהה אסרחדון בארצו, הוא ייצב את שלטונו והבטיח את העברתו המסודרת לאחר מותו בהשביעו בחודשים ניסן ואייר את סופריו ואת סגל הארמון, המשמר המלכותי וקבוצות אחרות (ראה SAA II 6:664–665; שטרק, עמ׳ 2–3 וכן SAA X 6, 7[17]) וכן ארגן את הצבא לקראת המבצע הגדול של כיבוש מצרים במסע השני נגדה, והשווה אל פעילותו המצומצמת של נבוכדנאצר אחרי כישלון מסעו למצרים (אפעל [לעיל, הערה 8], עמ׳ 183–185).

ד Chron. 1 iv 23; השווה כיו״ב Chron. 14:25; Frt. F obv. 10

ה Chron. 1 iv 24–25; Chron. 14:26. לפי הכרוניקה הבבלית, הוכה צבא מצרים בשלושה קרבות־שדה בימים ג׳, ט״ז, י״ח בתמוז, ואילו בכרוניקת אסרחדון מדובר בתבוסה מצרית גדולה ביום ג׳ בתשרי. מן ההבדל בשמות החודשים נגזר משך הזמן שעמד לרשות אסרחדון כדי לצור על צור בדרך התקדמותו למצרים (על מצור זה ראה Frt. F obv. 12–14): לפי הנתון שבכרוניקה הבבלית אפשר להקצות למצור שבועיים-שלושה לכל היותר, ואילו לפי כרוניקת אסרחדון הוא יכול להימשך כמעט שלושה חודשים. ראוי לציין כי תאריך כתיבתה של מנסרה Nin. S, גם אם הוא תאריך ׳מכוון׳ (ראה להלן, עמ׳ 61), מאשש את נוסחת הכרוניקה הבבלית בנוגע למועד כיבוש מוף.

בפתיחה לשבר המנסרה Borger, Nin. E, col. ii = Nin. S 4 col. v מדובר בניצחון אסרחדון בקרב שהיה במצרים ביום ג׳ בחודש ששמו לא שרד. לפי אסטלת זנג׳ירלי (שורות 37–43), ארכה ההתקדמות מאִשְׁחֻפְּרִ עד מוף 15 יום. מצירוף שני הנתונים הכרונולוגיים הללו מסתבר, שהקרב הנזכר בשבר המנסרה הנדון נערך באִשְׁחֻפְּרִ ביום ג׳ בחודש (תמוז), והקרב על מוף נערך ביום י״ח בתמוז (כנמסר בכרוניקה הבבלית).

מהפרש הזמן שבין קרב־השדה השלישי (י״ח בתמוז) ובין כיבוש מוף (ארבעה ימים אחר כך, לפי הכתוב בכרוניקה הבבלית) מסתבר שלא התפתח קרב מצור של ממש על מוף וכי בעצם לא היה בידי אסרחדון סיפק להתקין את אמצעי ההבקעה המפורטים באסטלת זנג׳ירלי (Mnm. A rev. 41–43). מתקבל יותר על הדעת שמחבר הטקסט שעל האסטלה, אשר כתב על לכידת מוף ב׳חצי יום׳, השתמש כאן בנוסחה טכנית מקובלת (המוכרת, למשל, מתיאור כיבושן של ערי יהודה בידי סנחריב; ראה לקנביל [להלן, הערה 19], עמ׳ 32–33, iii, שורות 21–23) והוסיף עליה את הביטוי המוגזם המאדיר את הניצחון שהושג בתוך זמן קצר ביותר.

16 על משך זמנם של מסעי הצבא הארוכים והשפעתם על המִנהל האימפריאלי עיין I. Ephʿal, 'On Warfare and Military Control in the Ancient Near Eastern Empires: A Research Outline', in H. Tadmor & M. Weinfeld (eds.), *History, Historiography and Interpretation*, Jerusalem 1983, pp. 99–101

17 על השבעת חיל המשמר המדי של אסרחדון ראה M. Liverani, 'The Medes at Esarhaddon's Court', *JCS*, 47 (1995), pp. 57–62

ו Chron. 1 iv 30–31; Chron. 14:28–29. אסרחדון חי עוד 28-31 חודש אחרי כיבוש מצרים (ההפרש נוצר מתוך ההבדל בין התאריכים הנקובים בכרוניקות באשר לחודש שבו נכבשה מצרים). כל הפעילות הספרותית והתעמולתית הקשורה לכיבוש מצרים התרחשה בתוך זמן קצר יחסית זה.

תעודות שבהן נכתב על כיבוש מצרים

מהדורת הדין וחשבון

זמן קצר אחרי כיבוש מצרים נכתב דין וחשבון שתוארו בו המסע למן היציאה מאשור וההתקדמות דרך פיניקיה, ארץ ישראל ומדבר סיני, הלחימה במצרים וכיבושה וכן הפעולות שנעשו אחרי הכיבוש (לקיחת שלל, הגליה וארגון השלטון האשורי באזור הכבוש). הדין וחשבון לא הגיע לידינו בשלמותו. מה ששרד ממנו רשום בטיוטה שחלק ממנה כתוב על לוח שבור (Borger, Frt. F) ובשברי מנסרה מתומנת (Nin. S).[18]

בלוח השבור Frt. F שרדו 36 שורות בלבד. מתוארת בהן בפירוט ובנוסח ספרותי נמלץ התקדמות אסרחדון וצבאו דרך ארץ ישראל ובמדבר סיני עד אִשְׁחֻפְּרִ, מקום הקרב הראשון במבואות מצרים. בחמש השורות שלפני תיאור המסע שרד סופו של תיאור הפעולה נגד שובריה.

שלושה משברי המנסרה Nin. S מכילים פסקאות על פעילותו של אסרחדון בשובריה ובמצרים. באחד מהם, בטור ה של המנסרה, תוארה המלחמה נגד שובריה (Nin. S 3, col. b = בורגר [להלן, הערה 45], עמ' 115). בשבר אחר, שאף הוא מכיל קטע של אותו הטור, התחיל תיאור המסע השני למצרים (Borger, Nin. E, col. ii = Nin. S 4, col. b). הקטע ששרד מתחיל ביום שבו התחולל הקרב הראשון של מסע זה על אדמת מצרים.[19] בשבר השלישי, שהכיל קטעים מטורים ו-ז של המנסרה, שרדו רשימות של קבוצות גולים ממצרים לפי מקצועותיהם, של מושלים אשורים אשר הופקדו על ערים מוסבות־שם במצרים וכן פירוט המס השנתי למלך אשור וההקצבות לקרבנות לאלים שהושתו על מצרים (Nin. S 5, cols. a–b = Borger, Frt. J).[20] משחזור זה של מנסרה Nin. S מתברר שתיאור המסע למצרים והפעולות שנעשו שם בעקבותיו היה מפורט ביותר ונכללו בו לא

18 על מנסרה Nin. S ושחזורה ראה H. Tadmor, 'An Assyrian Victory Chant and Related Matters', in G. Frame (ed.), *From the Upper Sea to the Lower Sea: Studies on the History of Assyria and Babylonia in Honor of A.K. Grayson*, Leuven 2004, pp. 273–276. חלקי המנסרה מצוינים להלן לפי שיטת תדמור.

19 תיאור יציאתו של אסרחדון לקרב בשורות 1-19 דומה במידה ניכרת לתיאור הספרותי הנמלץ של יציאת סנחריב לקרב חֲלוּלֶה (השווה אל D.D. Luckenbill, *The Annals of Sennacherib*, Chicago 1924, 44:63ff.).

20 תעתיק ותרגום וכן הערות על שבר כתובת זה ראה גם H. Onasch, *Die assyrischen Eroberungen Ägyptens*, Wiesbaden 1994, pp. 31–37

פחות מ־200 שורות (מספר השורות הממוצע במנסרה אשורית מתומנת הוא 95).[21]

בסוף המנסרה רשום תאריך כתיבתה והוא מנוסח בסגנון חגיגי: 'חודש ^{itu} ^{d}MAḪ (זה לוגוגרם המציין את החודש העילמי בשביל תמוז[22]), ה־*lim*[*mu*] של..., בשנה שבה [נלכדה מוף ו]שללה [ני]שא'. אם נשלים כאן את שם האפונים [כַּנֻנַי] (הוא האפונים של שנת 10 לאסרחדון, 671/70 לפסה"נ), יהיה עלינו לומר שהפעולות במצרים המפורטות במנסרה (ובכללן ארגון ההגליה וביצועה, מינוי המושלים ולקיחת השלל המסודרת, כמתואר בכתובת), וכן הסבת שמותיהן של ערי מצרים נעשו בתוך שמונה ימים אחרי כיבוש מוף (שתאריכו, כ"ב בתמוז, נקוב בכרוניקה הבבלית). בתוך זמן קצר זה, כמובן, אף היה צריך לכתוב את המנסרה במצרים (אחר כך היה צריך להביאה לנינוה, ששם נתגלו שבריה). כיוון שלא ייתכן שכל הפעולות היו עשויות להסתיים בתוך ימים ספורים, יש להעלות את הסברה שהתאריך הנקוב לכתיבת המנסרה אינו אמִתי כי אם 'מכוון', אידאלי, בדומה לנוסחת 'שנת מלכו' של אסרחדון שנרשמה כתאריך חיבורה של 'כתובת בבל' שלו (Bab. A–G) כדי ליצור רושם כי שיקם את העיר בבל החרבה ובנאהּ מיד משהיה למלך.[23] דרך אחרת לפתרון הקושי היא לראות במילים 'בשנה שבה [נלכדה מוף ו]שללה [ני]שא' ביטוי עמום מבחינה כרונולוגית, שמשמעותו 'כאשר', כמצוי בתעודות כלכליות נֵאו־אשוריות, ולהשלים את השם החסר בנוסחת התאריך [שֻׁלְמֻ־בֵּלִי־לַשְׁמֶ], שהיה האפונים של שנת 11 לאסרחדון (670/69 לפסה"נ).[24]

עוד ראוי להזכיר כאן טבלה קטנת ממדים ופגומה בחלקה, K 8692, שבה נרשמה בסגנון אנאליסטי לקיחת שלל עצום וגולים 'שעורם שחור כזפת', בני משפחתו של שליט ששמו לא שרד בטקסט שבידינו.[25] לכתוב בטבלה זו לא נמצאה מקבילה בכתובות אסרחדון ואשורבניפל.

המונומנטים

בעקבות כיבוש מצרים וכתיבת הדין וחשבון עליו הוצבו במקומות פומביים מונומנטים של אסרחדון ועליהם כתובות אשוריות אשר הושתתו על הדין וחשבון הזה (אין ספק שנמעניהם של מוצרי תעמולה מובהקים אלו היו רבים

21 כתובות זנג'ירלי ונהר אל־כלב מכילות פסקאות שלא שרדו בשברי מהדורת הדין וחשבון שהגיעו לידינו (ראה Mnm. A rev. 40–46; Mnm. C 7–23). בהנחה שפסקאות אלו מושתתות על הדין וחשבון, אפשר להשתמש אף בהן לשחזורו.

22 ראה E. Reiner, 'Inscription from a Royal Elamite Tomb', *AfO*, 24 (1973), p. 100

23 ראה M. Cogan, 'Omens and Ideology in the Babylonian Inscription of Esarhaddon', in Tadmor & Weinfeld (above, note 16), pp. 85–87

24 ראה ח' תדמור וא' וייסרט, אצל תדמור (לעיל, הערה 18), עמ' 276.

25 ראה W.G. Lambert, 'Booty from Egypt?', *JSS*, 33 (1982), pp. 61–70. לשאלת שיוכו של טקסט זה למסעו השני של אסרחדון למצרים ראה גם אונש (לעיל, הערה 20), עמ' 25–28.

מן הקוראים הפוטנציאליים של הלוחות והמנסרות). כמה מן המונומנטים הללו נתגלו במערב האימפריה: שתי אסטלות נתגלו בתֵל ברסיפ (כיום תל אחמר), אחת בזנג׳ירלי (בירת שַׂמְאַל), תבליט של אסרחדון ועליו כתובת נמצא מגולף בסלע ליד שפך נהר אל־כלב (10 ק״מ מצפון לבירות) ושבר מצבה נתגלה בקקון (6 ק״מ מצפון־מערב לטול־כרם).[26]

אסטלות אסרחדון מזנג׳ירלי ומתל ברסיפ הן הגדולות שבאסטלות המלכים האשוריות: גובה אסטלת זנג׳ירלי 322 ס״מ (בתוספת הכן שעליו הוצבה התנשאה האסטלה לגובה 346 ס״מ). גובה אסטלות תל ברסיפ הוא 380 ו־330 ס״מ בהתאמה. שלוש האסטלות דומות במתארן: נראה בהן אסרחדון עומד, מעליו סמלי אלים ולפניו שני אנשים שקטנים ממנו (באסטלת זנג׳ירלי הם מגיעים עד ברכיו, באסטלות תל ברסיפ עד מותניו) בתנוחות תחינה. האחד – מזוקן ועל ראשו כובע קוני – עומד, והאחר – טיפוס נגרואידי חסר־זקן, על ראשו אוּרֵאוּס – כורע. באסטלות תל ברסיפ הדמויות שלפני אסרחדון מתוארות בתנועות כניעה רגילות, ואילו באסטלת זנג׳ירלי אסרחדון מתואר אוחז חבלים המחוברים בחחים לשפתותיהן, וידיה ורגליה של הדמות הנגרואידית נתונות באזיקים.[27] מקובל לזהות את הכורע עם אֶשַׁנְחֻרֻ בן תרהקה, אשר הוגלה בידי אסרחדון, כמצוין בכתובת זנג׳ירלי (שורה 43) ובכתובת נהר אל־כלב (שורה 12). אשר לדמות השנייה, העומדת, סבר תירו־דנז׳ן – על סמך הזכרת עבדמלכת בתחתיתה של אסטלת תל ברסיפ – כי זה עבדמלכת מלך צידון. אולם על־פי העדויות המפורשות שעבדמלכת

26 אסטלת זנג׳ירלי (Borger, Mnm. A): תעתיק ותרגום של הקטע הנוגע לכיבוש מצרים ולפעולות שנעשו בעקבותיו (אחור, שורות 37–50) וכן הערות ראה גם אצל אונש (לעיל, הערה 20), עמ׳ 24–29. ציור הכתובת, תעתיקה ותרגומה ראה E. Schrader, 'Inschrift Asarhaddon's, Königs von Assyrien', in von Luschan (below), pp. 30–43. לפרטים טכניים על האסטלה (כגון מקום הימצאה, גובהה ומשקלה) ראה F. von Luschan, *Ausgrabungen in Sendschirli*, I: *Einleitung und Inschriften*, Berlin 1893
אסטלה A מתל ברסיפ (Borger, Mnm. B): ציור האסטלה ופרטים טכניים עליה וכן תעתיק הכתובת ותרגומה ראה F. Thureau-Dangin & M. Dunand, *Til-Barsib*, Paris 1936, pp. 151–155. על אסטלה B ראה שם, עמ׳ 155–156.
כתובת נהר אל־כלב (Borger, Mnm. C): תצלום המונומנט וציור הכתובת וכן תעתיקה ותרגומה ראה F.H. Weissbach, *Die Denkmäler und Inschriften an der Mündung des Nahr El-Kelb*, Berlin–Leipzig 1922
על כתובת קקון ראה להלן, הערה 38.

27 אסרחדון מתואר בכתובת זנג׳ירלי (שורה 24) אוחז שליטים זרים בחח (*mukīl ṣerret maliki*). על הובלת שבויים בחבלים שבקצותיהם טבעות (חחים) המושחלות בשפתותיהם ראה גם P.E. Botta & M.E. Flandin, *Monument de Niniveh*, Paris 1849, Pl. 83. וריאנט של תיאור זה מופיע בתבליט־הסלע של אַנֻבָּנִנִ מלך הלֻלֻבִּ, שבו אֵלָה מובילה את האויבים בחחים המושחלים באפיהם; ראה J. Börker-Klähn, *Altvorderasiatische Bildstelen und vergleichbare Felsreliefs*, Mainz 1982, No. 31 (זמנו של התבליט שנוי במחלוקת החוקרים). לעניין התיאור המילולי של מה שנראה בתבליטים הנזכרים השווה אל הכתוב על מנשה בדה״ב לג:יא. על השחלת חבל בלחייו המנוקבות של אויב שנלכד (וַיְתַ׳ע בן בִּרְדַד מלך הערבים) והצגתו לראווה ראה כתובות אשורבניפל A ix 106–107 והשווה אל איוב מ:כה–כו.

נמלט מפני מלך אשור וכי ראשו הוסר מעליו והובא לאשור (Nin. A ii 71–74, iii 32–34 וכן Chron. 1 iv 67; Chron. 14:14) קשה לזהותו עם דמות המתחנן לפני מלך אשור שבתבליט. לפיכך יש הסבורים כי זה בעל, מלך צור, אשר במהלך המסע לכיבוש מצרים הושם עליו מצור מפני שבטח בתרהקה מלך מצרים ושיתף עמו פעולה (ראה Frt. F obv. 12–14). אולם ראוי לציין שבכתובות אסרחדון לא נאמר כי בעל נלכד או הוכנע. כידוע, הוא הוסיף למלוך על צור גם בימי אשורבניפל (ראה C i 24).[28]

על כל פאה משני הצדדים של אסטלות זנג׳ירלי ותל ברסיפ מגולפת דמות אדם עומד: הדמות בצד ימין מתוארת בסגנון אשורי, ואילו זו שבצד השמאלי מתוארת בסגנון בבלי. אל נכון אלה הם בניו של אסרחדון שנועדו לרשת את מלכותו: אשורבניפל ימלוך על אשור והאימפריה, ושַמַש־שֻם־אֻכִּן – על בבל.[29] שרי אשור ואנשיה הושבעו להם אמונים בניסן ובאייר, שנת 9 לאסרחדון, עשרה חודשים לפני היציאה למסע השני למצרים.[30]

באסטלת זנג׳ירלי חקוקה הכתובת מלפנים ומאחור. על אחת מאסטלות תל ברסיפ (אסטלה A אצל תירו־דנז׳ן ודינאן [לעיל, הערה 26]) חקוקה כתובת רק מלפנים, ונראה שלא הושלמה.[31] על אסטלת תל ברסיפ השנייה (אסטלה B, שם) לא נכתב דבר בוודאי מפני שאסרחדון מת קודם שהספיקו לחקוק כתובת על גבי התבליט.[32]

28 להשקפה שאין הכרח לחפש קשר ישיר בין הדמויות המתחננות שבאסטלות זנג׳ירלי ותל ברסיפ ובין התרחשויות צבאיות מסוימות במערבה של האימפריה בימי אסרחדון (ולפיכך אין צורך לזהות את הדמויות הללו עם אישים ידועים) וכן שהאסטלות מעיקרן לא נועדו להטיל מורא על הנתינים אשר במערב האימפריה ולהרתיעם מלמרוד אלא להראות באופן מרשים את עצמת אסרחדון בעיני האופוזיציה הפנימית לשלטונו ולהבטיח את ירושת המלוכה בין בניו אשורבניפל ושַמַש־שֻם־אֻכִּן – להשקפה זו ראה P.A. Miglus, 'Die Stelen des Königs Asarhaddon von Assyrien: Siegesdenkmäler oder ein politisches Vermächtnis?', *BaM*, 31 (2000), pp. 195–209. לבחינת תקפותה של השקפה זו ראוי להביא בחשבון כי האסטלות הוכנו זמן רב יחסית לאחר שהוסדרה ירושת המלוכה: השבעת הנאמנות לאשורבניפל ולאחיו הייתה באייר 672, ואילו עשיית האסטלות לא התחילה לפני סוף 671 (אחרי כיבוש מצרים ואחרי התגבשות הכתיבה המלכותית על ארגון השלטון במצרים). עצם הדבר שאין כל כתובת על אסטלה B מתל ברסיפ מקרב אל הדעת שהאסטלות נעשו סמוך למות אסרחדון (במרחשוון 669) ולפיכך לא הושלמו. ועוד זאת: אשורבניפל ושַמַש־שֻם־אֻכִּן לא הוזכרו כלל בכתוב באסטלות.

29 אשורבניפל ממוקם מימין, כיאה למעמדו הבכיר, ושַמַש־שֻם־אֻכִּן – משמאל; השווה אל SAA X 185:5–12.

30 ראה לעיל, עמ׳ 59, הערה ג. בהכללת דמויותיהם של בני אסרחדון באסטלות הנדונות אין לראות את הסיבה העיקרית להצבתן. כאמור, אין הם מוזכרים כלל בטקסטים החקוקים על האסטלות.

31 רק 19 מתוך כ־34 השורות שנחקקו בצד הפנים של האסטלה קריאות. מן השורה החקוקה בשוליים השמאליים של האסטלה מתקבל לכאורה רושם שהיא סוף הטקסט (השווה שורה זו אל הכתובת שבאסטלת זנג׳ירלי, אחור, שורות 50, 52). אמנם עדיין חסרות נוסחות הברכה והקללה למטפלים בכתובת לעתיד לבוא.

32 בחפירות זנג׳ירלי נתגלתה עוד אסטלה מלכותית אשורית (ראה פון לושאן [לעיל, הערה 26], עמ׳ 28–29). היפגעותה החמורה משרפה ומפגעי מזג האוויר הניעה את

גובה הגומחה המגולפת בסלע אשר בשפך נהר אל־כלב 189 ס״מ ובה דמותו של אסרחדון עומד ומעליו סמלי אלים (בדומה לאסטלות זנג׳ירלי ותל ברסיפ). על גבי התבליט נחקקה כתובת בת כ־40 שורות. אין כאן דמויות האנשים המתחננים ואף לא בניו, אולם ההקשר התוכני והכרונולוגי של המונומנט מתברר מן הכתובת שבו, שעניינה כניסת אסרחדון למוף, תיאור השלל שנלקח שם והרכב הגלות שהוגלתה ממצרים.

לעומת הזהות הכמעט מוחלטת במתאר של אסטלות זנג׳ירלי ותל ברסיפ ולעומת הדמיון הרב בין דמות המלך (וגם רוב סמלי האלים) בתבליט נהר אל־כלב ובין התיאורים הסטנדרטיים של מלכי אשור[33] הכתובות שעל גבי המונומנטים הללו אינן זהות: לכתובת תל ברסיפ (אסטלה A) אופי של כתובת סיכום: אסרחדון מוצג בה כמי שפעל נגד הערבים,[34] חִלַּכֻּ, אֶלְפִּ וּבְּרְנַכִּ,

---

החופרים להשאירה באתר. מתוך הקבלה לזוג האסטלות מתל ברסיפ סברה ברברה פורטר כי אסטלה זו הייתה בת זוגה של אסטלת אסרחדון (Mnm. A) ולכן שיערה כי הייתה עליה כתובת ארמית או פיניקית וכי שתיהן נועדו לשני סוגי קהל שנבדלו בלשונותיהם, האחת – לקוראי אשורית והאחרת – לקוראי הלשון המקומית (B.N. Porter, 'Language, Audience and Impact in Imperial Assyria', *IOS*, 15 [1995], pp. 51–72, notes 3, 9). השערה זו נראית שגויה: אסטלת אסרחדון היא של אבן דולריט, גובהה 322 ס״מ והייתה מוצבת בשער העיר, ואילו האסטלה הפגומה הייתה של אבן גיר, גובהה 190 ס״מ בלבד והייתה מוצבת בארמון הצפוני־מזרחי במרחק 320 מטר מחברתה (ראה פון לושאן [לעיל, הערה 26], עמ׳ 10). אין לשער שאחת האסטלות טולטלה אחרי כיבוש שַׁמְאַל והורחקה מן המקום שבו הוצבה (משקלה של אסטלת אסרחדון היה כ־6 טונות ושל האסטלה האחרת – כמחצית המשקל הזה). זאת ועוד. כתובות דו־לשוניות נתגלו והן חקוקות על אותה האבן או על אבנים הסמוכות זו לזו. אין טעם לשער כי אסטלות שהיו מרוחקות זו מזו (גם בתל ברסיפ היה המרחק שבין הכתובות יותר מ־600 מ׳) היו כתובות בשתי לשונות ונועדו לשני קהלי קוראים.

בהבחינה בהבדלים שבתיאורים החזותיים שבאסטלות זנג׳ירלי ותל ברסיפ פורטר סוברת כי הם נבעו מן הכוונה להתאימם לקהלי יעד שונים זה מזה לפי ההיסטוריה הפוליטית של כל אחד מן המרכזים שבהם הוצבו האסטלות, תל ברסיפ ושַׁמְאַל (פורטר, שם, עמ׳ 51–72 וכן: N.B. Porter, '"For the Astonishment of All Enemies": Assyrian Propaganda and Its Audiences in the Reigns of Ashurnasirpal II and Esarhaddon', *Bulletin of the Canadian Society for Mesopotamian Studies*, 35 [2000], pp. 7–18; idem, 'Assyrian Propaganda for the West: Esarhaddon's Stelae for Til Barsip and Samʾal', in G. Bunnens [ed.], *Essays on Syria in the Iron Age*, Louvain–Paris–Sterling, Va. 2000, pp. 143–176). לדעתי, הנתונים שבידינו אינם מספיקים להגדרת עמדתם הפוליטית של תושבי שַׁמְאַל ותל ברסיפ באופן שיוכל להסביר את ההבדלים החזותיים בתבליטים. כפי שנראה להלן מעיון בכתובות נהר אל־כלב וקקון, הטקסטים החקוקים על האסטלות אינם תומכים בסברת פורטר. נראה יותר שההבדלים החזותיים נבעו מעשייתם בידי אומנים שונים איש איש לפי טעמו, אם כי על־פי מתאר אחד.

33 למשל, ניכר דמיון בין המונומנט של אסרחדון בנהר אל־כלב ובין חמשת המונומנטים האשוריים האחרים החצובים באותו האתר, שבשאלת זהות המלכים שדמויותיהם מונצחות בהם הדעות חלוקות, אך אין ספק שאינן של אסרחדון; ראה ברקר־קלהן (לעיל, הערה 27), עמ׳ 211–212.

34 פרשיות הנוגעות לערבים באות ברוב הטקסט ששרד בכתובת (שורות 7–19). אולי גם כמה מן השורות שקדמו לשורה 7, שלא שרדו, נוגעות לערבים.

מני ואשכנז, גִּמר וחֶבֶשְׁנַ (ובתחתית האסטלה חקוק שמו של עבדמלכת מלך צידון). פעולות אלו התרחשו במרוצת כמה שנים שקדמו לשנת 673 לפסה״נ, לפני המסע הראשון והכושל למצרים. אין בכתובת זכר לכיבוש שובריה ומצרים, אולם בהתחשב שהכתובת לא הושלמה, ייתכן שגם כיבוש שובריה ומצרים נועד להיכלל בה.

כתובת זנג׳ירלי שונה בתכלית: היא כתובה בגוף ראשון ורשומים בה תוארי אסרחדון, שבחיו בהיותו בחיר האלים, גבורתו (בעזרת האלים) והיותו ירא האלים ופועל בשמם. זה טקסט רווי אדיקות, ולאלים (ולא לאסרחדון) יש בו מקום מרכזי. מכלל האירועים הצבאיים שהתרחשו בימי מלכותו של אסרחדון הוזכרו במפורש רק פעולותיו במצרים במסעו השני עליה. תיאורן בא ב־14 שורות בלבד מתוך 92 השורות שבכתובת (אחור, שורות 37–50). הוא מתחיל בהבסת חילו של תרהקה וברדיפה אחריו מֵאִשְׁחֻפְּרִ עד מוף, מהלך 15 יום.[35] בהמשך נאמר כי מוף נלכדה בתוך חצי יום במצור באמצעות מנהרות ופרצים, הוחרבה והועלתה באש. אשת תרהקה ופילגשיו, יורש העצר אֻשַׁנְחֻרֻ ויתר בניו ובנותיו של תרהקה הוגלו אשורה. רכושו, סוסיו, בקרו וצאנו הרבים לאין מספר נתפסו. ׳שורש׳ כוש נעקר ממצרים, הופקדו עליה מלכים, פחות, סגנים ופקידים למיניהם והוטלו עליהם מסים ומנחות קבועים שנועדו לאל אשור ולאלים הגדולים. מטרת המונומנט מתבררת מן הכתוב בשורות 50–53 כי אסרחדון ציווה לעשות את המצבה ולכתוב עליה את גבורות האל אשור ואת מעשי גבורתו הוא (בעזרת האל) למען יראו האויבים לעד. הכתובת מסתיימת בבקשה מן השליט לעתיד לבוא (*rubû arkû*) אשר יראה את שמו של אסרחדון חקוק בה כי לכשיקראו באוזניו את הכתוב במצבה, ימשח אותה בשמן, יקריב קרבן ויגדל את שמו של האל אשור (אחור, שורות 56–57). נראה אפוא כי המסר של האסטלות בשביל הבאים בשערי זנג׳ירלי ותל ברסיפ היה בראש ובראשונה חזותי ונבע מגודל התבליטים וממה שמתואר בהם, ואילו לכתוב באסטלות יוחדה חשיבות משנית בלבד.[36]

הדיווח ההיסטורי בכתובת נהר אל־כלב נפתח בכניסת אסרחדון למוף הכבושה (שורות 7–8) בלי תיאור המסע במדבר ובלא הזכרת קרבות. אחר כך בא פירוט נרחב (יותר מן הפירוט שבכתובת זנג׳ירלי) של השלל

35 בשלוש השורות הקודמות לקטע הנדון (אחור, שורות 35–37) נאמר כי ׳אחרי שאשור והאלים הגדולים, אדוני, ציווני התקדמתי בבטחה ובשלום (ב)דרכים רחוקות, הרים נישאים, חולות עצומים, מקום צמא׳. אפשר לראות בכך רמז סתמי לקשיי ההתקדמות במדבר סיני, אבל הוא הולם גם אזורים קשים אחרים שבהם נע צבא אסרחדון בשנים הקודמות כגון המסע לארץ בָּזוּ, והשווה אל Nin. A iv 53–60.

36 במילים אחרות אפשר לומר שהתבליט היה מכוון לבני אותו הזמן, ואילו הטקסט נועד בעיקר לבני הדורות הבאים. על משניות המסר התעמולתי של הכתוב באסטלת זנג׳ירלי אפשר ללמוד גם מדרך הצבתה: חלקה האחורי, שעליו נחקק רוב הטקסט, היה סמוך לקיר השער וספק אם אפשר לקרוא אותו; ראה נתוני פון לושאן (לעיל, הערה 26), עמ׳ 11 ואילך.

שנלקח מתרהקה (שורות 9–22) ושל הגולים ממצרים ובהם בני משפחתו של תרהקה ובעלי מקצועות נחשבים (שורות 23–27).[37] שורות 30–40 פגומות ביותר, ושרדו בהן שמות של שליטים שכנראה, שיתפו פעולה עם תרהקה: שורה 30: ...בן בְּנְזֶק...; שורה 31: .... אשקלון; שורה 32: של תרהקה ומבצריהם...; שורה 33: .... צור. שורה 34: .... 22 מלכים. שורות 35–40 לא שרדו.

כאמור, שבר של עוד כתובת נמצא בקקון. הוא מכיל 20 שורות, ובכל אחת מהן שרדו סימנים מועטים בלבד.[38] בכתובות זנג'ירלי ונהר אל־כלב נמסרו השתלטות אסרחדון על מצרים ופעולותיו לאחר קרב־השדה (הראשון) בה, ואילו בקטע מקקון מתואר מהלך מוקדם יותר של המבצע הצבאי: למן היציאה מן העיר אשור, הפעילות נגד בעל, מלך צור (ששיתף פעולה עם תרהקה), וההתקדמות אל דרום הארץ ומשם במדבר סיני על קשייו ומוראותיו (השווה אל Frt. F obv. 10–rev. 8). כיוון שברור שתיאור השלב הראשוני של המסע לבדו אין בו כדי למלא כתובת היסטורית, יש מקום להניח שתיאור המסע בכתובת קקון היה ארוך ומפורט יותר מבשאר המונומנטים וכלל גם את כיבוש מצרים והפעולות שנעשו בעקבותיו. בכך קרובה כתובת קקון למהדורת הדין וחשבון הנרחבת של Frt. F ומנסרה Nin. S יותר מלמונומנטים הגדולים. השוני בין כתובת קקון ובין המונומנטים ניכר גם בגודלם של סימני כתב היתדות החקוקים בהם.[39] לפיכך וכיוון שיש יחס ישיר בין גודל המונומנט ובין גודל סימני הכתב, מתברר שכתובת קקון אינה שייכת לסדרת המונומנטים הגדולים. המסר התעמולתי של כתובת קקון לא נבע אפוא מגודלה כי אם מעצם הצבתה באזור שלא רבו בו קוראי האשורית.

לסיכום העיון בדיווח על כיבוש מצרים: בולטת בו האינטנסיביות של הכתיבה ושל הכנת המונומנטים כאובייקטים של תעמולה במערב האימפריה. כאמור, מאמץ תעמולתי זה לגילוייו המגוונים נעשה בתוך שנתיים ימים לכל היותר.

37 רשימת בעלי המקצועות המוגלים נמשכה אל נכון גם בשורות 28–29, שאינן קריאות כיום, השווה אל Frt. J i 9–17.

38 הכתובת עתידה להתפרסם בידי אלנתן וייסרט, ואני מודה לו על שהעמיד לרשותי את נוסחה המשוחזר. בכתובת זו נשתמר נתון יחיד שאין לו זכר ביתר כתובותיו של אסרחדון אשר בידינו: נמסר בו כי צבא אשור חצה את מדבר סיני בעזרת בני מבשם (על קבוצת נוודים זו ראה בר' כה:יג). הזכרת בני מבשם כאן יחידאית היא בכלל המקורות האשוריים הידועים (ב־Frt. F rev. 1–2 בעלי הגמלים שעליהם הוטענו נאדות מים אשר נועדו להשקיית חיל אשור בעת התקדמותו בצפון מדבר סיני צוינו בשם העצם הכללי 'ערבים').

39 גובה השורות באסטלת זנג'ירלי הוא 43 מ"מ בקירוב, באסטלת תל ברסיפ 37 מ"מ בקירוב, בכתובת נהר אל־כלב 31 מ"מ בקירוב ובכתובת קקון 17 מ"מ בקירוב.

הסבת הטופונימים

טופונימים שהרכבם Kār/Dūr RN/DN היו נהוגים למכביר במסופוטמיה מתחילת התקופה הבבלית הקדומה ואילך. החידוש שחל בתקופה הנאו־אשורית אינו אפוא בעצם קריאת יישובים בשמות שזה הרכבם כי אם בשימוש בטופונימים מסוג זה להסבת שמותיהן של ערים כבושות (להבדיל מערים שנוסדו זה מקרוב ביזמה ממלכתית) כדי להמחיש ולבטא את השלטון האשורי.[40]

בכתובות המלכים הנאו־אשוריות שבידינו רשומות 50 ערים ששמותיהן הוסבו בעקבות כיבושן בידי צבא אשור החל בימי אשורנצרפל השני וכלה בימי אסרחדון. 41 מהן נכללות במחקרה של פונגרץ־לייסטן ועליהן יש להוסיף 9 ערים במצרים ששמותיהן הוסבו עם כיבושה בידי אסרחדון בשנת 671 לפסה"נ אך נשמטו מדיונה.[41] דבר הסבת שמותיהן בידי אסרחדון של ערים כבושות ששימשו מרכזי שלטון במצרים צוין גם בכתובות אשורבניפל.[42] שני שלישים של הטופונימים החדשים (33 במספר) ניתנו בימי אסרחדון. מבחינה ממוקדת יותר של נסיבות נתינתם מתברר כי 32 מהם נוצרו בתוך פחות משנתיים (בין כיבוש שובריה ובין חיבור הדין וחשבון על כיבוש מצרים).

שמות המקומות שהוסבו לפני ימי אסרחדון נבדלים הבדל ניכר מאלה שהוסבו בימיו: עד ימי אסרחדון נגזרו רובם ככולם במתכונת Kār/Dūr RN/DN.[43]

40 B. Pongratz-Leisten, 'Toponyme als Ausdruck assyrischen Herrschaftsanspruchs', in B. Pongratz-Leisten, H. Kühne & P. Xella (eds.), *Ana šadī Labnāni lū allik* (Festschrift W. Röllig), Neukirchen-Vluyn 1997, pp. 325–343

41 את רשימת הערים שהושמטו ראה אצל בורגר Frt. J ii 2'–11' (=Bu 91-5-9,218); הרשימה באה גם אצל אונש (לעיל, הערה 20), עמ' 31. נראה שתחילתה קטועה. משרידי שורות 8', 10' של Frt. J ii עולה כי נכללו בהן עוד טופונימים. כדי להעריך את מספר הטופונימים שנכללו ברשימה בשלמותה ראוי להשוותה עם רשימת מרכזי השלטון במצרים שבכתובות אשורבניפל, שבהן נרשמו (בשמותיהן המצריים) 21 ערים לצד שמותיהם של 20 'מלכים' שהופקדו עליהן בידי אסרחדון אחרי כיבוש מצרים (A i 90–109; C ii 87–92; ראה אצל אונש [לעיל, הערה 20], עמ' 36. פֶּרֶט [H. Verreth, 'The Egyptian Eastern Border Region in Assyrian Sources', *JAOS*, 119 (1999), pp. 234–247] סובר כי הרשימה שבכתובות אשורבניפל מורכבת וכי כמה ערים הוזכרו בה פעמיים). שתיים מהן מוזכרות ב'לוחות חרן' של אשורבניפל בשמותיהן המצריים והאשוריים כאחד (חַתְחַרִבַּ/אתריביס = Limmer-iššakku-Aššur, ראה Streck, Harran obv. 65 והשווה אל אונש, שם, עמ' 42; סאיס = Kār-Bēl-mātāti, ראה Borger, Smlt. obv. 25; Streck, Harran obv. 61 וכן אונש, שם, עמ' 35). יש מקום לשער שגם שמותיהן של שאר הערים הוסבו. מספרן הכולל של הערים ששמותיהן הוסבו בידי אסרחדון יהיה אפוא 43 לפחות (כר־אסרחדון, שקמה על חורבות צידון + 21 ערים בשובריה + 21 ערים במצרים).

42 ראה A.C. Piepkorn, *Historical Prism Inscriptions of Ashurbanipal*, Chicago 1933, Prism E i 14–15

43 ראה פונגרץ־לייסטן (לעיל, הערה 40), עמ' 331–335.

למן ימיו נגזרו רובם ככולם (31 מתוך 32 ששרדו בידינו) במתכונת של סִסמאות המזכירה מאוד את שמותיהם של רבים משעריהן של ערי אשור הגדולות.[44] סִסמאות אלו מביעות את מעמדו הריבוני של מלך אשור, בלי לנקוב בשמו, ואת זיקתו לאל אשור כגון 'אל תפר את דבר המלך', 'יאיר בא־כוחו (ה־*iššākku*) של (האל) אשור',[45] את גודלו ועצמתו של אשור, האל הלאומי כגון 'מי ישווה ל(אל) אשור', '(האל) אשור הרחיב את (מוטת) עולו', 'יאריך ימים המשמח את לב(ו של האל) אשור' וכן סִסמאות 'פטריוטיות' כגון 'השבתי ל(אל) אשור את ארצו', 'תגדל (הארץ ו)אל תקטן'. מתכונת מרשימה כזאת לשמות ערים היא בבחינת חידוש באימפריה האשורית ובמידה רבה במזרח הקדום כולו.[46] עוד אפשר להבחין כי בשנת 4 למלכותו עדיין נקט אסרחדון את המתכונת הישנה שלפיה הוכלל שם המלך בטופונים המוסב (כזה הוא שמה של כר־אסרחדון, העיר שנבנתה על חורבות צידון בשנת 676 לפסה"נ). נראה אפוא שהשינוי הבולט בנוהג זה החל עם המסע נגד שובריה ונמשך עם כיבוש מצרים בהיותו פעילות תעמולתית מכוונת וכוללת.

בקרב הטופונימים התאופוריים שנגזרו במתכונת Kār/Dūr DN, שקדמו לימי אסרחדון, אנו מוצאים את שמות האלים אשור, נרגל, נבו, סין, אדד, אשתר ואנליל,[47] ואילו בטופונימים התאופוריים החדשים אשור תופס את חלק הארי ומקדים באופן מוחלט את יתר האלים. שמו משמש רכיב ב־14 מתוך 17 הטופונימים התאופוריים. היתר הם: בֵּל־מַתַתִי,[48] מרדוך ובֵּנִת=אשתר, כל אחד בטופונים אחד.

כידוע, מדיניותו של אסרחדון כלפי בבל למן ראשית מלכותו הייתה פיוס והתקרבות ומנוגדת ניגוד גמור למדיניות אביו סנחריב. מגמתו של אסרחדון להתקרב אל הבבלים, לחזק את מעמדו כמלך בבל (בד בבד עם היותו מלך אשור) ולקרב את בני שתי האומות לכלל חטיבה אחת מובעת ברבות מכתובותיו, והיא באה לידי ביטוי בהאדרת מרדוך ובקידום מעמדו בכתובות

44 חריג יחיד מכלל זה הוא הטופונים דור־אסרחדון, שניתן לאחת מערי שובריה הכבושות ונגזר לפי המתכונת הישנה. לשמות שערים בצורת סִסמאות ראה, למשל, A.R. George, *Babylonian Topographical Texts*, Louvain 1992, pp. 67, 177

45 לתוארו זה של אסרחדון עיין R. Borger, 'Die Inschriften Asarhaddons (AfO Beiheft 9)', *AfO*, 18 (1957–1958), p. 113, #10ª, 9

46 דוגמה יחידה קודמת למתכונת זו היא הטופונים Ana-Aššur-utēr-aṣbat (='השבתי לאשור (ו)לכדתי') שניתן לעיר 'אשר אנשי ארץ חת יקראוה פִּתְרֻ' והוזכר בכתובות שלמנאסר השלישי (RIMA 3, 23:85–86; 51–52:40–43; 64–65:38–40). בשם זה משתקף שהעיר ישבה באזור מריבה שעליו נאבקו האשורים והארמים. משמעותו ההיסטורית של הטופונים האשורי מתבררת מסמיכות הזכרתה של אנ־אשור־אתר־אצבת לצד '(העיר) מֻתְכִּנֻ אשר בעבר הנהר פרת – אשר יישב תגלת־פלאסר (הראשון, 1114–1076 לפסה"נ) (ו)בימי אשור־רבי (השני, 927–1012 לפסה"נ) מלך אשור לכד מלך הארמים בכוח'. ערים אלו השיב לאשור שלמנאסר השלישי (RIMA 3, 19:35–38).

47 ראה פונגרץ־לייסטן (לעיל, הערה 40), עמ' 331–335.

48 Bēl-matāti בכתובות מלכים אשוריות הוא כינוי לאל אשור; ראה K.L. Tallqvist, *Akkadische Götterepitheta*, Helsinki 1938, p. 48

אלו.[49] כך נקבע מעמד מכובד למרדוך גם בתיאורי מלחמותיו של אסרחדון בשובריה ובמצרים: ב׳מכתב לאל׳ נקשר נס ההכרעה בקרב על אֻפֻּמֶ, בירת שובריה, במרדוך ׳מלך האלים׳, אשר הטה את כיוון הרוח בעת ששילחו הנצורים אש בסוללת המצור שבנו חיילי אסרחדון על העיר ומתוך כך אחזה האש בחומת העיר ושרפה אותה לעפר.[50] ובמהדורת הדין וחשבון על המסע למצרים דרך מדבר סיני נאמר כי ׳מרדוך האדון הגדול [בא] לעזרתי ... החיה את חילותי׳.[51] לאור הבחנה זו בולטת העובדה שמגמת האדרתו של מרדוך אינה ניכרת בטופונימים המוסבים של ערי שובריה ומצרים. כאמור, כאן שמור לאשור המקום הראשון במעלה, ואילו שמו של מרדוך מופיע בטופונים אחד בלבד (Bīt-Marduk). מסתבר שבדינים והחשבונות הספרותיים על הפעולות הצבאיות בשובריה ובמצרים מזה ובהסבת הטופונימים מזה משתקפות שתי מערכות אידאולוגיה שונות זו מזו, האחת הופנתה כלפי הבבלים ונועדה לזכות באהדתם והאחרת הייתה אשורית בלבדית. מכאן שראוי לראות בהסבת הטופונימים ובחיבור הדינים והחשבונות פעולות שנעשו בשתי סְפֵרות שונות זו מזו.

49 ראה B.N. Porter, *Images, Power, and Politics: Figurative Aspects of Esarhaddon's Babylonian Policy*, Philadelphia 1993, passim, esp. pp. 141–142

50 Gbr. II ii 3–9. בפסקה זו מרדוך מכונה בתואר ׳מלך האלים׳ (שורה 5), ואילו בפסקאות אחרות באותו החיבור ׳מלך האלים׳ הוא אשור; ראה Gbr. II i 1, 18

51 Frt. F rev. 9–10. מוטעה הוא ייחוס תשועה נוספת למרדוך שייחס לבט (ובעקבותיו פורטר) – תשועה על־ידי הורדת גשם לחיילי אשור הצמאים במסעם למצרים (ראה R. Labat, 'Rapports sur les conférences: Assyrien', *Annuaire 1973–1974. École pratique des hautes études, IVe section: Sciences historiques et philologiques*, 1974, p. 65; פורטר [לעיל, הערה 49], עמ׳ 141): בשבר הכתובת 79-7-8,196, המוזכר אצל לבט (הוא אצל בורגר Frt. G), אין מדובר בהשקיית הצבא האשורי על־ידי נס (שעשה כביכול מרדוך) כי אם בהובלת המים על גבי גמלים (בדומה לכתוב ב־Frt. F).

הגלגל המכונף

סמל של אלים ראשיים בתקופת האימפריה האשורית

מאת

טלי אורנן

עצמתה המדינית והתפשטותה הטריטוריאלית של האימפריה האשורית יצרו דפוסים תרבותיים דומים ולעתים אחידים ברחבי המזרח הקדמון במהלך המחצית הראשונה של האלף הראשון לפסה״נ. יש שטענו שהמצע המשותף אשר כונן בתקופת האימפריה, בייחוד מאמצע המאה השמינית לפסה״נ בימי תגלת־פלאסר השלישי, יצר את התשתית שעליה התבסס ברבות הימים ההלניזם.[1] בכוונתי לעמוד כאן על דפוסים כאלה שהתקיימו ברחבי האימפריה האשורית באמצעות אחד הסמלים הדתיים השכיחים באותה התקופה – הגלגל המכונף, הידוע לעתים בכינוי המתאים לזיהויו במולדתו מצרים – גלגל החמה המכונף.

אני מבקשת לזרוע אור על משמעות הגלגל המכונף המופיע בהיצגים חזותיים בארצות קדמת־אסיה כסמל שייצג אלוהויות אחדות – לאו דווקא אלוהויות שמשיות – שכמה מהן מילאו תפקיד של אלוהויות ראשיות. זאת אנסה להדגים על־ידי סקירת הופעותיו של הגלגל המכונף באמנות האשורית והבבלית, במבע החזותי של ממלכות החסות האשוריות בצפון סוריה, בייחוד בממצאי זנג׳ירלי, ובאמנות הארץ־ישראלית משלהי המאה השמינית. פרק הזמן שבו יתמקד הדיון משתרע מן המאה התשיעית עד המאה השישית לפסה״נ, אחרי נפילת האימפריה.

מוצאו של הגלגל המכונף הוא בימי השושלת החמישית של הממלכה הקדומה במצרים, שאז שימש אחד מהיצגיו של רע, אל השמש מהליופוליס.[2] כבר בראשית הצגתו באמנות של ארצות קדמת־אסיה, בחותמות־גליל מעובדים בסגנון הסורי מאמצע המאה השמונה־עשרה לפסה״נ ובחרפושיות מקומיות מארץ ישראל מתקופת הברונזה התיכונה,[3] נבדל הגלגל המכונף

1 H. W. Saggs, 'The Assyrians', in D. J. Wiseman (ed.), *Peoples of the Old Testament*, Oxford 1973, pp. 161–162

2 R. H. Wilkinson, *Reading Egyptian Art*, London 1996, p. 101

3 חותמה של מתרונה בת אֲפְּלַחַנְדַ מלך כרכמיש נחשב לחותם־הגליל הסורי המתוארך הקדום ביותר שבו מופיע גלגל מכונף; ראה A. Otto, *Die Entstehung und Entwicklung der Klassisch-Syrischen Glyptic*, Berlin – New York 2000, pp. 35, 270.

שמקדמת־אסיה מן האב־טיפוס המצרי, ובאופן הצגתו ניכרים שינויים מרובים בצורתו, בהקשריו ובמשמעויותיו. בהיצגיו של הגלגל המכונף בחותמות־גליל סוריים בדרך כלל הוסרו שני נחשי האוּרֵאוּס שהיו חלק מן הסמל המצרי, והוסרו גם טופרי הנשר שנראו לפעמים מתחת לגלגל החמה המצרי, ולעתים נוספה במרכז הגלגל שמקדמת־אסיה וַרְדָּה גדולה (ציור 1). גם ההקשר התְּמוני שבו הסמל מופיע השתנה במהלך אימוצו במבע החזותי של ארצות קדמת־אסיה. כבר בהופעותיו ברבע הראשון של האלף השני בחותמות־גליל סוריים הוצג מעל לעץ מסוגנן, שלעתים נראה כעמוד דמוי עץ (ציור 1). יתרה מזו, מראשית תיאוריו באמנות של מערב אסיה קוּשר

ציור 1: גלגל מכונף וורדה מעל עמוד דמוי עץ, חותם־גליל סורי, המוצא אינו ידוע, המאה השמונה־עשרה לפסה"נ
מתוך טסייה (הערה 4), מס' 189 • באדיבות OBO פריבורג, שווייץ

הגלגל המכונף, כמו שהראתה רות אופיפיציוס, לא רק לאלוהויות שמש לפי מקורותיו המצריים אלא גם לאלוהויות שמים אחרות שייצגו תופעות טבע שמימיות רבות ומגוונות, כגון המטר, הרעם והברק.[4] שינוי זה בהחלט התאים לתנאי הסביבה החדשים של סמל זה בקדמת־אסיה.

על הגלגל המכונף בחרפושיות מקומיות מארץ ישראל ראה D. Ben-Tor, 'The Absolute Date of the Montet Jar Scarabs', in L.H. Lesko (ed.), *Ancient Egyptian and Mediterranean Studies in Memory of William A. Ward*, Providence 1998, p. 7

4 R. Mayer-Opificius, 'Die geflügelte Sonne Himmels- und Regendarstellungen im alten Vorderasien', *Ugarit-Forschungen*, 16 (1984), pp. 190–236; B. Teissier, *Egyptian Iconography on Syro-Palestinian Cylinder Seals of the Middle Bronze Age*, Fribourg–Göttingen 1996, pp. 95–100, 158

כיוון שבמולדתו היה הסמל קשור לאל רע של הליופוליס, שנחשב לאביו של המלך המצרי, במצרים נקשר לעתים דימוי חזותי זה עם המלכות או עם נושא המשרה שלה, הוא המלך.[5] אולם אין ודאות גמורה שמאפיין זה של הסמל היה קיים באמנות של ארצות מערב אסיה. אף על פי שהשימוש במגדיר האלוהי לצד שמו של אל השמש (^{d}UTU) נקשר גם בשמם של שליטים מסופוטמיים כגון שֻׁלְגִ וחמורבי,[6] אין בידינו הוכחות חד־משמעיות המזהות את התואר הזה עם הגלגל המכונף, ועל כן מוטב שלא להסיק שסמל זה ייצג דמויות של מלכים במסופוטמיה. כך נחשף לפנינו עוד שוני, תוכני, בין הגלגל המכונף האסיאתי ובין האב־טיפוס המצרי שלו.

ההנחה שהגלגל המכונף במסופוטמיה ובאזורים הסמוכים לה לא ייצג את השליט[7] מסתייעת גם בהערכה שבדרך כלל באמנות של מסופוטמיה ושכנותיה נדחתה הצגת המלך כדמות על־טבעית: בהופעה חד־משמעית שלו כאֵל (שלא כמסתמן בתקופות מסוימות במבע הכתוב המסופוטמי) או בהצגתו באמצעות בעל חיים או יצור כלאיים.[8]

במהלך המחצית השנייה של האלף השני נפוץ הגלגל המכונף לאזורים אחרים ברחבי המזרח הקרוב הקדום ונעשה שכיח בטביעות של חותמות־גליל מנוזי, בחותמות־גליל מגולפים בסגנון מיתני ובחותמות־גליל מאשור מן המאה הארבע־עשרה וראשית המאה השלוש־עשרה, שבאמצעותם עבר הסמל לאמנות האשורית בת האלף הראשון.[9] הופעתו הראשונה של הגלגל

5 R.H. Wilkinson, *Symbol and Magic in Egyptian Art*, London 1994, p. 213; פרנקפורט מגדירו סמל של הורוס, אל השמים המסומל בבז, המייצג גם את המלך (H. Frankfort, *Art and Architecture of the Ancient Orient*[5], New Haven–London 1996, pp. 134–135, 215). ראה גם טסייה (לעיל, הערה 4), עמ' 101.

6 S. Dalley, 'The God Salmu and the Winged Disk', *Iraq*, 48 (1986), p. 98

7 אלא לעתים באמנות החתית, וראה D. Beyer, *Emar IV, Les sceaux*, Fribourg–Göttingen 2001, pp. 341–342; D. Parayre, 'Carchemish entre Anatolie et Syrie à travers l'image du disque solaire ailé (ca. 1800–717 avant J.-C.)', *Hethitica*, 8 (1987), pp. 329–327

8 בתקופת ההגמוניה של השושלת השלישית של אור, למשל, שאז העדות הכתובה מורה על האלהת השליט, העדות התמונית אינה משקפת מגמה זו באופן חד־משמעי. כך, למשל, בחותמות־הגליל בני התקופה אמנם המלך מחקה את דמותו של האל, אולם אין הוא חבוש בכתר הקרניים, שהוא המגדיר האלוהי המובהק ביותר; וראה I.J. Winter, 'The King and the Cup: Iconography of the Royal Presentation Scene on Ur III Seals', in M. Kelly-Buccellati et al. (eds.), *Insight Through Images: Studies in Honor of Edith Porada*, Malibu 1986, pp. 253–268

9 מאייר־אופיפציוס (לעיל, הערה 4), עמ' 192, 195; H. Frankfort, *Cylinder Seals*, London 1939, pp. 208, 275–276; E.D. van Buren, *Symbols of the Gods in Mesopotamian Art*, Rome 1945, pp. 94–95; U. Seidl, *Die babylonischen Kudurru-Reliefs*, Fribourg–Göttingen 1989, p. 99; W. Orthmann, 'Eine Wandmalerei aus Halawa und die Darstellung der Sonne in der vorderasiatischen Kunst', in D.J.W. Meijer (ed.), *Natural Phenomena, Their Meaning, Depiction and Description in the Ancient Near East*, Amsterdam 1992, p. 220

המכונף באמנות האשורית המונומנטלית הייתה באובליסק השבור מימיו של אשור־בֵּל־כַּל (1073–1056; ציור 2).[10]

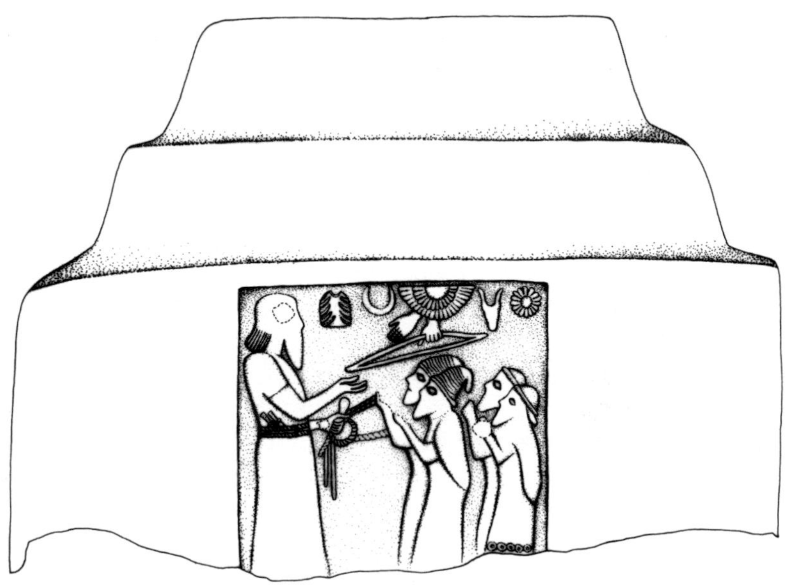

ציור 2: גלגל מכונף שממנו מוגשים קשת וחצים למלך, האובליסק השבור, נינוה
ציירה פנינה ארד על־פי J. Curtis, 'The Broken Obelisk', *Iraq*, 69 (2007), Figs. 1–4

שני שינויים בהצגת הגלגל המכונף, המרמזים על מאפייניו העתידיים, משתקפים במונומנט זה. הראשון הוא שתי הזרועות האנושיות המגיחות מן הגלגל אשר התפתחו ברבות הימים באמנות האשורית החדשה לדמותו של האל הנראית בתוך הגלגל המכונף. השינוי השני משתקף בקשת הנמסרת למלך באמצעות זוג הידיים. עצם הענקת כלי הנשק הזה מגדירה את האלוהות המיוצגת בסמל כאלוהות לוחמת, וכך מונומנט זה מבשר את אחת מתכונותיו הבולטות של האל שיסומל בגלגל המכונף באשור באלף הראשון – תכונת הלחימה. שני המאפיינים הללו משתקפים היטב כבר בלבנה מזוגגת

10 J. Börker-Klähn, *Altvorderasiatische Bildstelen und vergleichbare Felsreliefs*, Mainz 1982, p. 178, No. 131; T. Ornan, 'Who is Holding the Lead Rope? The Relief of the Broken Obelisk', *Iraq*, 69 (2007), pp. 59–72 (ושם ספרות); A.K. Grayson, RIMA 2, pp. 99–105

מימי תֻּכֻּלְתִּ־נִנֻרְתַ השני (890–884; ציור 3)[11] ובייחוד בתבליטי־הקיר של אשורנצרפל השני (883–859) בארמון הצפון־מערבי בנִמרוד (למשל, ציור 4). הפן הלוחמני המיוצג בגלגל המכונף כפי שהופיע באמנות האשורית וכמוהו מקומו המרכזי של הסמל וקרבתו הפיזית למלך מלמדים שבמקרים אלו הוא ייצג את האל אשור, שעמד בראש הפנתאון של ממלכת אשור.[12]

ואולם זיהוי זה מעורר קשיים, שכן בכתובות החקוקות על כמה מונומנטים – כגון האסטלה של בֵּל־חַרַן־בֵּל־אֻצֻר מתל אַבְּטָה, האסטלה של סרגון השני מלרנקה ותבליטי־הסלע של סנחריב מבַּוִיָּן ומג'ודי־דאג – הגלגל המכונף מזוהה עם האל שַׁמַש דווקא,[13] ואילו זיהויים כתובים מעין אלה אינם בנמצא בכל הנוגע לאל אשור. באסטלה של אשורנצרפל, שכוננה לרגל חנוכת הארמון הצפון־מערבי בשנת 879 אפשר, כנראה, לזהות את הסמל עם שַׁמַש בגלל העיטור שבתוך לוחית הגלגל, המחקה את סמל השמש הבבלי (ציור 5; והשווה לציור 11 להלן).[14] זיהוי הגלגל המכונף עם שני אלים אולי מעיד על מגבלותיו של המחקר המודרני. אולם הוא מרמז שהסמל היה עשוי לייצג שני אלים שונים זה מזה גם במציאות העתיקה. מסקנה זו מסתייעת בהצעתו של למברט שסבר שכאשר הופיע הסמל לבדו עם המלך במונומנטים הוא ייצג את האל אשור, ואילו כאשר הוא הוצג בלוויית סמלים אחרים, ובייחוד בתבליטי־סלע ובאסטלות מלכותיות (דוגמת האסטלה שבציור 5) הוא ייצג את האל שַׁמַש.[15]

11 W. Andrae, *Coloured Ceramics from Ashur and Earlier Ancient Assyrian Wall-Paintings*, London 1925, p. 27, Pl. 8

12 פרנקפורט (לעיל, הערה 9), עמ' 205–210; S. Parpola, 'The Assyrian Tree of Life: Tracing the Origins of Jewish Monotheism and Philosophy', *JNES*, 52 (1993), p. 185

13 זיידל (לעיל, הערה 9), עמ' 235.

14 על זיהוי הגלגל המכונף עם שַׁמַש ראה מאייר־אופיפיציוס (לעיל, הערה 4), עמ' 198–201; P. Calmeyer, 'Das Zeichen der Herrschaft ... ohne Šamaš wird es nicht gegeben', *Archäologische Mitteilungen aus Iran*, 17 (1984), pp. 140–141; J.E. Reade, 'Shikaft-I Gulgul: Its Date and Symbolism', *Iranica Antiqua*, 12 (1977), pp. 38–39; S. Herbordt, *Neuassyrische Glyptik des 8.–7. Jh. v. Chr. unter besonderer Berücksichtigung der Siegelungen auf Tafeln und Tonverschlüssen*, Helsinki 1992, p. 98; D. Collon, *Catalogue of the Western Asiatic Seals in the British Museum, Cylinder Seals V, Neo-Assyrian and Neo-Babylonian Periods*, London 2001, p. 79

15 למברט סבור שהסמל ייצג בתחילה את שַׁמַש ובתקופה האשורית החדשה גם את אשור. הגלגל המכונף הוא הסמל שאותו עבדו, ואילו העץ שמתחתיו מייצג את הברכה שהאל מעניק; ראה W.G. Lambert, 'Trees, Snakes and Gods in Ancient Syria and Anatolia', *Bulletin of the School of Oriental and African Studies*, 48 (1985), p. 439, note 27

ציור 3: האל אשור יורה בקשת מתוך גלגל מכונף, לבנה מזוגגת, אשור
מתוך J.B. Pritchard, *The Ancient Near East in Pictures Relating to the Old Testament*, Princeton 1954, No. 536 · באדיבות הוצאת אוניברסיטת פרינסטון

ציור 4: האל אשור בתוך הגלגל המכונף מחזיק בקשת, תבליט־קיר מן הארמון הצפון־מערבי, נִמרוד
מתוך A.H. Layard, *Monuments of Nineveh*, I, London 1849, Pl. 21

ציור 5: גלגל מכונף וסמלי אלים, אסטלת חנוכת הארמון הצפון־מערבי, נִמרוד
מתוך ברקר־קלהן (הערה 10), מס׳ 137b • באדיבות המכון הבריטי לחקר עירק (BISI), לונדון

כפל זהותו של הגלגל המכונף באמנות האשורית החדשה משתקף גם בחותמות־גליל אשוריים. בחותמות המציגים את הסמל מעל לעץ מסוגנן, בדומה להופעתו בתבליטי־הקיר שבארמון הצפון־מערבי, הוא ייצג, כנראה, את האל אשור (ציור 6), ואילו במקרים אחרים – בעיקר כשהופיע עם גרמי שמים אחרים ייצג את שַׁמַש (ציור 7). בדוגמה האחרונה הגלגל מזוהה עם שַׁמַש גם משום הצבתו מעל איש־עקרב (גִּרְתַּבְּלֻלֻ), ברייה דמוית אדם עומדת על שתיים בעלת זנב־עקרב. זיהוי כזה מתאפשר גם במקרים שבהם הגלגל המכונף נראה מעל איש־פר עומד על שתיים (כֻּסריכֻּ; ציורים 8, 9), שכן שני היצורים הללו נקשרו לאל השמש כבר באמצע האלף השלישי לפסה״נ.[16]

16 F. A. M. Wiggermann, 'Mischwesen', *RLA*, 8, 1994, p. 226

ציור 6: גלגל מכונף מעל עץ, חותם־גליל אשורי של מֵשֵׁזִב־נִנֻרְתַּ, תַּרְבִּצֻ
מתוך L. Jakob-Rost, *Die Stempelsiegel im Vorderasiatischen Museum,* Mainz 1997,
p. 12, Fig. 1

ציור 7: גלגל מכונף נתמך בידי איש־עקרב ולצדו סמלים של גרמי שמים, חותם־גליל אשורי של ניסאנה, המוצא אינו ידוע
מתוך U. Winter, *Frau und Göttin*, Fribourg–Göttingen 1983, Fig. 501 · באדיבות OBO פריבורג, שווייץ

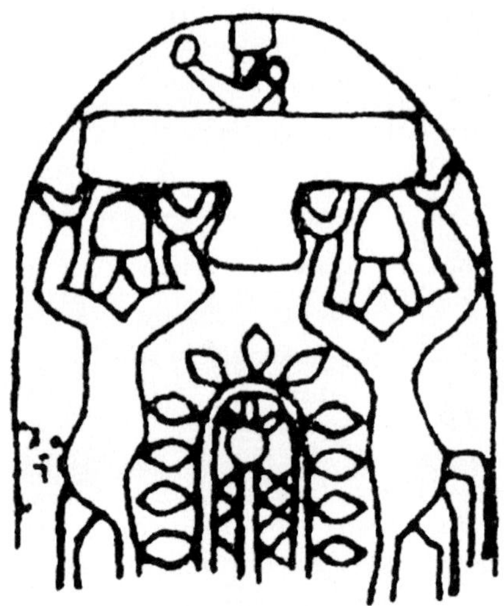

ציור 8: גלגל מכונף נתמך בידי אנשי־פר, טביעת חותם, לרסה
מתוך T. Ornan, 'A Complex System of Religious Symbols: The Case of the Winged-Disc in First-Millennium Near Eastern Imagery', in C.E. Suter & Ch. Uehlinger (eds.), *Crafts and Images in Contact: Studies on Eastern Mediterranean Minor Art of the 1st Millennium BCE*, Fribourg–Göttingen 2005, Fig. 8 • באדיבות OBO פריבורג, שווייץ

ציור 9: גלגל מכונף נתמך בידי אנשי־פר, תבליט־אבן, תל חלאף
מתוך אורנן (לעיל, ציור 8), ציור 23 • באדיבות OBO פריבורג, שווייץ

גם כאשר הוצג הגלגל המכונף מעל לסוס הוא סימן, כנראה, את האל שַׁמַש (למשל, ציור 10).[17] כפל זהותו של הגלגל המכונף תואם גם את הצעתה של סטפני דאלי אשר שלא כלמברט סבורה שהוא ייצג ברוב המקרים את שַׁמַש, אך בדומה לתואר ^{d}UTU היה עשוי לייצג גם אלוהויות אחרות, בייחוד כאשר עמדו בראש פנתאון.[18]

ציור 10: אלוהות מכונפת ניצבת על סוס, חותם־גליל אשורי, המוצא אינו ידוע
מתוך שרואר (הערה 17), ציור 107 • באדיבות OBO פריבורג, שווייץ

דומה שלא במקרה נבחר הגלגל המכונף לייצג את האל אשור שכידוע, היה חסר מסורת חזותית משל עצמו ו'שאל' את זהויותיו התמוניות מאלוהויות אחרות.[19] אכן, הבחירה בסמל זה להצגתו של אשור מילאה את הנדרש בהיותו דימוי חזותי של אלוהויות שמים גדולות בצפון מסופוטמיה ובסוריה כבר באלף השני לפסה"נ. הצגתו של אשור באמצעות סמל שהיה מזוהה עם אלוהויות גדולות, ובהן שַׁמַש, משקפת את תהליך הבנייתו של אל ראשי, ראש פנתאון, המגלם בדמותו דמויות של אלים אחדים. תהליך זה נרמז

17 הרבורדט (לעיל, הערה 14), עמ' 227, מס' 87; R.M. Boehmer, 'Die Neuassyrischen Felsreliefs von Maltai (Nord Irak)', *Jahrbuch des Deutschen Archäologischen Instituts*, 90 (1975), p. 52; S. Schroer, *In Israel gab es Bilder, Nachrichten von darstellender Kunst im Alten Israel*, Fribourg–Göttingen 1987, pp. 282–382

18 דאלי (לעיל, הערה 6).

19 W.G. Lambert, 'The God Aššur', *Iraq*, 45 (1983), pp. 82–86

במקורות כתובים לעניין שני ראשי הפנתאון המסופוטמי באלף הראשון: אשור ומרדוך.[20]
שלא כשכיחותו של הגלגל המכונף באשור, בבבל היה זה סמל נדיר. את האל שַׁמַשׁ באמנות הבבלית ייצג הגלגל נטול-הכנפיים שבתוכו כוכב בעל ארבע קרניים וביניהן ארבע קבוצות של קווים גליים, המכונה נִפְחֻ או שַׁמְשָׁתֻם.[21] הגלגל נטול-הכנפיים הופיע באמנות של דרום מסופוטמיה למן התקופה האכדית ברבע השלישי של האלף השלישי ועד התקופה הבבלית החדשה, והוא זוהה כסמלו של שַׁמַשׁ בכתוביות על 'אבני גבול' (כֻּדֻרֻ) מימי מֶלִשִׁחֻ שמן הרבע הראשון של המאה השתים-עשרה לפסה"נ ובלוח האל שַׁמַשׁ מסיפַּר (ציור 11).[22]

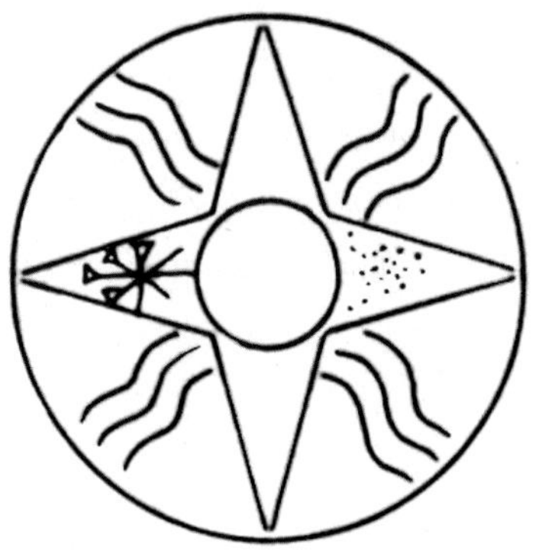

ציור 11: סמל האל שַׁמַשׁ, לוח האבן של האל שמש, סיפר
ציירה פנינה ארד על-פי T.N.D. Mettinger, *No Graven Image? – Israelite Aniconism in its Ancient Near Eastern Context*, Stockholm 1995, p. 48, Fig. 2.7

20 W.G. Lambert, 'The Historical Development of the Mesopotamian Pantheon: A Study in Sophisticated Polytheism', in H. Goedicke & J.J.M. Roberts (eds.), *Unity and Diversity: Essays in the History, Literature, and Religion of the Ancient Near East*, Baltimore–London 1975, pp. 197–199; S. Parpola, SAA IX, pp. xviii–xxi, and notes 13, 16; idem, 'Assyria's Expansion in the 8th and 7th Centuries and Its Long-Term Repercussions in the West', in W.G. Dever & S. Gitin (eds.), *Symbiosis, Symbolism, and the Power of the Past: Canaan, Ancient Israel, and Their Neighbors from the Late Bronze Age through Roman Palestine*, Winona Lake, Ind. 2003, p. 105 (ושם ספרות).

21 U. Seidl, 'Göttersymbole und -attribute', *RLA*, 3, 1971, p. 485; J.A. Brinkman, 'A Note on the Shamash Cult of Sippar in the Eleventh Century B.C.', *RA*, 70 (1976), pp. 183–184; CAD, Š/1, s.v. *šamšatu* 1, pp. 332–334

22 זיידל (לעיל, הערה 9), עמ' 98–100; D. Collon, *Catalogue of the Western Asiatic Seals in the British Museum, Cylinder Seals III, Isin-Larsa and Old Babylonian Periods*, London 1986, p. 48; על לוח האבן של האל שַׁמַשׁ מסיפַּר ראה ו"א הורוויץ, '"לוח גלגל-החמה" של נבובלאדן מלך בבל (BBSt 36)', ארץ-ישראל, כז (תשס"ג), עמ' 91–109.

אולם בכמה היקרויות מופיע הגלגל המכונף גם באמנות הבבלית שמן האלף הראשון. מדובר במעט חותמות־גליל בבליים מן המאות התשיעית–השמינית, המחקים חותמות אשוריים בני הזמן,[23] ובכמה חותמות־טביעה בבליים המיוחסים בדרך כלל לתקופה שלאחר נפילת אשור (למשל, ציור 12).[24] בגלל ההקשר התרבותי־ההיסטורי של חותמות מעין אלה לא סביר במקרים האלה לזהות את הגלגל המכונף עם האל אשור. לפיכך קשה להחליט אם בדוגמאות אלו היה הגלגל המכונף סמל כללי של אלוהות המעניקה את חסותה למתואר מתחתיה או סימל את שַמַש או אולי אף היה עשוי לייצג את מרדוך, ראש הפנתאון הבבלי.

ציור 12: מאמין לפני גלגל מכונף, חותם־טביעה נאו־בבלי מיובא, עין גדי
מתוך אורנן (לעיל, ציור 8), ציור 12 · באדיבות OBO פריבורג, שווייץ

הגלגל המכונף מופיע פעמיים באמנות הבבלית המונומנטלית מימי נבונאיד: הוא נמנה עם שלושת הסמלים שלפניהם ניצב המלך באסטלה שמוצאה בחרן והשמורה היום במוזאון הבריטי (ציור 13) ובתבליט־סלע שנתגלה לא מכבר בקלעת־סלע (פטרה) המיוחס לנבונאיד בעיקר על־פי שרידי התמונה החקוקה עליו.[25] הצגת הסמל בשני מונומנטים אלו מדגימה אימוץ סממנים

23 E. Porada, *Corpus of Near Eastern Seals in North American Collections*, I: *The Pierpont Morgan Library*, Washington 1948, p. 88, Nos. 726–731; A. Moortgat, *Vorderasiatische Rollsiegel: Ein Beitrag zur Geschichte der Steinschneidekunst*, Berlin 1940, Nos. 632, 634; B. Wittmann, 'Babylonische Rollsiegel des 11.–7. Jahrhunderts v. Chr.', *BaM*, 23 (1992), p. 223, Nos. 152–157

24 B. Mazar & I. Dunayevsky, 'En-Gedi, Fourth and Fifth Seasons of Excavations, Preliminary Report', *IEJ*, 17 (1967), pp. 133, 139, Pl. 31:2; ראה גם חותם משומרון: J.W. Crowfoot et al., *Samaria-Sebaste* III: *The Objects from Samaria*, London 1957, p. 87, Pl. 15:19

25 ברקר־קלהן (לעיל, הערה 10), מס' 266. א' רז וט' אוצ'יטל, 'סלע אדום', קתדרה, 101 (תשס"ב), עמ' 31–37; S. Dalley & A. Goguel, 'The Selaᶜ Sculpture: A Neo-Babylonian Rock Relief in Southern Jordan', *Annual of the Department of Antiquities of Jordan*, 51 (1997), pp. 169–176; B.L. Crowell, 'Nabonidus, as-Silaᶜ, and the Beginning of the End of Edom', *BASOR*, 348 (2007), pp. 80–83

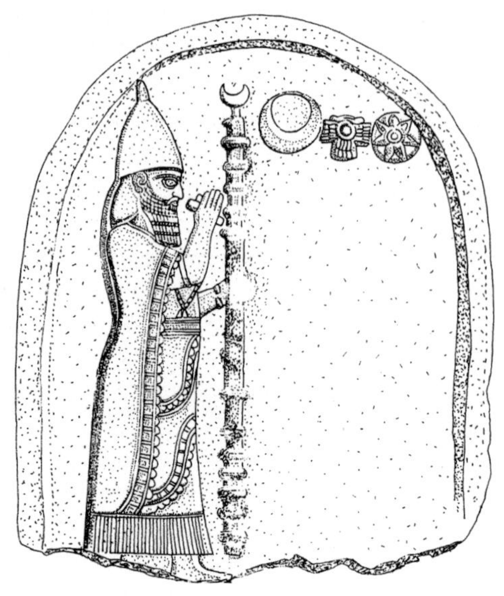

ציור 13: גלגל מכונף בין כוכב לסמלי ירח, אסטלה של נבונאיד שמוצאה בחרן
מתוך ברקר־קלהן (הערה 10), מס׳ 266

חזותיים אשוריים בידי נבונאיד, אימוץ המשתקף גם בלבושו של המלך באסטלה מחרן. ניכוס דגמים אשוריים בידי מלכי בבל המאוחרת לא ייחד רק את נבונאיד. בזאת קדם לו נבוכדנאצר השני, שבתבליטי־הסלע שלו בוואדי בריסה שבלבנון הוצג באמצעות שתי הנוסחאות החזותיות האשוריות האופייניות ביותר: המלך הנלחם באריה והמלך הניצב לצדי עץ.[26] אימוץ בבלי זה של נוסחה אשורית מלכותית ידועה נעשה, קרוב לוודאי, כדי לזכות ביוקרה שיוחסה למלך אשור. לפיכך אין להתפלא שדימוי כזה שימש את מלך בבל רק לאחר נפילתה של אשור, ולא במקרה הוצגו חידושים איקונוגרפיים כאלה מחוץ לארץ בבל עצמה.

במונומנטים הללו של נבונאיד הגלגל המכונף הוא במרכז, משמאל לו נראה הסמל המשולב של הסהר והירח ומימינו הכוכב, המזוהה עם אשתר. השימוש בשלושה סמלי אלים בלבד ולא ברבים יותר, כמקובל במונומנטים האשוריים, אפיין את המונומנטים הבבליים באלף הראשון. אולם בבבל, בלוח מסיפַּר הנזכר לעיל (ציור 11), למשל, חקוק בַּמרכז גלגל החמה הבבלי נטול־הכנפיים. הוספת הכנפיים לסמל הבבלי המסורתי בימיו של נבונאיד משקפת אימוץ של סמל אשורי שכיח, שנועד לזכות את המשתמשים בו ביוקרה ובכוח שיוחס לסמל הזה. היא תואמת את שאיפתו של נבונאיד

26 ברקר־קלהן (לעיל, הערה 10), מס׳ 259–260, ואולי גם מס׳ 268.

ל'חידושים' חזותיים במבע התמוני הבבלי בן הזמן, כמשתקף בשיר השנינה שבו הואשם המלך ביצירת דימויים חזותיים שלא נודעו קודם לכן.[27] אולם ניכוס סמל זה למערכת הסמלים הדתית של בבל בימיו של נבונאיד התאפשר קרוב לוודאי גם מפני שהיה איקון חזותי רב־משמעי, והיה עשוי לייצג דמויות של כמה אלים.

אפשר שבאסטלות של נבונאיד ייצג הגלגל המכונף את שַׁמַש בדומה לאב־טיפוס של האסטלות האשוריות שממנו, כנראה, הושפעו. אולם בגלל מעמדו המיוחד של אלוהי הירח בתקופת שלטונו של נבונאיד אולי אפשר לטעון שהגלגל המכונף במונומנטים אלו ייצג את אל הירח, אף שלעתים באסטלות הללו אלוהות זו מסומלת גם באיקון המשולב של לוחית הלבנה והסהר. הצגת אל הירח, בדומה להצגת שַׁמַש ואשור, באמצעות גלגל מכונף מתועדת בממצא החזותי: בחותם־גליל המלווה בכתובת ארמית של ברכהדד (ציור 14), לדוגמה, סין נראה בדמותו האנושית, מוכתר בסהר וניצב בתוך גלגל מכונף בדומה לתיאוריו השכיחים של אשור. היציגם כאלה מופיעים גם

ציור 14: אל הירח בתוך סהר מכונף, חותם־גליל של ברכהדד, המוצא אינו ידוע ציירה נגה זאבי על־פי חותם־גליל 34.208, המוזאון לאמנות, בוסטון · צויר באדיבות המוזאון

27 T.-G. Lee, 'The Jasper Cylinder Seals of Aššurbanipal and Nabonidus' Making of Sîn statue', *RA*, 87 (1993), pp. 131. הגלגל המכונף מופיע במונומנטים מתימא שבחצי האי ערב, מן המאה החמישית, שהושפעו מן האמנות הבבלית בימי נבונאיד. בהתבססה על כתובת החקוקה על אחד המונומנטים הללו – אסטלה השמורה במוזאון הלובר – הציעה דאלי (לעיל, הערה 6], עמ' 85–86) לזהות את הסמל עם האל צַלְמ, הנזכר בכתובת שעל אסטלה זו כאלוהות שהוצבה בתימא. אולם אף שאין בידינו מקורות יתדיים המקשרים בין צַלְמ ובין הפר (שם, עמ' 88) זיקה אפשרית של הכתובת לתבליט שעל האסטלה מרמזת שבמקרה זה צַלְמ עשוי להתייחס לפר הגדול הנראה במרכז. וראה E.A. Knauf, 'The Persian Administration in Arabia', *Transeuphratène*, 2 (1990), p. 212, note 49

על אסטלות שמוצאן בצפון סוריה ובדרום־מערב תורכיה שבהן אל הירח מוצג באמצעות סמלו, הסהר. באסטלה מתֵל ברסיפ, למשל, הסהר עוטף את הגלגל בחלקו התחתון ונעשה חלק בלתי נפרד מן הסמל עצמו (ציור 15).[28] האיקון המכונף מסמל פה את אלוהות הירח ואולי גם את אלוהות השמש, ונוסף על כך הוא רומז פה, כפי שמלמד ההקשר התמוני, לדימוי אלוהי שלישי – אל הסערה הניצב מתחתיו.

ציור 15: לוחית סהר מכונפת מעל לאל הסערה, תֵל ברסיפ
מתוך אורנן (לעיל, ציור 8), ציור 18 • באדיבות OBO פריבורג, שווייץ

28 G. Bunnens, *A New Luwian Stele and the Cult of the Storm-God at Til Barsib – Masuwari*, Paris 2006

מיזוג כמה רכיבים חזותיים לסמל אחד המשתקף בגלגוליו של הגלגל המכונף באמנות של האלף הראשון עשוי לעתים להיות מורכב יותר ואף לרמז לדמויותיהן של עוד אלוהויות. בתבליט מסַקצֶ׳גֶזוּ, למשל, נוספת על רכיבי הסמל – הכנפיים, הגלגל והסהר – ורדה (ציור 16). שילוב הוורדה בתוך הגלגל שיקף, כאמור, את אחד השינויים שחלו בסמל עם אימוצו במערב אסיה בראשית האלף השני (לעיל, ציור 1). במאגר המוטיבים החזותיים של אמנות המזרח הקדום נודעה הוורדה כבר בתקופת אֶרֶךְ בשלהי האלף הרביעי כמייצגת אלוהות נשית, אולי אִנַנָ. היא מופיעה גם בתיאורים חתיים של הגלגל המכונף, וסביר שהצגתה במונומנטים מן האלף הראשון מצפון סוריה ומדרום־מזרח תורכיה הושפעה גם מהם. זיהוי האלוהות המיוצגת בוורדה בהיצגים מן האלף הראשון לא תמיד נהיר, אולם ברור למדיי שלפחות בהקשרים חזותיים מסוימים היא מייצגת אלוהות נשית.[29] באסטלה

ציור 16: סהר־ורדה מכונף, תבליט־קיר, סַקצֶ׳גֶזוּ
מתוך אורנן (לעיל, ציור 8), ציור 19 • באדיבות OBO פריבורג, שווייץ

29 I.J. Winter, 'Carved Ivory Furniture Panels from Nimrud: A Coherent Subgroup of the North Syrian Style', *Metropolitan Museum Journal*, 11 (1976), p. 46; לקשרים קדומים יותר בין הוורדה ובין דמויות נשיות ראה E.D. van Buren, 'The Rosette in Mesopotamian Art', *ZA*, 45 (1939), pp. 99–107; E. Porada, 'A Cylinder Seal with a Camel in the Walters Art Gallery', *The Journal of the Walters Art Gallery* (*Essays in Honor of Dorothy Kent Hill*), 36 (1977), pp. 1–6; ראה גם את הוורדות בשנהב ה'חתי' ממגידו, המרמזות לדמותה של האלה שַׁאְשְׁכַּ המיוצגת באישה הערומה שבמרכז, והשווה אל R.L. Alexander, 'Šaušga and the Hittite Ivory from Megiddo', *JNES*, 50 (1991), p. 161

ממלטיה, למשל, נראית ורדה מכונפת מעל שתי אלוהויות שהחשובה – זו היושבת – היא אלה (ציור 17).[30] פרח בעל ארבעה עלים המשולב בגלגל מכונף נראה גם בלוח ברונזה ששימש לעיטור מצח של סוס הנושא כתובת של חזאל מלך ארם, שנחשף במתחם האלה הֶרָה שבסמוס (ציור 18). הפרח במקרה זה מלווה בארבע חריטות עדינות המזכירות לכאורה את גלגל השמש הבבלי, אולם כיוון שמתחתיו מוצגות רק דמויות של נשים, כנראה אלות, דומה שגם כאן מופיעה ורדה בתוך גלגל מכונף.[31] הדוגמאות הללו ממחישות שהגלגל המכונף שימש לא רק לייצוג אלים גדולים אלא חצה את גבולות המִגדר השמימיים וייצג גם דמויות של אלות גדולות.

מן הנסקר עד כה עולה שהגלגל המכונף שימש באמנות של קדמת־אסיה באלף הראשון סמל כללי של אלוהויות. כך היה עשוי לייצג דמויות של אלים גדולים, כגון שַמַש או סין, או אלים ראשיים שעמדו בראש הפנתאון, כגון אשור. זהותה של האלוהות שיוצגה בגלגל סומנה לעתים על־ידי תוספת סמן מייחד כגון סהר הירח או הוורדה. סיוע להמחשת מורכבותו של הגלגל המכונף והצגתו כסמל של אלוהות ראשית לא רק באשור אלא גם בממלכות החסות שלה או במדינות שהיו נתונות להשפעתה נמצא בשלושה מונומנטים מלכותיים מזנג׳ירלי: אורטוסטט חקוק בכתובת פיניקית של כְּלַמֻוַ מן המאה התשיעית (ציור 19) ושני אורטוסטטים כתובים ארמית של בררכב, בן זמנו של תגלת־פלאסר השלישי במחצית השנייה של המאה השמינית (ציור 20 וציור 21, שבו נראים רק סמלי האלים שנחקקו על המונומנט).[32]

לזיהוי סמלי האלים של המונומנטים מזנג׳ירלי נדרשו כמה חוקרים, אולם לטעמי, פרשנותו של יגאל ידין היא המתאימה ביותר, שכן היא משתלבת בראייה הכללית של שחזור מקומו של הגלגל המכונף במבע החזותי במחצית הראשונה של האלף הראשון לפסה״נ. ידין הציע שהגלגל במונומנטים של מלכי שַמְאַל היה אחד משני הסמלים שייצגו את רכבאל, האל הפטרון של השושלת השליטה בשַמְאַל, הידוע רק על־פי ממצאי זנג׳ירלי. בייצגו את האל ששמו או תוארו רכבאל לווה הגלגל המכונף בעול, סמל אלוהי

30 W. Orthmann, *Untersuchungen zur späthethitischen Kunst*, Bonn 1971, Pl. 42:f; J.D. Hawkins, *Corpus of Hieroglyphic Luwian Inscriptions*, I/1–3, Berlin–New York 2000, Pl. 164; T. Ornan, 'The Lady and the Bull: Remarks on the Bronze Plaque from Tel Dan', in Y. Amit, E. Ben Zvi, I. Finkelstein & O. Lipschits (eds.), *Ancient Israel in Its Near Eastern Context: A Tribute to Nadav Naaman*, Winona Lake, Ind. 2006, pp. 303–307 (ושם ספרות). על תנוחת הישיבה המסמנת חשיבות באמנות של המזרח הקדום ראה וינטר (לעיל, הערה 8), עמ׳ 255–256.

31 D. Parayre, 'A propos d'une plaque de harnais en bronze découverte à Samos: Réflexions sur le disque solaire ailé', *RA*, 83 (1989), pp. 45–51; I. Ephʿal & J. Naveh, 'Hazael's Booty Inscriptions', *IEJ*, 39 (1989), pp. 192–200 (ושם ספרות).

32 J. Tropper, *Die Inschriften von Zincirli*, Münster 1993, pp. 5, 24–26

ציור 17: ורדה מכונפת, אסטלה, מלטיה
מתוך הוקינס (הערה 30), ציור 164 · באדיבות פרופ׳ דייוויד הוקינס, לונדון

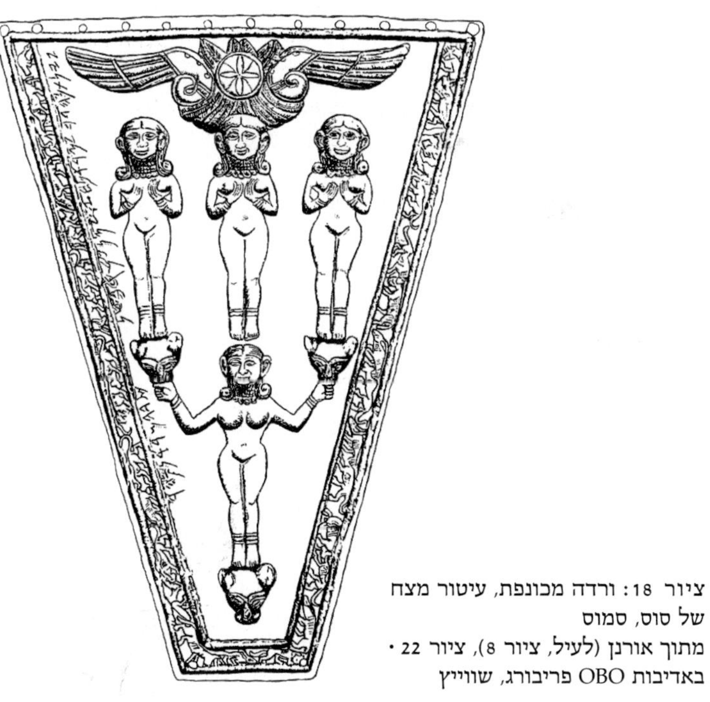

ציור 18: ורדה מכונפת, עיטור מצח של סוס, סמוס
מתוך אורנן (לעיל, ציור 8), ציור 22 · באדיבות OBO פריבורג, שווייץ

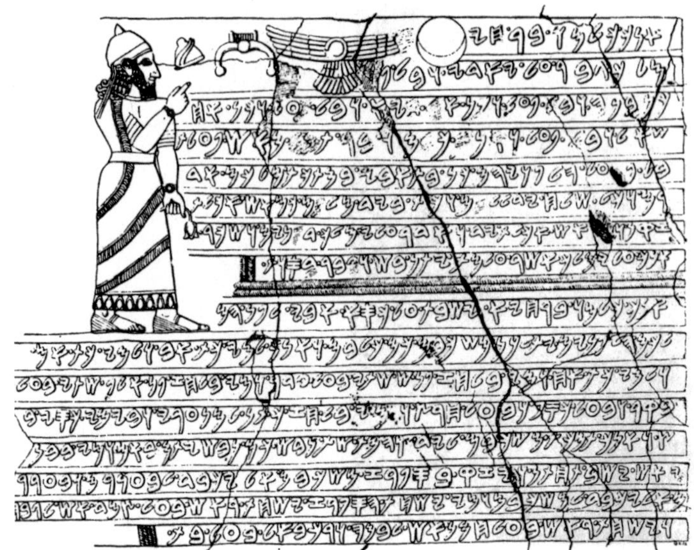

ציור 19: גלגל מכונף לצד סמלי אלים, אורטוסטט של כלמו, זנג׳ירלי
מתוך אורנן (לעיל, ציור 8), ציור 24 • באדיבות OBO פריבורג, שווייץ

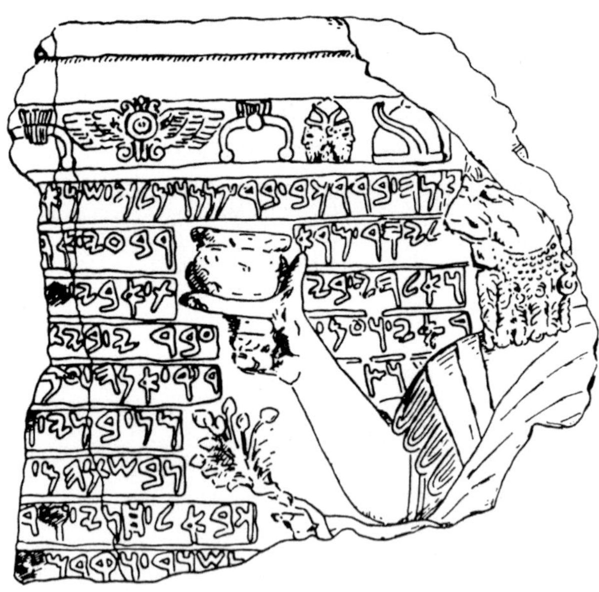

ציור 20: גלגל מכונף לצד סמלי אלים, אורטוסטט של בררכב, זנג׳ירלי
מתוך נ׳ נאמן וח׳ רבין, הערך ׳שמאל׳, אנציקלופדיה מקראית, ח, ירושלים 1982, טור 319

ציור 21: סמלי אלים על אורטוסטט של בררכב, זנג׳ירלי
ציירה פנינה ארד על־פי ידין (הערה 33), ציור 4

יחידאי באמנות של המזרח הקדום, שעד כה גם הוא מתועד רק בממצאי זנג׳ירלי.[33]

הבחירה בשני סמלים אלו לייצוגו של האל הראשי של שַׁמְאַל משקפת מיזוג של סממנים מקומיים ואשוריים, המאפיין את ההיגד החזותי של ממלכות החסות של אשור. הבחירה בגלגל המכונף לתיאורו של ראש הפנתאון המקומי מבטאת חיקוי מקומי לייצוגה של אשור שבהתחשב במקומה של ממלכת שַׁמְאַל בתחומי השליטה החתיים לשעבר גם הושפע ממסורת חתית קדומה יותר. כנגד זה הבחירה בעול משקפת את הייחוד המקומי. מיזוג זה של העתקת דימויים אשוריים לצד קיום או יצירה של דגמים מקומיים בא לידי ביטוי במונומנטים של זנג׳ירלי לא רק במבחר הסמלים אלא גם במאפיינים אחרים. הצגת השליט ניצב לפני קבוצה של סמלים דוממים, למשל, מחקה בלא ספק את האב־טיפוס האשורי הנפוץ באסטלות ובתבליטי־סלע שכוננו בכל רחבי האימפריה, ובהם הוצג מלך אשור ניצב לפני סמלי אלוהיו. אולם תנוחת המחווה של שליטי שַׁמְאַל וכמוה הסְמָנים המלכותיים שהם מחזיקים בידיהם – הפרח והגביע – נבדלים ממחוות ההערצה האשוריות במאות התשיעית והשמינית, והם משקפים מסורת סורית מקומית שראשיתה בתחילת האלף השני.[34] מסקנתו של ידין שהגלגל המכונף והעול ייצגו את

33 י׳ ידין, ׳על סמלי האלים בשמאל (זינג׳ירלי) בקארתאגו ובחצור׳, ידיעות, לא (תשכ״ז), עמ׳ 35–34 (ושם, עמ׳ 33–32 לתולדות המחקר של פענוח הסמלים); A. R. Millard, 'An Israelite Royal Seal?', *BASOR*, 208 (1972), p. 8. אך ראה טרופר (לעיל, הערה 32), עמ׳ 22 שאמנם מזהה את העול עם רכבאל אך את הגלגל המכונף הוא מזהה עם שַׁמַשׁ.

34 ע׳ ציפר, ׳גלגולים, תמורות ומהפכות בסממני השלטון באמנות המזרח הקדום: המגבת, הפרח והקערה׳, חיבור לקבלת התואר דוקטור לפילוסופיה של אוניברסיטת תל־אביב, 1999, עמ׳ 126–133, 195–196. במחווה האשורית ׳הושטת האצבע׳ *ubānu tarāṣu*, האופיינית למאות התשיעית והשמינית, הסוגד מצביע באצבע ימינו לעבר מושא הפולחן ושמאלו מושטת פתוחה לפנים; ראה U. Magen, *Assyrische Königsdarstellungen: Aspekte der Herrschaft, eine Typologie*, Mainz 1986, pp. 45–55

האל הראשי של שושלת שַׁמְאַל מסתייעת גם בטביעת חותם המלכות של ברכב, שבה נראים רק שני סמלים אלו (ציור 22). בדומה לחותם המלכות האשורי, שהציג את המלך מכניע אריה, גם תמונת חותמו של ברכב שולבה בתעמולה הממלכתית שהשתמשה בדימויים חזותיים נבחרים ומגוונים כדי להפיץ את ההיגד המלכותי: במקרה זה – החסות האלוהית של רכבאל, האל של מלכי שַׁמְאַל, ובעקבותיה אשרור סמכותו השלטונית של המלך ברכב.

הצגת הגלגל המכונף כאחד מסמלי האל הפטרון של השושלת השַׁמְאַלית ותפקידו בתעמולה הממלכתית מניעים אותנו לבחון עוד דוגמה ששולב בה סמל כזה במִנהל של מדינת חסות אשורית. הכוונה, כמובן, לממלכת יהודה ולתפקידו של הגלגל המכונף בתעמולה השלטונית המקומית על־פי הצגותיו בטביעות על קנקני 'למלך' משלהי המאה השמינית (ציור 23).[35] צורתו וסגנונו

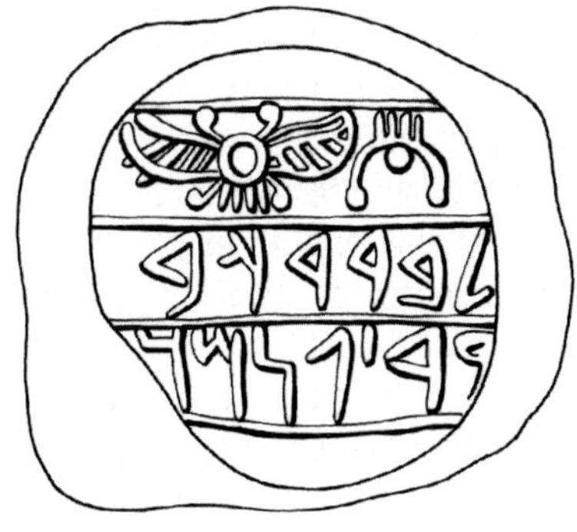

ציור 22: גלגל מכונף ועול, טביעת חותמו של ברכב, זנג'ירלי
ציירה פנינה ארד על־פי ידין (הערה 33), ציור 2

ציור 23: גלגל מכונף, טביעות 'למלך', לכיש ורמת רחל מתוך פראר (הערה 36), לוח 9, מס' 103, 104 • באדיבות פרופ' דומיניק פראר, צרפת

35 A.G. Vaughn, *Theology, History, and Archaeology in the Chronicler's Account of Hezekiah*, Atlanta 1999, pp. 81–82 (ושם ספרות).

המיוחד של הגלגל המכונף שנטבע בחותמות 'למלך' ובעיקר עיקולן מעלה של קצות הכנפיים מזכירים את הצגותיו בצפון סוריה, בייחוד בזנג'ירלי.[36] השימוש בחותם זה במִנהל ממלכת יהודה, המסתבר מעצם הופעת התיבה 'למלך', מעלה על הדעת שחותם המלכות היהודאי חיקה את האב־טיפוס בן הזמן המתוחכם יותר של חותם המלכות האשורי.[37] המסקנה שבעת ששולב הגלגל המכונף בתעמולת המִנהל של ממלכת יהודה הוא ייצג באשור ובצפון סוריה אלוהות אינה עולה בקנה אחד עם ההנחה שהייתה מקובלת במחקר, והיא שביהודה דווקא הוא ייצג את המלכות.[38] טענה זו נגזרה מן הדגם החתי בן האלף השני לפסה"נ שעל־פיו, כפי שצוין למעלה, היה הגלגל המכונף עשוי לייצג לעתים הן את אלוהות השמש הן את המלך. אולם, כאמור, בארצות מערב אסיה בדרך כלל לא שימש הגלגל המכונף סמל של מלכות.[39] נוסף על כך מדוע להרחיק לממלכה החתית באלף השני לפסה"נ כדי ללמוד על יהודה במאה השמינית כאשר בידינו הקבלות בנות הזמן שעל־פיהן ייצג הגלגל המכונף אלוהות? יש להדגיש שאף על פי שבידינו עדויות מקראיות שאמנם לעתים הן מאוחרות מן הממצא החזותי הנידון כאן, המדגישות את ייחודה של התפיסה התְּמונית הישראלית העתיקה – אף על פי כן המבע החזותי של ממלכות יהודה וישראל צריך להיבחן בראש ובראשונה על־פי אמות המידה התקֵפות לכלל המזרח הקדום. רק אחרי הדגשת הדומה והמשותף בין המבע החזותי של ממלכות יהודה וישראל ובין המבע החזותי של שכנותיהן העתיקות ישורטט ויודגש הייחוד הישראלי הקדום. הופעת הגלגל המכונף בשלהי המאה השמינית ביהודה זמן קצר לאחר הצגתו בזנג'ירלי, שבה סימל את האלוהות הראשית של הממלכה, מחזקת את ההצעה שגם ביהודה הוא ייצג את האלוהות הראשית של השושלת המקומית – יהוה – שממצאים כתובים חוץ־מקראיים בני הזמן מאשרים את שכיחות פולחנה בפרק הזמן הנידון.[40] עצם הדבר שעדויות לאימוץ הסמל לתעמולה השלטונית נמצאו עד כה רק באשור

36 A. D. Tushingham, 'A Royal Israelite Seal (?) and the Royal Jar Handle Stamps (Part Two)', *BASOR*, 201 (1971), p. 33; D. Parayre, 'Les cachets ouest-sémitiques à travers l'image du disque solaire ailé (perspective iconographique)', *Syria*, 67 (1990), pp. 290–291

37 מילארד (לעיל, הערה 33), עמ' 8.

38 בהתאם מילארד (לעיל, הערה 33) שולל גם את ההצעה לראות בחרפושית המכונפת סמל של מלכות (וראה להלן).

39 מאייר־אופיפיציוס (לעיל, הערה 4), עמ' 189. משום כך אף קשה לקבל את הצעתה של דאלי ([לעיל, הערה 6], עמ' 99) שלעתים באלף הראשון ייצג הגלגל המכונף גם דמות שלטונית בת־תמותה.

40 וראה, למשל, ש' אחיטוב, אסופת כתובות עבריות מימי בית־ראשון וראשית ימי בית־שני, ירושלים תשנ"ג, עמ' 19–22 (כתף הינום), 34–52 (אוסטרקונים מס' 2–6, 9 מלכיש), 70–72, 74–77 (אוסטרקונים מס' 16, 18, 21, 40 מערד), 153–160 (פיתסים וציור קיר מכונתילת עג'רוד), 111–113 (חורבת אל־קום), 116–117 (כתובת במערה באזור עין גדי), 251, 258 (כתובת מישע) ושכיחות התוספת התאופורית 'יהו' 'יו' בשמות עבריים.

ובסוריה מסייע לראות בהופעת הסמל ביהודה פועל יוצא של התפשטות האימפריה האשורית.

הבחירה בגלגל המכונף לאחד משני הסמלים ששימשו את השושלת הירושלמית משתקפת מחד גיסא במיעוט היקרויותיו בכלל החותמות העבריים ומאידך גיסא בהצגתו בחותם של שבניו עבד עזיו, הנמנה עם החותמות הספורים המזכירים שם של מלך מיהודה (ציור 24).[41] בכך מסתמנים היטב חשיבותו של דגם זה במערכת הסמלים המלכותית ומקומו הרם בהיירכיה של הסמלים היהודאיים. בדומה לשַׂמְאַל גם ביהודה לוותה הצגת האלוהות הראשית באמצעות הגלגל המכונף עוד בסמל אחד – חרפושית מכונפת – שגם היא קרוב לוודאי ייצגה את האלוהות הראשית.[42] אולם שלא כהצגת צמד הסמלים של האלוהות הראשית בשַׂמְאַל ביהודה הם מופיעים בנפרד בטביעות 'למלך'. על-פי ממצאי זנג'ירלי, גם באימוץ הגלגל המכונף ביהודה בשלהי המאה השמינית אפשר לראות פרי של השראה אשורית, ואילו בשילובה של החרפושית כנראה יש לראות ביטוי מקומי לשאילת דגם מצרי, אולי בתיווך פיניקי.

שכיחותו של הגלגל המכונף במוצרים פיניקיים, שמקצתם נתגלו גם בארץ ישראל, לכאורה מלמדת שמקור הסמל המוצג בטביעות 'למלך' היה במוצרים

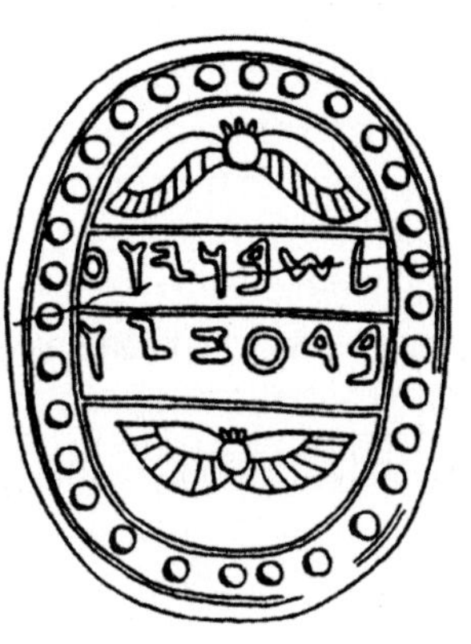

ציור 24: היצג כפול של גלגל מכונף, חותם שבניו עבד עזיו, המוצא אינו ידוע
מתוך קיל ואילינגר (הערה 45), ציור 263b • באדיבות פרופ' אותמר קיל ופרופ' כריסטוף אילינגר

41 לחותם זה מצטרפים חותמיהם של פקידי מלכי יהודה אשנא עבד אחז, אביו עבד עזיו וכן החותם הישראלי של שמע עבד ירבעם B. Sass, 'The Pre-exilic Hebrew Seals: Iconism vs. Aniconism', in B. Sass & Ch. Uehlinger (eds.), *Studies in the Iconography of Northwest Semitic Inscribed Seals*, Fribourg–Göttingen 1993, pp. 238–239. בחותמו של אשנא נראה גלגל חמה מצרי מלווה בשני נחשי אוּרֵאוּס. על חותמות של אנשים פרטיים שבהם גלגל מכונף ראה N. Avigad & B. Sass, *Corpus of West Semitic Stamp Seals*, Jerusalem 1997, Nos. 298, 343, 685

42 מילארד (לעיל, הערה 33), עמ' 6. גם טיילור מציין ששני הסמלים שיקפו מסר דומה; ראה J.-G. Taylor, *Yahweh and the Sun: Biblical and Archaeological Evidence for Sun Worship in Ancient Israel*, Sheffield 1993, p. 46

פיניקיים.[43] אולם כאמור, הדמיון הצורני שבין הגלגל המכונף של טביעות 'למלך' ובין הופעותיו בזנג'ירלי מסייע לראות את מקור ההשראה לגלגל היהודאי באמנות בת הזמן ששגשגה בצפון סוריה. מסקנה זו מתחזקת גם על סמך הזיקה האיקונוגרפית של ממצאים אחרים מיהודה ומשפלת יהודה לתגליות מזנג'ירלי, כגון בולה מעוטרת בסהר מעיר דוד ולוחית כסף מתל מקנה.[44] קשרים בין יהודה ובין אחת מממלכות סוריה שהתקיימו בחסות האימפריאלית האשורית מהדהדים גם בסיפור המקראי על אחז והחידושים הדתיים שהביא מדמשק (מל"ב טז:י–יח).

גם את התפיסה הרואה בגלגל היהודאי חיקוי ישיר לדגם המצרי עתיק היומין קשה לקבל כפשוטה,[45] שהרי בתקופה הנידונה, בשלהי המאה השמינית לפסה"נ, היה סמל זה שכיח במאגר החזותי של ארצות קדמת־אסיה ובהן ארץ ישראל כבר יותר מאלף שנים. במרבית הופעותיו בארץ ישראל, כגון בכן החרס מתענך, הוא מזוהה עם רכיבים, סגנון ותוכן שמקורם באמנות החזותית שפרחה מצפון לארץ ישראל.[46] העיתוי שבו נבחר הגלגל המכונף לייצג את אלוהות בית המלוכה הירושלמי – בשלהי המאה השמינית לפסה"נ – בשיא התפשטותה של האימפריה האשורית ובשיאם של המגעים בין מדינת החסות הקטנה ובין האימפריה – מחזק את ההשערה שאכן, האב־טיפוס האשורי הוא שהשפיע על הצגתו ועל משמעותו של הסמל הירושלמי.

43 D. Parayre, 'Deux chapiteaux hathoriques à Amathonte: Étude des disques solaires ailés', *Bulletin de correspondance hellénique*, 114 (1990), pp. 220–233. לעוד דוגמאות להצגת הגלגל המכונף במוצרים פיניקיים ממזרח וממערב הים התיכון שזמנם עד המאה החמישית ראה S. Moscati (ed.), *The Phoenicians – Exhibition Catalogue*, Milan 1988, pp. 108, 117, 159, 305, 307, 319, 376, 409, 442, 516, 528

44 B. Brandl, 'Bullae with Figurative Decoration', in D.T. Ariel (ed.), *Excavations at the City of David 1978–1985*, VI: *Inscriptions*, Jerusalem 2000, p. 64; T. Ornan, 'Ištar as Depicted on Finds from Israel', in A. Mazar (ed.), *Studies in the Archaeology of the Iron Age in Israel and Jordan*, Sheffield 2001, pp. 246–248

45 פראר (לעיל, הערה 36), עמ' 293–294; O. Keel & Ch. Uehlinger, *Gods, Goddesses, and Images of God in Ancient Israel*, Minneapolis 1998, pp. 275–276; אולם ראה פראר, שם, עמ' 295. טיילור ([לעיל, הערה 42], עמ' 42–58) סבור שמקור הגלגל היהודאי הוא בפולחנו של הורוס מאדפו, אף על פי שהוא מציע (עמ' 45) שמבחינה צורנית הדגם הסורי הוא שהשפיע על עיצוב הסמל בטביעות 'למלך'.

46 פ' בק, 'כני הפולחן מתענך: לבירור המסורת האיקונוגרפית של כלי הפולחן שנתגלו בארץ בתקופת הברזל א'', בתוך נ' נאמן וי' פינקלשטיין (עורכים), מנוודות למלוכה: היבטים ארכיאולוגיים והיסטוריים על ראשית ישראל, ירושלים 1990, עמ' 420, 435. וראה לדוגמה, גלגל מכונף בחותמות־גליל מן האלף השני אצל קיל ואילינגר (לעיל, הערה 45), עמ' 40, ציור 31b (תל פארעה הצפוני); P. Beck, 'Cylinder Seals from the Temple in Area H', in Y. Yadin et al., *Hazor* III–IV, Jerusalem 1989, pp. 311, 312–313, 316, 318, Pl. 319: 1, 2; Pl. 320: 1, 3; B. Parker, 'Cylinder Seals from Palestine', *Iraq*, 11 (1949), Nos. 102, 113

אולם מן הנאמר לעיל אין להסיק שהגלגל המכונף ביהודה לא היה טעון גם משמעות שמשית. היבט שמשי זה של הסמל משתקף, למשל, כבר בהצגתו לצד חרפושית מכונפת על חותם דמוי חרפושית משומרון (ציור 25) במַחְבָּר שהשראתו, כפי שציין טיילור, היא בקמעות נוביים משלהי המאה השמינית.[47] יתרה מזו, זיקתו הכפולה של סמל זה לאלוהות ראשית

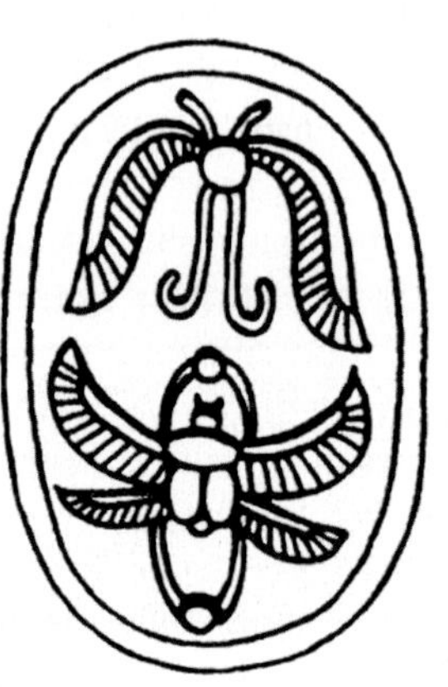

ציור 25: גלגל מכונף מעל חרפושית מכונפת, חותם־טביעה דמוי חרפושית, שומרון
מתוך קיל ואילינגר (הערה 45), ציור 258a • באדיבות פרופ׳ אותמר קיל ופרופ׳ כריסטוף אילינגר

ולאלוהות השמש בשני מקרי הבוחן שמחוץ לארץ ישראל הנידונים כאן מרמזת שגם ביהודה היה הסמל טעון משמעות כפולה. באשור, כפי שנזכר למעלה, ייצג הגלגל המכונף את האל אשור או את שַׁמַש לפי ההקשרים החזותיים שבהם הופיע. כפל משמעות כזה מסתמן גם בגלגל המכונף בזנג׳ירלי באמצעות הכינוי רכבאל. אף על פי שכינוי זה מרמז שלכאורה מדובר ברכב של האל אֵל, עדויות הקושרות את שַׁמַש עם מרכבה מצביעות על זיקה לאֵל.[48] וכך גם בשַׁמְאַל – בעקבות מסורת חתית שראתה בגלגל המכונף סמל שמשי ובהשראת הדגם האשורי – ייצג הגלגל המכונף אלוהות ראשית מקומית הטעונה מסר שמשי. תפיסה כפולה כזאת של הסמל ביהודה אינה מפתיעה, שכן יהוה, המסומל בגלגל המכונף, מיזג בהיותו אל ראשי, בדומה למרדוך ולאשור, מאפיינים של אלוהויות גדולות אחדות ובהן אלוהות השמש.[49] אמנם נדירות הופעתו של הרכיב ׳שמש׳ בשמות פרטיים מארץ ישראל ומסוריה במקורות חוץ־מקראיים במחצית הראשונה של

47 קיל ואילינגר (לעיל, הערה 45), עמ׳ 274, ציור 258a; טיילור (לעיל, הערה 42), עמ׳ 51, ציור 6.

48 E. Lipiński, 'Shemesh', DDD 2nd edition, p. 765

49 טיילור (לעיל, הערה 42), עמ׳ 257–260; F.M. Cross, *Canaanite Myth and Hebrew Epic*, Cambridge, Mass.–London 1997, pp. 50, 72, 247; K. van der Toorn, 'Yahweh', DDD 2nd edition, pp. 916–918

האלף הראשון עשויה לרמז שפולחן אלוהות השמש לא היה נפוץ באזורים אלו ומשום כך לא בהכרח ייצג הגלגל המכונף גם את האלוהות הזאת. ואולם סממנים שמשיים בפולחנו של יהוה דוגמת הסוסים הנזכרים בספר מלכים ב כג:יא או המרכבה, הסוסים והאש בסיפורי אליהו במלכים ב ב:יא–יב מרמזים על היבטים של אור ושמש בפולחנו של יהוה[50] ומחזקים את זיהוי הגלגל המכונף עם סמל של יהוה כאל ראשי הטעון גם משמעות שמשית. דימוי מקראי מאוחר הממחיש את הזיקה של הגלגל המכונף ליהוה והמחבר בין יהוה ובין שמש, מרפא וצדק – הסממן המאפיין ביותר של אלוהות האור – משתקף בדברי מלאכי 'וזרחה לכם יראי שמי שמש צדקה ומרפא בכנפיה' (ג:כ).

סיכום ומסקנות

בתקופת התפשטותה של האימפריה האשורית שימש הגלגל המכונף סמל אלוהות כללי שהיה עשוי לייצג דמויות של אלים ואלות גדולים, כגון שַׁמַש או סין. כך יכול דימוי חזותי זה לשמש גם סמל של אלים ראשיים, למשל, רכבאל בשַׂמְאַל או יהוה ביהודה, ולעתים הוא ייצג אלים שהוצבו בראש פנתאון, דוגמת אשור. מסקנה זו מסתייעת בהופעותיו של הגלגל המכונף בימי שלטון פרס לאחר נפילת האימפריות של אשור ובבל, שאז ייצג את אַהֻרַה־מַזְדָה, האל הראשי של השושלת האחמנית.[51]
דומה שלאופן הצגת הגלגל המכונף בחלקה העליון של התמונה היה תפקיד בבחירתו לייצג כמה אלים, שכן במבע החזותי של המזרח הקדום יוחד מרום התמונה לרכיבים החשובים ביותר שלה. לפיכך מיזוג סמלים של אלים בגלגל המכונף הביא לידי שדרוג מעמדם של האלים שיוצגו בסמל זה. בזאת התאים האיקון רב־הזהויות של הגלגל המכונף לשמש סמל של אלים גדולים, אלים ראשיים או ראשי פנתאון.
הצגתם של אלים ראשיים בתחומיה ובגבולותיה של האימפריה האשורית כגון בשַׂמְאַל וביהודה באמצעות הגלגל המכונף חיקתה את ייצוגו של האל אשור בסמל זה וביטאה את השפעתה התרבותית של אשור על מדינות החסות שלה.[52] הבחירה מחדש בסמל עתיק יומין שנודע בקדמת־אסיה

50 על הרכיב 'שמש' בשמות פרטיים ובשמות מקומות במקרא ראה טיילור (לעיל, הערה 42), עמ' 92–98, וכן על הרמזים האחרים לפולחן שמשי־יהוויסטי שם, עמ' 118, 120, 127–128, 147, 163. ליפינסקי (לעיל, הערה 48), עמ' 765–766. ון־דר תורן (לעיל, הערה 49), עמ' 917–918.

51 M. Cool Root, *The King and Kingship in Achaemenid Art: Essays on the Creation of an Iconography of Empire*, Leiden 1979, pp. 169–173; פרפולה (לעיל, הערה 20), עמ' 105 (ושם ספרות).

52 השווה אל S. Mazzoni, 'Syria and the Periodization of the Iron Age: A Cross-Cultural Perspective', in G. Bunnens (ed.), *Essays on Syria in the Iron Age*, Louvain–Paris–Sterling 2000, pp. 49–50, 53

כבר בראשית האלף השני לפסה"נ בממלכות הקטנות שהתקיימו בתחומי האימפריה האשורית משקפת תהליך היסטורי־תרבותי מוכר של תְּרבות שבמהלכו הנחות והחלש מאמץ את מאפייניו של הגדול והחזק מתוך התאמה לצרכיו – כדי להידמות לו ולהיות שותף להצלחותיו.

גם תהליך המיזוג של כמה ישויות אלוהיות לאחת, שהודגם כאן באמצעות הגלגל המכונף, אינו בלתי קשור להוויה המדינית שבתחומיה התפתח סמל דתי זה, היינו האימפריה האשורית, שכן עם שגשוגה והעלאתה של האימפריה – מדינת־העל שכללה ערב רב של עמים, תרבויות ואמונות – שודרג גם מעמדו של האל הראשי שאותו עבדה השושלת המושלת באימפריה.[53] אחד הביטויים לשדרוג כזה היה האצת התהליך שבו הוטמעו בדמותו של האל הראשי דמויות של אלוהויות רבות אחרות, וקרוב לוודאי שבכך הותוותה הדרך להתפתחותה של האמונה באל יחיד.

כיוון שמרום התמונה יוחד, כאמור, לרכיביה החשובים ביותר, ייתכן שעצם מיקומו הגבוה של הגלגל המכונף בהיצג החזותי תרם להיותו סמל שייצג אלוהויות גדולות. האפשרות שאופן הצגתו של דימוי תמוני היה עשוי להשפיע על תפקידו ועל משמעותו ובעקבות זאת לגבש את הרעיון הדתי שייצג מדגישה את תפקידו של המבע החזותי בשחזור ההיסטוריה הדתית. שכן אם ייצג סמל חזותי אחד אלוהויות מספר, אפשר לשער שתופעה זו הייתה עשויה לתרום ואולי אף לזרז היווצרות של תפיסות דתיות שמיזגו לאחת כמה דמויות אלוהיות. התפתחות זו, שהייתה בוודאי אטית מאוד וכללה שלבי ביניים רבים, מחזקת את ההכרה שהאמונה באל אחד ובאלוהות יחידה הייתה תוצאה של תהליך התפתחותי ארוך ולא הייתה פרי התפרצות אמונית חד־פעמית.

53 ראה ב"א לוין, "'הוי אשור שבט אפי' (יש' י: טו) – אמונת הייחוד המקראית באספקלריה מדינית־בינלאומית: פתח דבר', ארץ־ישראל, כז (תשס"ג), עמ' 136–142.

כתובות נציבי סוחו
בראי ההיסטוריוגרפיה האשורית

מאת

נדב נאמן

מבוא

בשנים 1983-1978 נערכו חפירות הצלה באזור חַדִיתָה שבחבל הפרת התיכון לרגל הקמת סכר חדש על נהר פרת (סכר קַדִיסִיָה). הסכר תוכנן באופן שיציף מאה ושלושים ק״מ לאורך הנהר בתחום שיש בו אתרים קדומים רבים ובכללם האי אל־קלעה שעליו שכנה עֲנַת, בירת מחוז סוחו. אתרים רבים נחפרו בידי משלחות שהגיעו מכמה ארצות, מקצתם בהיקף רחב ורבים אחרים בהיקף בינוני או קטן.[1] במהלך החפירות נחשפו כתובות בכתב היתדות שנכתבו על לוחות חומר או נחרתו על אבן בידי שני נציבים שכיהנו במחוז סוחו במאה השמינית לפסה״נ. עשרים מן הכתובות נמצאו בחפירות שנערכו בסוּר גַ׳רְעָה, השוכנת לגדות נהר פרת, עוד ארבע כתובות נתגלו בחפירות האי עֲנָה וכתובות מעטות נתגלו בשלושה אתרים אחרים. שבע שנים לאחר תום החפירות פרסמו קביניו ואיסמעיל פקסימילה, תעתיק ותרגום של כל הכתובות בצירוף מבוא שבו הציגו את הטקסטים ודנו בקצרה בתרומתן של הכתובות למחקר וכן במבנן ובייחודן הספרותי והלשוני.[2] הכתובות מסוחו עובדו ותורגמו לאחר זמן גם בידי פריים במהדורת הכתובות של מלכי אשור ובבל שמפרסמת אוניברסיטת טורונטו, וציטוט הכתובות להלן הוא על־פי מהדורה זו.[3] במחקרים שהתפרסמו בעשר השנים האחרונות דנו חוקרים בתרומתן של הכתובות לחקר הגאוגרפיה ההיסטורית של אזור הגֶ׳זִירָה, ההרכב האתני־לשוני של תושבי האזור ובכללם שבטי

1 J.N. Postgate & P.J. Watson, 'Excavations in Iraq, 1977–78', *Iraq*, 41 (1979), pp. 148f, 155, 159; M.D. Roaf & J.N. Postgate, 'Excavations in Iraq, 1979–80', *Iraq*, 43 (1981), pp. 192–198; R. Killick & M.D. Roaf, 'Excavations in Iraq, 1981–82', *Iraq*, 45 (1983), pp. 199–224; S.J. al-Shukri, 'The Salvage of the Antiquities of the Qadissiya Dam Basin', *Sumer*, 42 (1986), pp. 9–11

2 A. Cavigneaux & B.K. Ismail, 'Die Statthalter von Suḫu und Mari im 8. Jh. v. Chr. Anhand neuer Texte den irakischen Grabungen im Staugebiet des Qadissiya-Damms', *BaM*, 21 (1990), pp. 321–456

3 G. Frame, *Rulers of Babylonia from the Second Dynasty of Isin to the End of Assyrian Domination (1157–612 BC)*, RIMB 2, Toronto 1995, pp. 275–331

הארמים ששכנו בו, סחר השיירות הערבי שהתנהל בחבל הפרת התיכון ובמידה מעטה בתרומתן גם לחקר המקרא.[4]

מפעליו של שַׁמַשׁ־רֵשׁ־אֻצֻר היו ידועים לחוקרים זה שנים רבות, שכן מצבה שלו נמצאה בראשית המאה העשרים בחפירות בבל ונידונה מאז פעמים רבות.[5] ואולם עד לחפירות החדשות הייתה זו עדות מבודדת. כתובות מלכי אשור מזכירות אף הן את מחוז סוחו, אבל מרבית ההזכרות הללו שייכות למאה התשיעית לפסה"נ, ואילו על תולדות המחוז במאה השמינית לפסה"נ נמסרות בכתובות רק ידיעות מעטות. גילוי הכתובות החדשות העמיד את המחקר על בסיס חדש ושפך אור על השלטון, העיור, המִנהל, החברה והפולחן בחבל הפרת התיכון באמצע המאה השמינית לפסה"נ.

בעולם האידאולוגי של מסופוטמיה ראו במסעות מלחמה ובפעולות בנייה פרי יזמה של השליט, ולכן גם הצבת מצבות המנציחות אותם נחשבה לזכות מלכותית בלבדית. כך הדבר גם כאשר בפועל הונהג המסע או נעשה מפעל הבנייה בידי אחד מנתיני המלך. זו הסיבה שאך מצבות מעטות הוצבו בידי שרים ונציבים אשוריים. כתובות לא מלכותיות ידועות בעיקר מסוף המאה התשיעית ומן המאה השמינית לפסה"נ,[6] תקופה שנחלש בה השלטון המרכזי

4 M. Liverani, 'Early Caravan Trade between South-Arabia and Mesopotamia', *Yemen*, 1 (1992), pp. 111–115; idem, 'Raṣappu and Hatallu', *SAAB*, 6/2 (1992), pp. 35–40; M. Fales, 'Mari: An Additional Note on "Raṣappu and Hatallu"', *ibid.*, pp. 105–107; P.E. Dion, 'Les Araméens du Moyen-Euphrate au VIIIe siècle à la lumière des inscriptions des maîtres de Suhu et Mari', *Supplement to* Vetus Testamentum, 61 (1995), pp. 53–73; R. Zadok, 'The Ethno-Linguistic Character of the Jezireh and Adjacent Regions in the 9th–7th centuries (Assyria Proper vs. Periphery)', in M. Liverani (ed.), *Neo-Assyrian Geography*, Rome 1995, pp. 228–230; E. Lipiński, *The Aramaeans: Their Ancient History, Culture, Religion*, Leuven 2000, pp. 105–107, 425–428; B. Pongratz-Leisten, 'Genealogien als Kulturtechnik zur Begründung des Herrschaftsanspruchs in Assyrien und Babylonien', *SAAB*, 11 (1997), pp. 96–98

5 ראה את הספרות המצוטטת אצל פריים (לעיל, הערה 3), עמ' 279; R. Mayer-Opificius, 'Das Relief des Šamaš-rēš-uṣur aus Babylon', in M. Dietrich & O. Loretz (eds.), *Vom Alten Orient zum Alten Testament: Festschrift für Wolfram Freiherrn von Soden zum 85. Geburtstag*, Kevelaer–Neukirchen-Vluyn 1995, pp. 333–348

6 דיונים מסכמים ושם ספרות נוספת ראה A.K. Grayson, 'Assyrian Officials and Power in the Ninth and Eighth Centuries', *SAAB*, 7 (1993), pp. 19–52; idem, 'Studies in Neo-Assyrian History II: The Eighth Century B.C.', in E. Robbins & S. Sandahl (eds.), *Corolla Torontonensis: Studies in Honour of Ronald Morton Smith*, Toronto 1994, pp. 73–84; idem, 'The Struggle for Power in Assyria: Challenge to Absolute Monarchy in the Ninth and Eighth Centuries B.C.', in K. Watanabe (ed.), *Priests and Officials in the Ancient Near East: Papers of the Second Colloquium on the Ancient Near East – The City and its Life held at the Middle Eastern Culture Center in Japan*, Heidelberg 1999, pp. 253–270; F. Blocher, 'Assyrische Würdenträger und Gouverneure des 9. und 8. Jh.: Eine Neubewertung ihrer Rolle', *AoF*, 28 (2001), pp. 298–324

ועלה כוחם של פקידים ונציבים, והם נטלו לידם סמכויות מלכותיות ובכללן גם הצבת מצבות.[7]
הקורפוס הגדול ביותר של כתובות לא מלכותיות שנתגלה עד כה במסופוטמיה בתקופת ההגמוניה האשורית הוא של נציבי סוחו. יש להדגיש כי סוחו לא סופחה לאשור, אל נכון בשל קרבתה לממלכת בבל והחשש האשורי מעימות עם בבל על השליטה בחבל הפרת התיכון, והשלטון האשורי בסוחו היה בדרך כלל רופף למדיי.[8] לכאורה יכלו נציבי סוחו להציב מצבות בכל זמן שהוא, אבל עצם הדבר שכל המִצבות שנתגלו נכתבו בתוך פרק זמן קצר מלמד שהלכה לחוד ומציאות לחוד. נראה שמלכי אשור לא ראו בעין יפה הצבת מצבות בידי שרים ונציבים, ואלה נמנעו מלהתגרות בהם. דומה אפוא שנציבי סוחו ניצלו את חולשתה של אשור ברבע השני ובראשית הרבע השלישי של המאה השמינית לפסה״נ כדי לחזק את כוחם ולהרחיב את סמכויותיהם, ואף כתבו כתובות והציבו מצבות המנציחות את פועלם.
רוב הכתובות שבידינו הן של נִנֻרְתַ־כֻּדֻרִ־אֻצֻר, ורק כתובות מעטות נכתבו בידי אביו, שַׁמַשׁ־רֵשַׁ־אֻצֻר. שניהם נושאים את התואר ׳נציב הארצות סוחו ומארי׳, ואולם מארי לא נכללה במחוז הכפוף להם. מסתבר שלפנינו תואר רשמי מסורתי, המשקף את מצב הדברים שהיה בעבר, ונציבי סוחו הוסיפו להחזיק בו על אף הנסיבות המשתנות. רוב הכתובות נכתבו על טיט ורק מעטות נכתבו על אבן, ויש מקום להניח שהראשונות שימשו טיוטה לאחרונות. פרשת המלחמה בארמים נזכרת בלוחות שנתגלו בשני אתרים – סוּר גַ׳רְעָה וַדַוַלִי, ומכאן שמצבות שנזכרה בהן פרשה זו נכתבו והוצבו במקומות אחדים במחוז.[9] בכתובת על לוח טיט שנמצאה בסוּר גַ׳רְעָה מתוארת בניית מקדש בעיר ענת.[10] יש אפוא מקום לשער שבאתר זה, שבו

7 יש להטיל ספק בטענה של בלוכר (לעיל, הערה 6) שהתחזקות השרים והנציבים האשוריים אינה מעידה על חולשת השלטון המרכזי באשור וכי יזמותיהם ומפעליהם שירתו נאמנה את חצר המלוכה האשורית. תהליך של ביזור ומעבר הכוח מן המרכז אל בעלי שררה שפעלו בפריפריה הביא בלי ספק לידי החלשת המרכז, גם אם כלפי חוץ הוסיפו השרים והנציבים לשמור על נאמנותם לאשור. אין ספק שהצבת מצבות בידי פקידים, לעתים מתוך התעלמות מן השלטון המרכזי, פגעה ביוקרתו של השלטון המרכזי ובאידאולוגיה שניסה להפיץ בקרב תושבי הממלכה. ראיה לכך היא העובדה שלאחר שעלה תגלת־פלאסר השלישי לשלטון לא הוצבו עוד מצבות בידי שרים ונציבים ואף מקצת מצבות שהוצבו בתקופה הקודמת הושחתו, ויש לתלות זאת במדיניות של השליט החדש. ייתכן שפעולות הבנייה והפיתוח של השרים והנציבים שירתו את האינטרס האשורי אך במחיר אבדן שליטה על חלקים מן הממלכה, ויש להטיל ספק בהנחה שאכן, מציאות זו הייתה רצויה לחצר המלוכה האשורית.

8 על יחסי סוחו עם אשור ראה J.A. Brinkman, *A Political History of Post-Kassite Babylonia 1158–722 B.C.*, Rome 1968, pp. 184–187, 201; A.K. Grayson, 'Studies in Neo-Assyrian History: The Ninth Century B.C.', *Bibliotheca Orientalis*, 33 (1976), p. 137; N. Háklár, 'Die Stellung Suḫis in der Geschichte: Eine Zwischenbilanz', *Oriens Antiquus*, 22 (1983), pp. 29–31; M. Liverani, *Studies in the Annals of Ashurnasirpal II*, II: *Topographical Analysis*, Rome 1992, p. 114

9 פריים (לעיל, הערה 3), עמ׳ 309–311.

10 פריים (לעיל, הערה 3), עמ׳ 318–319, כתובת 10.

נתגלו רוב הכתובות ובכללן גרסאות רבות המתארות את אותה הפרשה, ישבו הסופרים שחיברו את הטיוטות ואת המצבות.
רבות מן הכתובות שנמצאו קטועות ושבורות, אבל כיוון שפרשיות רבות חוזרות ומופיעות באותו הנוסח עצמו בכתובות אחדות, אפשר לשחזר את הטקסט של רבות מהן.

הכרונולוגיה של נציבי סוחו

כתובותיו של הנציב האשורי נֵרְגַל־אֶרֶש מלמדות שבראשית המאה השמינית נכללה 'העיר ענת של סוחו' בנציבות הגדולה שהקים ואשר הקיפה את המחוזות ששכנו בחבל הפרת התיכון ומצפון לו עד למשולש נהר חבור.[11] נִנֻרְתַ־כֻּדֻרִ־אֻצֻר מספר כי 'האשורי' שלט חמישים שנה בעיר ענת, בירת סוחו, וכי רק בראשית ימי אביו, שַׁמַשׁ־רֵשַׁ־אֻצֻר, חזרה העיר לידי נציבי סוחו (מס' 9 במהדורת פריים). נראה שהכינוי 'האשורי' מכוון לנֵרְגַל־אֶרֶש,[12] שהחזיק בבירת המחוז, ואילו במחוז שלטו אז נציבי סוחו תַבְּנֵאַ, אִקִשַׁ־מַרְדוּךְ ונַסְחִר־אַדַד. נֵרְגַל־אֶרֶש כיהן כאפונים (*līmu*, תואר של בעל שררה אשורי שבשמו נקראה השנה) בשנת 775, ולאחר שנפטר או ירד מגדולתו בזמן לא ידוע שבה העיר לידי נציבי סוחו. שַׁמַשׁ־רֵשַׁ־אֻצֻר החל אפוא לכהן ברבע השני של המאה השמינית לפסה"נ.
באחת מכתובותיו נִנֻרְתַ־כֻּדֻרִ־אֻצֻר מזכיר את סין־שַׁלִמַנִי, נציב פחוות רֶצַפֶּ. הוא נזכר ברשימת האפונימים האשוריים כנציב רֶצַפֶּ/רַצַפַּ בשנת 747, וידוע שהחל לכהן לאחר שנת 775 וסיים את כהונתו לפני שנת 737. אף ידוע שתגלת־פלאסר השלישי (745–727) שם קץ לתופעת הפקידים והנציבים רבי־הכוח ובימיו שב השלטון המרכזי והטיל את מרותו על נציבי הפחוות שכיהנו ברחבי האימפריה. יש להניח שזמן־מה לאחר שעלה תגלת־פלאסר לשלטון הצטמצמה גם עצמאותם של נציבי סוחו. על סמך זאת ראוי אפוא לקבוע שכהונתם של שַׁמַשׁ־רֵשַׁ־אֻצֻר ושל נִנֻרְתַ־כֻּדֻרִ־אֻצֻר הייתה ברבע השני ובראשית הרבע השלישי של המאה השמינית לפסה"נ.
כתובות נציבי סוחו מיוחדות מפני שהן מזכירות את אבות השושלת דורות רבים. שַׁמַשׁ־רֵשַׁ־אֻצֻר מזכיר שבעה מקודמיו ונִנֻרְתַ־כֻּדֻרִ־אֻצֻר 'מסתפק' בחמישה דורות. להלן שחזור שורות הפתיחה המופיעות בשתיים מכתובותיו של שַׁמַשׁ־רֵשַׁ־אֻצֻר:

> אני שַׁמַשׁ־רֵשַׁ־אֻצֻר, נציב הארצות סוחו ומארי, בן אִקִשַׁ־מַרְדוּךְ, כנ"ל; אִקִשַׁ־מַרְדוּךְ הוא בן אֻיַמֻ, כנ"ל; אֻיַמֻ הוא בן [פלוני], כנ"ל; [פלוני] הוא

11 בשורה 25 של הכתובת מסַבַּאָה יש לתרגם: 'ארצות לַקֶ וחִנְדַנֻ, הערים ענת של סוחו ו(אַנַ)־אַשּׁוּר־אֻתִר־אַצְבַּת' ולא כפי שתרגם גרייסון. ראה RIMA 3, 209:25. לעניין היקף המחוז ששלט בו נֵרְגַל־אֶרֶש ראה ליוורני, 'סחר השיירות' (לעיל, הערה 4), עמ' 38–39; גרייסון, 'פקידים אשורים' (לעיל, הערה 6), עמ' 27–28, הערות 29–32; בלוכר (לעיל, הערה 6), עמ' 302–303, הערות 28–32.

12 השערה זו העלו קביניו ואיסמעיל (לעיל, הערה 2), עמ' 325, הערה 22.

בן אֲדַד־נַדִן־זֵר, כנ"ל; אֲדַד־נַדִן־זֵר הוא בן כֻּדֻרֶ, כנ"ל; זרע מדורי דורות (*zēru dārû*) של חמורבי מלך בבל. של תֻנַמִסַח, נצר רחוק (*līpu rūqu*) אבותיי רבים הם. לא רשמתי [את שמותיהם מתֻנַמִסַח? עד] כֻּדֻרֶ.[13]

כֻּדֻרֶ, הנזכר ברשימה, היה נציב סוּחוּ בשנה השישית לאשורנצרפל השני (878), ובנו, אֲדַד־נַדִן־זֵר, נזכר במכתב שנמצא בחפירות תל חמה ואשר שלח אותו מַרְדוּךְ־אַפְּל־אֻצֻר מסוּחוּ אל רֻדַמֻ/אֻרְתַמִס, יורשו של אִרְחוּלֵנִ בחמת.[14] פרפולה העלה את ההשערה שסוּחוּ נחלקה אז בין שני שליטים, מַרְדוּךְ־אַפְּל־אֻצֻר, ששלט בעיר הבירה ענת ובאזור שמסביב לה, ואֲדַד־נַדִן־זֵר, שתוארו היה נציב, והוא שלט במחוז. באחת מכתובותיו מספר נִנֻרְתַ־כֻּדֻרִּ־אֻצֻר על מצב דומה שנתהווה בתקופה מאוחרת יותר, כאשר ניתק ה'אשורי' את ענת ממחוז סוּחוּ ושלט בעיר בעוד אִקִשַׁ־מַרְדוּךְ, הנזכר ברשימת אבות השושלת, מכהן כנציב סוּחוּ. יש בכך כדי לאשש את השערה שהעלה פרפולה בדבר מדיניות אשורית שבאה להחליש את כוחם של נציבי סוּחוּ באמצעות ניתוק עיר הבירה מן המחוז שבשליטתם.[15] שיטה זו של שלטון באתרי מפתח בתוך מרחב עצמאי במידה רבה ידועה היטב מתולדות אשור למן המאה האחת־עשרה לפסה"נ ואילך, ונראה לי שכך יש לפרש גם את הזכרת העיר ענת בכתובותיו של נֵרְגַל־אֵרֶשׁ ובכתובות מסוּחוּ.[16] לאור זאת אפשר להניח ששושלת נציבי סוּחוּ מימי כֻּדֻרֶ, שכיהן בימי אשורנצרפל, ועד לימי נִנֻרְתַ־כֻּדֻרִּ־אֻצֻר, שכיהן בראשית ימי תגלת־פלאסר השלישי, ידועה לנו בשלמותה.[17]

13 פריים (לעיל, הערה 3), עמ' 283, כתובת 2, שורות 1–4; עמ' 284, כתובת 3, שורות 1–4. הטקסט המתורגם הוא פרי שילוב של שתי הכתובות. דיון בשושלת מסוּחוּ ראה במאמרה של פונגרץ־לייסטן (לעיל, הערה 4), עמ' 96–98.

14 S. Parpola, 'A Letter from Marduk-Apla-Usur of Anah to Rudamu/Urtamis, King of Hamath', in P.J. Riis & M.-L. Buhl (eds.), *Hama – Fouilles et recherches 1931–1938, II/2: Les objects de la période dite Syro-Hittite (Âge du Fer)*, Copenhagen 1990, pp. 257–265

15 מַרְדוּךְ־אַפְּל־אֻצֻר, הנזכר בין מעלי המס ב'אובליסק השחור' של שלמנאסר השלישי, היה אפוא שליט ענת ולא נציב סוּחוּ. ראה RIMA 3, p. 150

16 על שיטת השלטון בחבלים רחבים באמצעות החזקת נקודות מפתח ושליטה בדרכי התחבורה המקשרות ביניהן ראה M. Liverani, 'The Growth of the Assyrian Empire in the Habur/Middle Euphrates Area: A New Paradigm', *SAAB*, 2 (1988), pp. 81–98; H. Kühne, 'The Assyrian in the Middle Euphrates and the Habur', in M. Liverani (ed.), *Neo-Assyrian Geography*, Rome 1995, pp. 69–79. ביקורת על הפרדיגמה המוצעת ראה J.N. Postgate, 'The Land of Assur and the Yoke of Assur', *World Archaeology*, 23 (1991), pp. 255–257

17 באחת מכתובותיו (פריים [לעיל, הערה 3], עמ' 316, כתובת 9, שורות 22–24) הזכיר נִנֻרְתַ־כֻּדֻרִּ־אֻצֻר שלושה נציבים שכיהנו בסוּחוּ בעת ש'האשורי' החזיק בעיר ענת. מביניהם רק אִקִשַׁ־מַרְדוּךְ נזכר ברשימת אבות השושלת של שַׁמַשׁ־רֵשׁ־אֻצֻר. תַבְּנֵאַ, אשר נרצח בלכתו לאשור (שם, עמ' 315, שורות 6–8), היה, כנראה, בנו של אִיַּמֻ, ואִקִשַׁ־מַרְדוּךְ, אחיו, ירש אותו, ואילו נַסְחִר־אֲדַד היה אולי בנו של אִקִשַׁ־מַרְדוּךְ ואחיו של שַׁמַשׁ־רֵשׁ־אֻצֻר. ייתכן אפוא שעוד נציבים שלא הורישו את משרתם לצאצאיהם כיהנו בסוּחוּ בתקופה שבין אשורנצרפל השני לתגלת־פלאסר השלישי.

כֵּדֶרֶ מוצג כ׳זרע מדורי דורות׳ של תֻּנַמְסַח, ושלא כיתר נציבי סוחו הנזכרים בכתובות נושא שם כַּשִׁי.[18] הלה מוצג כמייסד השושלת של נציבי סוחו, ומסתבר שהמשרה של נציב סוחו צמחה בתקופה הכַּשִׁית ועברה מאב לבן מאות שנים. התואר ׳זרע מדורי דורות׳ (*zēru dārû*), שבו קשר הסופר את שושלת נציבי סוחו אל תֻּנַמְסַח, קשור לתואר ׳זרע מלכות מדורי דורות׳ (*zēr dārium ša šarrūtim*), הנזכר בפרולוג לחוקת חמורבי, ונבחר כדי להדגיש את קדמות השושלת וכדי ליצור קשר ספרותי עם חמורבי מלך בבל.[19] חמורבי מוצג בתור האב הקדמון של השושלת מסוחו, וזו דוגמה נאה לשושלת נציבים מקומית הנתלית באילן גבוה כדי להציג את ראשיתה.

בכתובותיו של נִנֻרְתַּ־כֻּדֻרִ־אֻצֻר השתמשו הסופרים שימוש גמיש בתארים ׳זרע מדורי דורות׳ ו׳נצר רחוק׳. לדוגמה: כתובת 2, שורות 3-2 וכתובת 11, שורות 14-13: ׳זרע מדורי דורות, נצר רחוק של תֻּנַמְסַח, בן חמורבי מלך בבל׳; כתובת 9, שורות 5-4: ׳זרע מדורי דורות של תֻּנַמְסַח, בן חמורבי מלך בבל׳; כתובת 10, שורות 14-12: ׳נצר רחוק של תֻּנַמְסַח, בן חמורבי מלך בבל׳.

על ייחודן של כתובות סוחו במסגרת הסוגה של כתובות מלכים

מחוז סוחו שכן בשוליים של שני מרכזי התרבות הגדולים של מסופוטמיה, אשור ובבל, ולא הייתה לו מסורת עצמאית של כתיבת כתובות רשמיות. שתי מסורות כתיבה היו ידועות לסופרים מסוחו – זו של אשור וזו של בבל. הדיון בכתובות מציב לפני החוקר את השאלות איזה משני הקטבים השפיע על מחברי הכתובות, כיצד סיגלו הסופרים את היסודות ששאלו ואם בכתובות שחיברו יש גם יסודות עצמאיים וייחודיים. בניסוח אחר: האומנם היו הסופרים משועבדים לדגמים ששאלו משתי התרבויות השכנות, או שעל־פי נורמות הכתיבה המקובלות פילסו לעצמם דרך עצמאית ועיצבו את כתובותיהם במתכונת השונה ממתכונת הכתיבה של שכניהם?

במה שאפשר לכנות ׳המסורת הספרותית׳ של מסופוטמיה הכתובות של נציבי סוחו מקיימות קשרים הדוקים עם כתובות מלכים אשוריות ובבליות. הכתב והלשון של הכתובות מסוחו הם בבליים לעומת הסגנון וחלק מאוצר הדימויים המושפעים מכתובות מלכי אשור, ואילו השילוב של תיאורי מלחמות ומפעלי בנייה, האופייני לכתובות מסוחו, הוא ביסודו אשורי ולא בבלי. יש לזכור כי רק כתובות מלכים מעטות מאוד נכתבו בבבל בראשית האלף הראשון לפסה״נ לעומת השפע הרב של כתובות שכתבו מלכי אשור. הקורפוס הגדול של כתובות מלכים שנמצא באשור ומעמדה ההגמוני של אשור במסופוטמיה במאות התשיעית-השמינית לפסה״נ נותנים מקום להניח

18 עוד טקסטים בבליים שנזכר בהם תֻּנַמְסַח מציין ברינקמן (לעיל, הערה 8), עמ׳ 254 והערה 1619.

19 דיון בביטויים ׳זרע מדורי דורות׳ (*zēru dārû*) ו׳נצר רחוק׳ (*līpu rūqu*) ראה אצל פונגרץ־לייסטן (לעיל, הערה 4), עמ׳ 97-98.

שכתובות מלכי אשור שימשו מקור השראה עיקרי להופעה הפתאומית של כתובות רשמיות באכדית בעמק הפרת התיכון ברבע השני של המאה השמינית לפסה"נ.

אמנם כתובות מלכי אשור שימשו דגם לכתיבה אך מבט חטוף בכתובות של נציבי סוחו מראה עד כמה הן נבדלות מיתר כתובות המלכים במסופוטמיה הידועות לנו. נמסרים בהן פרטים רבים על מלחמות ועל פעולות הבנייה והפיתוח של הנציבים ברחבי המחוז, ובהם נושאים הנראים פחותי ערך שלא נזכרו מעולם בכתובות מלכי אשור ובבל. פרשיות רבות מוצגות בפירוט חסר תקדים, ואילו המניעים למפעלים ולמעשים מוצגים באופן ישיר ובלתי מוסווה. התיאורים נחתמים תדיר בפנייה לבני הדורות הבאים מתוך כוונה להאדיר את שם הנציב ולהנציח את פועלו. כנגד זה בכתובות מלכי אשור מוטיב זה מופיע רק בחלק האחרון של הכתובת.

הכתובות מסוחו כולן כתובות סיכום ואף אחת מהן אינה ערוכה לפי סדר כרונולוגי. שלוש מן הכתובות של נִנֻרְתַ־כֻּדֻרִ־אֻצֻר הן כתובות הקדשה שנכתבו לרגל חנוכת מבנה ציבורי. אחת מהן, שנמצאה בחפירות האי עַנָה, פותחת בתוארי האלה ענת ונכתבה לרגל שיקום מקדש האלה בעיר ענת (מס׳ 10 במהדורת פריים). כתובת שנייה, שנמצאה בסוּר גַ׳רְעָה, פותחת בתוארי האל אדד ונכתבה לרגל שיקום מקדש האלים אדד ואַפְּלַאַדַּד בעיר ענת (מס׳ 11 במהדורת פריים), וכתובת שלישית, שנמצאה באי ענה, נכתבה לרגל חנוכת מקדש וארמון שנבנו בסמיכות זה לזה בעיר ענת (מס׳ 9 במהדורת פריים). תוכנן של שלוש הכתובות מכוון למפעל הבנייה החותם אותן. לעומת זאת בכתובות אחרות הנציבים מציגים מלחמות ומפעלי בנייה שעשו, ובולטת הופעת אותן הפרשיות בכמה מקומות בכתובות, וכך פרשה המופיעה בראשיתה של כתובת מסוימת עשויה להופיע באמצעה או בסופה של כתובת אחרת.[20] שלא כבכתובות מאשור ובבל, שבהן מפעל הבנייה חותם את תיאור מפעלי המלך ולאחריו מופיעה קללה למי שיפגע בכתובת, כמה מכתובות נציבי סוחו נחתמות בתיאורי מלחמה או פיתוח הממלכה. המצבה של שַׁמַשׁ־רֵשׁ־אֻצֻר, לדוגמה, נחתמת בפרשה על ביות דבורים (מס׳ 1 במהדורת פריים), ואילו כתובת של נִנֻרְתַ־כֻּדֻרִ־אֻצֻר נחתמת בפרשת שוד השיירה של בני תֵּימָא ושְׁבָא (מס׳ 2 במהדורת פריים). כתובות אחרות נחתמות בפנייה לשליט העתיד לבוא, פנייה המופיעה תדיר גם באמצע הכתובת. קללה מופיעה רק בכתובת אחת של שמש־רֵשׁ־אֻצֻר (מס׳ 1 במהדורת פריים), והיא שולבה באמצע הטקסט. כיוון שאין סיום קבוע לכתובות, לעתים קשה לקבוע את המטרה שלשמה נכתבו, ואולי אפשר לשער שמקצת הלוחות שימשו מעין אסופת פרשיות שבעת כתיבת מצבה חדשה היה אפשר ללקט מתוכן לפי בחירתו של הסופר.

על מרד בני רַאִיל כתב נִנֻרְתַ־כֻּדֻרִ־אֻצֻר כי ׳באשר לעניין זה לא שמתי לבי לכך ובתבליט לא חרתתי זאת׳. זו עדות שהכתובות לוו לעתים בתבליטים. חריתת תבליטים בארמון נזכרת גם בכתובת מס׳ 3 (iv 18). אכן, במצבה של

20 ראה את הלוח המשווה במאמרם של קביניו ואיסמעיל (לעיל, הערה 2), עמ׳ 334.

שַׁמַש־רֵש־אֻצֻר שנמצאה בבבל מופיע תבליט של הנציב הניצב לפני האלים אדד ואִשְׁתַר, ומאחוריו ניצבת האלה ענת. בכתובת אחרת על לוח אבן (מס׳ 10 במהדורת פריים) מוצג הנציב (נִנֻרְתַ־כֻּדֻר־אֻצֻר) בצד אחד של הכתובת והאלה ענת בצד האחר, ומעליהם מופיעים סמלי אלים. דומה שגם בשילוב מצבה ותבליטים חיקו נציבי סוחו את מלכי אשור ובבל, אבל עיצבו את המצבות בדרך המיוחדת להם.

בדומה לכתובות מלכים גם כתובות נציבי סוחו פותחות בלשון ׳אנוכי׳ או בהזכרת תואריו של האל שהכתובת הוקדשה לו. ואולם שורות הפתיחה דווקא מבליטות את ההבדלים ביניהם. מלכי אשור ובבל צירפו לשמותיהם שורה ארוכה של תארים רשמיים ואחריהם הזכירו אחד או שניים מאבותיהם, ואילו אצל נציבי סוחו מופיע תואר יחיד, ׳נציב הארצות סוחו ומארי׳, החוזר ומופיע פעמים אין ספור גם בגוף הכתובת. הם גם מציגים רשימה ארוכה של אבות השושלת, הפותחת במלך גדול קדום (חמורבי), ודומה שיש לראות בזה מעין ׳פיצוי׳ ספרותי על שאינם יכולים להתהדר בתארים דוגמת התארים של מלכי אשור, ולכן בחרו להציג את מוצאם משושלת עתיקה שראשיתה במלך הבבלי המפורסם והנכבד ביותר.

ואולם התמונה מורכבת יותר. באחת מכתובותיו הציג נִנֻרְתַ־כֻּדֻר־אֻצֻר את עצמו באופן הזה: ׳אשר האלים שמש, מרדוך, אדד ואַפְּלַאַדַד בשמחה ובנהרה הסתכלו עליי במלוא? פניהם המאירות, נתנו לי כוח רב, עוז ומלכות של ארץ סוחו, והעניקו לי צדק בגורלי׳ (כתובת 2 i 4-7). עוד בשתי כתובות הוא מציג עצמו במילים ׳אני נִ[נֻרְתַ־כֻּדֻר־אֻצֻר, נציב הארצות סוחו] ומארי, הנבחר, אשר האלים שמש, מרדוך, אדד ואַפְּלַאַדַד וכן אשתר מינו? [לפי? הוראת? שמש?] ומרדוך, ורוממו מעל מלכים חזקים ומעל נצי[בים רבי כוח?]׳ (כתובת 1, שורות 29–31; כתובת 4 i 1-3). בכתובת הקדשה לאלה ענת האלה מוצגת במילים ׳הנותנת הוראות לשליט הירא אותה׳ (כתובת 10, שורה 6). התארים הנקשרים בכתובות אלו לנציב סוחו משקפים אידאולוגיה מלכותית ונלקחו מכתובות מלכים ולא זו בלבד אלא שמחבריהן התעלמו מאי־התאמת מקצת התארים הללו למשרה של נציב.[21] בכתובת אחרת נִנֻרְתַ־כֻּדֻר־אֻצֻר מתאר את ראשית כהונתו במילים ׳שלושה חודשים בשנת מותו (של אבי), בראשית כהונתי כנציב, כאשר ישבתי על כיסא אבי׳ (כתובת 2 i 7-9), ואילו שַׁמַש־רֵש־אֻצֻר כותב ׳אני הצבתי את הכיסא ואת ההדום אשר בעיר רִיבַּנִיש׳ (כתובת 1 ii 40-44). מוטיב הישיבה על כס השלטון נלקח מכתובות מלכים והועבר לכהונת נציב, ואילו הביטוי ׳בראשית כהונתי כנציב׳ (*ina rēš šakinmātūtiya*), החוזר פעמים אחדות בכתובותיו של נִנֻרְתַ־כֻּדֻר־אֻצֻר, אינו אלא סיגול המונח הידוע ׳ראשית מלכות׳ (*rēš šarrūti*), המציין את פרק הזמן שלמן מותו של מלך ועד לראש השנה הבא, שאז מתחיל מניין שנים לשליט החדש.[22] בולטת אפוא היצירתיות של

21 פריים (לעיל, הערה 3), עמ׳ 295, כתובת 2, שורות 4–7.

22 על נטילת תארים מלכותיים בידי נציבי סוחו ראה דיון (לעיל, הערה 4), עמ׳ 60, הערה 46.

הסופרים שביקשו להאדיר את נציבי סוחו, ולשם כך בחרו ביטויים ותארים הלקוחים מלשונן של כתובות מלכי אשור ואשר לא תמיד הולמים את משרת הנציב.

מגמה זו להידמות למלכים באה לידי ביטוי גם במתן שמם של נציבי סוחו למקומות שיסדו. שַׁמַשׁ־רֵשַׁ־אֻצֻר כינה מצודה שיסד בשם דוּר־שַׁמַשׁ־רֵשַׁ־אֻצֻר, וייתכן שגם תעלה שחפר נקראה על שמו (כתובת 2, שורות 12, 15, 17; כתובת 3, שורה 13), ואילו נִנֻרְתַ־כֻּדֻרִּ־אֻצֻר כינה מצודה שיסד בַּשם דוּר־נִנֻרְתַ־כֻּדֻרִּ־אֻצֻר (כתובת 2 iii 16). נוהג זה אינו מיוחד רק לנציבי סוחו, וגם הכרוז בֵּל־חַרַן־בֵּל־אֻצֻר, שבנה מצודה באותו הזמן בערך במקום שאינו מרוחק ממרכזי השלטון האשוריים, כינה אותה בשמו, דוּר־בֵּל־חַרַן־בֵּל־אֻצֻר.[23]

לשון הכתובות מסוחו היא אכדית, והיא קרובה לבבלית יותר מלאשורית, אבל שולבו בה גם מטבעות לשון ייחודיים (*mannu arkû ša illâmma, idi/aḫ māti u idi/aḫ šadî* ועוד).[24] רבים מתושבי המחוז היו ארמים, ולפיכך אין לתמוה שרוב שמות המקומות הם שמיים־מערביים.[25] הביטויים המושפעים מארמית אינם רבים, וכולם מופיעים בכתובת 2 ובכתובות המשלימות קטעים החסרים בה.[26] עם אלה יימנו הביטוי 'לשים לפי חרב' (*ana pî patri*) (ii 7), השורש קו"ה (iii 11), המציין היקוות מים בבאר שנחפרה (*šakānu*), שמות העצם 'מחנות' (*karāši*), המציין התארגנות בחטיבות גדולות לשם יציאה למלחמה (i 10, 18), 'כנישתה' (*kinaltu*), המציין קבוצה שנאספה לשם ביצוע עבודה (iii 13), 'גדוד' (*gudūdu*), המציין חבורה שהתלכדה כדי לפשוט ולשלול שלל (iii 14) וכן *aṭīru*, שאולי יש לגזרו משורש עט"ר במשמעות 'חומה חיצונית' (iv 23-24).[27] קביניו ואיסמעיל שיערו שצורת הפועל *innaṭṭal* צמחה בהשפעת השורש הארמי נט"ל במשמעות 'לרחף מעל'.[28] אף ייתכן לשער שצורת הפועל *ašgug* ('לשאוג'), החוזרת בשתי כתובות, אינה אלא מיזוג של אכדית *šagāmu* ושל שמית־מערבית שא"ג.[29] לא מן הנמנע שהסופר שחיבר את הכתובת היה ממוצא ארמי, וכאשר לא נמצאו לו מונחים הולמים באכדית בחר במונחים ארמיים.

בסעיף הבא אציג כמה פרשיות הלקוחות מכתובות נציבי סוחו כדי להמחיש את אופיין ואת ייחודן לעומת כתובות מלכי אשור.

23 RIMA 3, pp. 241–243

24 ראה את רשימתם אצל קביניו ואיסמעיל (לעיל, הערה 2), עמ' 340.

25 צדוק (לעיל, הערה 4), עמ' 229–230.

26 רשימה חלקית הביא דיון (לעיל, הערה 4), עמ' 63, הערה 72.

27 במרבית המונחים דנו קביניו ואיסמעיל (לעיל, הערה 2), עמ' 351–357.

28 קביניו ואיסמעיל (לעיל, הערה 2), עמ' 355.

29 ראה פריים (לעיל, הערה 3), עמ' 308, כתובת 5, שורה 14; עמ' 310, כתובת 6, שורה 3. קביניו ואיסמעיל ([לעיל, הערה 2], עמ' 369) סברו שזו טעות של סופר.

ניתוח פרשיות המופיעות בקורפוס הכתובות של נציבי סוחו

הטקסט הראשון מתאר באריכות רבה את מלחמתו של נִנֻרְתַ־כֻּדֻר־אֻצֻר בבני שבטים ארמיים. בכתובות מוצגת הפרשה בגרסאות אחדות, לעתים בקיצור ולעתים בפירוט רב. התיאור המפורט לא שרד בשלמותו באף כתובת אחת, אבל מתוך צירופן של כתובות אחדות אפשר להשלים הרבה מן החסר. בתרגום נעשה מאמץ לצרף מקסימום קטעים לרצף אחד, ועל הקורא לתת את דעתו שהטקסט המקורי אולי היה שונה במקצת מן הטקסט האקלקטי המוצג כאן:[30]

(לאחר) שלושה חודשים בשנת מותו (של אבי), בראשית כהונתי כנציב, כאשר ישבתי על כיסא אבי, נאספו 2000 בני חַטַלֻ – (מ)בני סַרוּגֻ ועד בני לֻחֻיֻ – עם חיל הקשתים וראשי המחנות שלהם, וקבעו לעצמם קו פעולה משותף. מנהיגם הוא שַמְאַגַמְנִ, ה'כרוז' של בני סַרוּגֻ המעורב ב(מעשי) בגידה. הם יצאו כדי לפשוט על ארץ לַקֻ, ובהיותם בערבה נועצו כך: 'נציב ארץ סוחו אויב לנו. כיצד נעבור כדי לבוז בז מארץ לַקֻ?' שַמְאַגַמְנִ, ה'כרוז' של בני סַרוּגֻ, ויַאֵה בן בַּלְעַמֻ בן (שבט) אַמַתֻ, ראשי המחנות שלהם, אמרו כך: 'איש מאבותיו, נציבי ארץ סוחו, לא יצא ללחום נגד 1000 ארמים (Aramu). והנה כעת הוא יצא למלחמה נגד 2000 ארמים. ואכן, אם יעלה להילחם נגדנו, נצא נגדו ונהפוך את סוחו לארץ שלנו. ואם לא יעלה (נגדנו), נשלול שלל ונגייס אלינו אנשים (נוספים), ואז נלך ונעלה על בתי־האב של ארץ סוחו, נלכוד את היישובים שלו בערבה ונכרות את המטעים שלהם'.[31]
הם בטחו בכוחם ועברו אל ארץ לַקֻ, לכדו 100 יישובים מארץ לַקֻ, שללו שלל כבד מאוד והפכו את לַקֻ לעיים וחורבות. אַדַד־דַיַנֻ, נציב ארץ לַקֻ, בא אליי עם ארבע מרכבות ו־200 חיילים, נשק את הקרקע לרגליי והפיל תחנוניו. קיבלתי את תחינתו. ואילו סין־שַלְמַנִי, נציב ארץ רֻצַפֻּ, יצא נגדם עם כל צבא רֻצַפֻּ, [אך] בראותו אותם נבהל [ולא הסתער] עלי[הם].
[אני נִנֻרְתַ־כֻּדֻר־אֻצֻר, נציב הארצות סוחו ומארי, הנבחר, אשר] האלים שמש ומרדוך [...... רוממו מעל מלכים חזק]ים ומעל נציבים. [דרשתי את דב]ר האל אַפְלַאַדַד, האל 'חורץ הגורלות', [והוא הראה? לי] את [נתיב] ההליכה של החילות הללו ומסר לי את הוראתו. ואני [לא התר]שלתי, ובטחתי בדבר האל אַפְלַאַדַד, האדון הגדול, אדוני. גייסתי את משמר הארמון, רתמתי את מרכבתי ויצאתי נגדם למסע (כדי

30 פריים (לעיל, הערה 3), עמ' 293, כתובת 1, שורות 43–50; עמ' 296–298, כתובת 2, ii 7–36, iii 1–32; עמ' 305–306, כתובת 4, שורות 1–15; עמ' 308–309, כתובת 5, שורות 1–16. לוח משווה של פרשת המסע כפי שהשתמרה בטקסטים השונים הציגו קביניו ואיסמעיל (לעיל, הערה 2), עמ' 336; פריים (לעיל, הערה 3), עמ' 289.

31 יש דמיון ספרותי מסוים בין תיאור ההתייעצות בערבה לפני שפשטו בני חַטַלֻ על ארץ לַקֻ ובין דברי חושי הארכי לאבשלום בעת ההתייעצות בירושלים (שמ"ב יז:יא–יג).

לערוך) קרב ומערכה עם 105 מרכבות, 220 פרשים מנוסים, (רוכבי) סוסים מובחרים נאים, ו־3000 חיל רגלים. בחודש תמוז ישבתי יום ליד באר צֻמֵאַ, השוכנת בין באר מַכִּךְ לבאר גַלַבֻּ. ממול לבאר צֻמֵאַ יש ארבע מכלאות שאין בהן כבשים. ואני ידעתי שבבאר צֻמֵאַ ....
(קטע חסר במקום זה)

.... בשל נאמנות [לבי ......] מסור אותם [לידי. ... התפללתי?? ל]אל אַפְּלַאַדַד, האדון הגד[ול, אדוני, לאל שמש] ולאל מרדוך, האדון הגדול, [ולאלים הגדולים של השמים] והארץ (ש)ילכו [לצדי ...].
[... והוא (סין־שַלְמַנִי??) התקרב?] אל באר מַכִּךְ ובא לקראתי, ובבאר מַכִּךְ [הם ...] נערכו. ואנוכי נִנֻרְתַ־כֻּדֻרִ־אֻצֻר, נציב הארצות סוחו ומארי, אשר שמש ומרדוך, אדד ואַפְּלַאַ[דַד .....], לעזרתו ה[לכתי]. הצבתי [את משמר הארמון] מאחוריי ובמ[רכבתי, עם חייליי, מרכבותיי ופרשיי] יצאתי לפניהם. זעמתי על בנ[י ...], שאגתי כמו אריה עז ע[ל ...], ושטף [ענן] הבאתי עליהם, מתוך מרכבתי סחפתי אותם כ(סחוף) קני קש. החצים כמו ארבה עפו סביב המחנה שלי, אך איש מהמחנה שלי לא נפגע. אמנם נפגעו 38 איש מקרב המחנה שלי, אך איש מהם לא נפל בערבה. נפלתי לתוכם כמו להבה יוקדת ו־1616 איש מהם שמתי לפי חרב. ואילו ל־80 איש מביניהם הסרתי את זרועותיהם ואת שפתותיהם ושחררתי אותם כדי (להפיץ) את תהילתי. למן באר מַכִּךְ <עד> באר גַלַבֻּ ועד באר סֻרִבֻּ, ליד שלוש הבארות הנחלתי להם מפלה והבאתי לאבדנם. פיזרתי את חילות העזר הכבדים שלהם ופוררתי את מערכם. התגברתי על המנסים לברוח והזרמתי את דמם כמו מי נהר. נשרים ועיטים ריחפו מעל גוויותיהם. גולגולותיהם מילאו את ההרים והנחל(ים) כמו אבני הרים,[32] וציפורים קיננו בגולגולותיהם. 304 איש מביניהם הקדימו ונסוגו מפניי. בשל הקרב צמאו סוסיי וחייליי למים, ולכן לא רדפתי אחריהם. 40 איש מביניהם אבדו בצמא, 254 מביניהם חמקו, 1846 איש מהם הרגתי. זו המפלה היחידה שהנחיל נִנֻרְתַ־כֻּדֻרִ־אֻצֻר, נציב הארצות סוחו ומארי, לבני חַטַל. לכדתי במו ידיי את שַמְאַגַמְנִ, ה׳כרוז׳ של בני סַרוּגֻ, מנהיגם, עבד בוגדני אשר הארצות סוחו ואשור וכן אבותיי הרחיקו? אותו, הרגתי אותו ונח לבי. פשטתי את עורו כמו עור כבשה והצגתי לפני שער העיר גַבַּר־אִבְּנִ.
אני הנחלתי מפלה שכמוה איש <מאבותיי> לא הנחיל. אבותיי (אמנם) הכו עשר פעמים את האויב, אך לא השיגו (ניצחון) שלם כשלי. אני הנחלתי מפלה אחת שאיש מאבותיי לא השיג כמוה.

32 ד״ר נתן וסרמן הפנה את תשומת לבי למכתב שנשלח מסוחו לחמורבי, מלך בבל, בתקופה הבבלית הקדומה, ובו מצוטטת שבועה של שייח׳ אמורי: ׳(קללה תחול עליי) אם לא אמלא בגולגולות את גדות נהר פרת ואם לא אכסה(ו) בצואת סוסים כמו קני סוף׳. ראה W.H. van Soldt, *Letters in the British Museum*, II, Leiden 1994, No. 60, lines 11–12

מי שיעלה (לשלטון) בימים יבואו ויאמר כך: הכיצד זה הנחיל נִנֻרְתַּ־כֻּדֻּר־אֻצֻּר, נציב הארצות סוחו ומארי, את המפלה הזאת? לא בכוחי הנחלתי מפלה. בכוחם של האלים שמש, מרדוך, אדד ואַפְּלַאַדַּד, האלים הגדולים, אדוניי, הנחלתי את המפלה הזאת. מי שבימים יבואו יעלה (לשלטון) וישאל את זקני ארצו ואת זקני לַקֻ כך: הנכון הדבר שנִנֻרְתַּ־כֻּדֻּר־אֻצֻּר, נציב הארצות סוחו ומארי, הנחיל את המפלה בפקודת האל אַפְּלַאַדַּד, האל הגדול, אדוניו? זה היה מעשה ידיו של האל אַפְּלַאַדַּד, האל אדוני, [אשר ..., א]הב אותי ונתן בידי את המעשה הזה.

אף שהטקסט נכתב בלשון 'אני', לפי חוקי הסוגה, התיאור מצטיין בחיות רבה ומשקף יכולת סיפורית מרשימה. לתיאור מבנה מגובש: (א) הצגת האויבים ותכנית המתקפה שלהם; (ב) ביצוע השלב הראשון בתכניתם וחרדת הנציבים השכנים מעצמתם; (ג) השאלה באל וההכנות של נציב סוחו למסע נגד התוקפים; (ד) ההמתנה עד למתקפה; (ה) הקרב, הניצחון המכריע והשפטים שעשה באויבים; (ו) דגש חוזר ונשנה על גודל הניצחון.

התיאור בא להעצים את הניצחון, ולכן מודגשים עצמתו של האויב, העדר תקדים להתמודדות מוצלחת עם אויב חזק כל כך, הצלחת המתקפה הארמית על מחוז לַקֻ והחורבן שהמיטו עליו התוקפים ולבסוף חוסר האונים של הנציבים השכנים להתמודד עם עצמתם של התוקפים. בתיאור מודגשים יהירותו וביטחונו העצמי של האויב, הנשען על כוחו ועל עוצם ידו. לעומת זאת נִנֻרְתַּ־כֻּדֻּר־אֻצֻּר בטח באלי ארצו, ומעשהו הראשון הוא השאלה באל אַפְּלַאַדַּד, 'חורץ הגורלות'. בעקבות התשובה החיובית שקיבל מן האל גייס את צבאו ויצא לקדם את צבא האויב. הצבאות נפגשו בערבה, סמוך לגבול המערבי של סוחו, ונִנֻרְתַּ־כֻּדֻּר־אֻצֻּר נערך בבאר צֻמֻּאַ ומולו נערכו הארמים בבאר מַכִּרֻ. דומה שנִנֻרְתַּ־כֻּדֻּר־אֻצֻּר יזם את המתקפה, וחיל הקשתים שהציבו הארמים לא מנע אותו מלחדור למחנה האויב ולזכות בניצחון מוחץ. לדבריו, כמעט כל התוקפים נהרגו, מנהיגם נתפס והוצא להורג, ורק מעטים הצליחו להימלט. בסיום הפרשה חוזר הנציב ומדגיש שהאל אַפְּלַאַדַּד, ולא עוצם ידו, הוא שהביא לידי הניצחון.

התיאור מצטיין בחיוניות רבה וכולל שפע יסודות מקוריים, שאין להם מקבילות בספרות האכדית הידועה לנו. המחבר מכיר היטב את האויב הניצב מולו ומציג אותו בפירוט רב, וכן הוא מרבה בפרטים טופוגרפיים שלרוע המזל, אין ביכולתנו לזהותם. בתיאור משובצים ביטויים אירוניים כגון דמות הנציב השכן המבוהל שהגיע אליו עם צבא קטן, כריתת הזרועות והשפתיים של השבויים ושחרורם 'כדי (להפיץ) את תהילתי' ופשיטת עורו של מנהיג האויבים כעור כבשה לאחר קרב שנערך באזור של מכלאות צאן. אף שהכתובת מחקה כתובות מלכותיות נטל מחברה לעצמו חירות רבה וחרג מן הדפוסים הנוקשים של כתובות מלכותיות.

בשתי כתובות הקדשה שכתב נִנֻרְתַּ־כֻּדֻּר־אֻצֻּר מופיע תיאור מאלף של

תקופת השלטון האשורי בענת, בירת מחוז סוחו, ושל שחרור העיר וחזרתה לידי נציבי סוחו:[33]

(1) תַבְּנֶאַ, נציב ארץ סוחו, עלה לאשור עם מנחת ההתייצבות (לפני השליט)? שלו, ובאשור הרגו אותו. ותושבי העיר ענת מרדו נגד ארץ סוחו. הם הצטרפו ('נתנו ידיים') לאשורי והעלו את האשורי אל ענת. האשורי לכד את ענת בלי (שימוש) בכוח או במלחמה. האנשים, בני העיר, הם עצמם נתנו (את העיר) לאשורי. אחר כך הגלה האשורי אותם ופיזר אותם ברחבי הארצות. הוא הפך לעיים וחורבות את הבתים בצד הארץ ובצד ההר של העיר ענת. והאשורי הושיב את אנשיו שלו בענת.
מאז (ימי) שלושת הנציבים – תַבְּנֶאַ, אִקִש־מַרְדוּךְ ונַסְחִר־אַדַד – העיר ענת הייתה 50 שנה בידי האשורי. שלוש שנים [כנ"ל??], בימי שַׁמַש־רֵשַׁ־אֻצֻר, כנ"ל, אבי, עו[ד? ש..... לא ישב?] על כיסא אבי, כאשר הציב את האלים אדד ואַפְּלַאַ[דַד במקדש?], הם שבו ועשו את העיר ע[נת למקום? פורח?]. ב(מלאות?) ארבע [שנים] שהעיר ענת שג[שגה], לאחר [שאבי הל]ך לעולמו, אני [ישבתי] על כיסא אבי. [הגדלתי?] את מנחות הקבע והקר[בנות] וקבעתי את החגים של האלים אדד [ואַפְּלַאַדַד] לפי ההוראות של חמורבי, [מלך בבל, ושל?] אבי־מולידי. יישבתי [את העזובים??] ואת יושבי הקבע בעיר ענת בצד הארץ ובצד ההר של העיר. יישבתי את העיר ענת כמו לפנים, בצד הארץ ובצד ההר (של העיר). אני השבתי את האלים, אשר (שוכנים) בצד הארץ [ובצד ההר] של העיר ענת, ואשר בגלל האשורי הלכו אל העיר רִיבַּנִיש [וישבו בה??], וכמו לפנים הושבתי אותם במושביהם.

(2) בני ענת, תושבי העיר ענת, מרדו נגד ארץ סוחו. הם הצטרפו ('נתנו ידיהם') לאשורי והעלו את האשורי אל ענת. (אך) הוא (האשורי) חילל את העיר ענת ואת אלוהיה, חילל את הבגד הנאה של (האלה) ענת, את הזהב המובחר ואת האבנים היקרות, היינו את כל מה שיאה לאלוהותה. ואשר לה, הוא הושיבהּ במקום נסתר.
אני, נִנֻרְתַ־כֻּדֻרִי־אֻצֻר, נציב הארצות סוחו ומארי, עבד הירא את אלוהותה הגדולה, הוצאתי את (האלה) ענת ממקום סתר, [הכנתי?/ השבתי?] את הבגד הנאה, הזהב המובחר והאבנים היקרות [הל]לו?, פיארתי את אלוהותה והושבתי אותה ב[מושבה?]. ה[גדלתי?] את מנחות הק[בע] שלה וקבעתי (את החגים??) לפי הוראות חמורבי, מלך [בב]ל, אשר קדם לי.

שתי הכתובות נחלקות לשני חלקים ברורים: תחילה מוצגת בהן סקירה של מה שנפגם בעבר, ואחר כך מסופר כיצד מפעליו של מחבר הכתובות (נִנֻרְתַ־

33 פריים (לעיל, הערה 3), עמ' 315–316, כתובת 9 i 6–ii 19; עמ' 318, כתובת 10, שורות 15–32.

כֻּדֻר־אֻצֻר) הביאו לידי החזרת עטרה ליושנה. הכתובת הראשונה פותחת בסקירה מפורטת של השתלשלות הדברים בעיר ענת בתקופת השלטון האשורי. סקירות מפורטות מעין אלה ידועות לנו היטב מכתובות מלכי חת באלף השני לפסה״נ אך אינן שכיחות בכתובות מלכי אשור ובבל. לאחר מכן תיאר המחבר את המפנה שחל בגורלה של העיר עם חזרתה לידי נציבי סוחו ואת מפעליו המכוונים לשיקום העיר ולשגשוגה. הכתובת השנייה פותחת אף היא בסקירת גורלה של העיר בעבר, ויש סימטריה ברורה בין התיאור של מה שנפגם בעבר בחלק הראשון ובין השיקום והחזרת המצב לקדמותו בחלק השני.

לעיל הראיתי שהכינוי 'האשורי' מכוון לנֵרגַל־אֵרֵש וכי רק לאחר שירד מגדולתו חזרה ענת לידי נציבי סוחו. לדברי נִנֻרתַ־כֻּדֻר־אֻצֻר, העיר עברה לידי הנציב האשורי בעקבות פנייתם של תושבי העיר, ובשתי הכתובות בולט מוטיב החטא ועונשו: בני ענת משלמים את מלוא המחיר על בגידתם בנציבי סוחו. ואולם יותר מכול בולט בכתובות האופן השלילי שבו 'האשורי' מוצג. לפי הכתובת הראשונה, הוא החריב את העיר, הגלה את תושביה והביא אחרים תחתיהם, וגרם שאלי העיר ינטשו אותה ויעברו לעיר שכנה, ובעקבות זאת שובשו סדרי הקרבנות והחגים במקדשים. לפי הכתובת השנייה, 'האשורי' חילל את קודשי האלה ענת וגרם להפסקת פולחנה. רק לאחר ששבה העיר לשלטונם של נציבי סוחו היא שוקמה, תושביה יושבו מחדש, האלים הושבו למקדשיהם והפולחן שב וכונן כמו קודם. ביקורת בוטה מעין זו על האשורים אינה ידועה לנו משום מקור שנכתב במזרח הקדום בימי גדולתה של אשור, כמובן, חוץ מן המקרא. ואולם הטקסט המקראי נכתב בפריפריה של האימפריה האשורית, בשפה שהייתה זרה לאשור והיה נגיש רק לחוג מצומצם של סופרים. ואילו הכתובות מסוחו הן כתובות ראווה שנכתבו בשפה האכדית במחוז שאינו מרוחק מאשור, ואם הוצבו בפומבי, יכלו לקרוא אותן גם מלומדים אשוריים. דומה שהדבר מלמד על הביטחון העצמי של נציבי סוחו בעקבות הירידה בכוחה ובהשפעתה של ממלכת אשור ואולי גם על תקוות לשבירת כוחה של אשור שרווחו באותה העת.

לבסוף, התיאור משקף מידת־מה של חוסר ניסיון מצד מחבר שתי הכתובות. נִנֻרתַ־כֻּדֻר־אֻצֻר מספר ש'האשורי' פגע באלי העיר ובפולחנם, והם 'עזבו' את העיר ענת ועברו לעיר שכנה (רִיבַּנִיש). רק כאשר חזרה ענת לידי שַׁמַשׁ־רֵשׁ־אֻצֻר הוא שיקם את העיר החרבה והשיב את האלים למקדשיהם. מוטיב האלים הנוטשים את עירם או את ארצם לפני מפלה או חורבן ושבים אליה עם בוא התמורה בגורלה ידוע היטב מן המזרח הקדום. בדרך כלל לנטישה נלווה תיאור של חטא המביא לידי זעם האלים וגורם להם לעזוב את המקום. בכתובת נזכרת בגידתם של בני ענת בנציבי סוחו, אבל הזעם האלוהי אינו נזכר בה כלל, והאלים עוזבים את העיר בתגובה על מעשי האשורים. בלי להיות ער לדבר הציג המחבר את אלי סוחו כאלים חלשים הנתונים לשרירות לבם של בני אנוש. נראה שרצה להציג את האשורים באור שלילי כמחללי קדושתם של אלי העיר, ולא שם לב למשתמע מדבריו על כוחם של האלים.

אני נִנֻרְתַ־כֻּדֻר־אֻצֻר, נציב הארצות סוחו ומארי. בני תֵּימָא ושְׁבָא, אשר רחוק מקומם, שליחי(הם) לא באו לפניי ולא עברו אצלי. שיירתם עברה סמוך למימי באר מַרְתֻ ובאר חַלַתֻ, אך חלפה ונכנסה אל העיר חִנְדָנֻ. בעיר כַּר־אַפְּלַאַדַ, באמצע היום, שמעתי על הממכר שלהם ואסרתי את מרכבתי ('רתמתי את עולי'). חציתי בלילה את הנהר ולמחרת, עוד לפני הצהריים, הגעתי ליישוב אַזְלַיְנוּ. שלושה ימים ישבתי באַזְלַיְנוּ, וביום השלישי הם הגיעו. לכדתי במו ידיי 100 מהם בעודם בחיים. לכדתי במו ידיי 200 מגמליהם על מטענם – אריגים צבועים אדום, אריגים למסע?, ברזל, אבני־?? – סחורות מכל הסוגים. שללתי את שללם הכבד והבאתיו אל תוך ארץ סוחו.[34]

בחרתי להביא את הפרשה הזאת משום שהיא ממחישה עוד קו היכר של הכתובות מסוחו: העדר הסוואה למניעי הנציבים בעת שנקטו קו פעולה מסוים. ספרות רבה נכתבה על התעמולה האשורית ועל מתן צידוק למלחמות ולכיבושים של מלכי אשור.[35] הסופרים האשוריים גילו רגישות רבה לאופן הצגת פעולותיהם, ובתיאוריהם מובאים הנמקות והסברים רבים ומגוונים למסעות המלחמה, לכיבושים ולפעולות העונשין שנקטו נגד הארצות שכבשו. בקטע שלפנינו חסרה הנמקה למתקפה על השיירה הערבית חוץ מהימנעותם מלהתייצב לפני הנציב ולעבור בתחומו. השיירה עברה בחִנְדָנֻ, ממערב לסוחו, והנציב חצה את הגבול וארב לה בתחומה של נציבות שכנה, תקף אותה במפתיע באופן שמנע את המשמר מלהגן עליה, שבה שבויים ולקח שלל רב.

לעניין זה יש להדגיש כי סחר היה אינטרס של כל הצדדים וכי הממלכות המעורבות וכמותן המעצמות הגנו על השיירות ועל הסוחרים שעברו בתחומן. השיירה שנשבתה הייתה בדרכה צפונה אל תחום השלטון האשורי, ובכל זאת לא נמנע נִנֻרְתַ־כֻּדֻר־אֻצֻר מלתקוף אותה ולשלול את שללה, ובכתובתו הוא מתגאה במעשיו. יש בכך עוד עדות לחולשה הרבה של אשור באותה העת ולביטחון העצמי של נציב סוחו שלא יימצא מי שיעניש אותו על הפגיעה בסחר השיירות הבין־לאומי.

אני נִנֻרְתַ־כֻּדֻר־אֻצֻר, נציב הארצות סוחו ומארי, גיליתי בראש המצוק קרקע ראויה לעיבוד ולבי מלאני לבנות עליה עיר. שפכתי יסוד מאבנים וחיזקתי (אותו), בניתי עליו עיר וקראתי שמה כַּר־אַפְּלַאַדַ. הושבתי בה 50 אנשי־??, תושבי ארץ סוחו, אשר פנו אל נִנֻרְתַ־כֻּדֻר־אֻצֻר, נציב הארצות סוחו ומארי, לשם ישיבה בעיר לאמור: 'הושב אותנו בעיר שלך'. נטעתי בקרבתה מטע. בניתי מקדש לאל אַפְּלַאַדַ והושבתי בו

34 פריים (לעיל, הערה 3), עמ' 300, כתובת 2 iv 26–38; S.W. Cole, 'On the Existence and Meaning of a Term *šīmūtu* in Early Neo-Babylonian', *N.A.B.U.* 1995, No. 109

35 B. Oded, *War, Piece and Empire: Justifications for War in Assyrian Royal Inscriptions*, Wiesbaden 1992, ושם גם ספרות מוקדמת יותר.

[כוהן?] של אַפְּלַאַדַד, תושב העיר ענת. קבעתי למנחתו (של האל) סאה לחם (סאה = 6 ליטר בקירוב) ובירה מובחרת [....], והענקתי (זאת) לבאי המקדש (*ērib bīti*) ולשר העיר (*ḫazannu*). בניתי בה ארמון לנציב. חיברתי סוללה מנהר פרת, הגבהתי אותה ובניתי עליה [......].[36]

מבין פעולות הבנייה והשיקום הרבות שמזכירים נציבי סוחו בכתובותיהם בחרתי בקטע זה, שבו סיפר נִנֻרְתַ־כֻּדֻּרִי־אֻצֻר על ייסוד יישוב חדש, שנקרא כַּר־אַפְּלַאַדַד ('מעגן האל אַפְּלַאַדַד'). מוטיב פיתוח הארץ ואִכלוסה אינו שכיח בכתובות מלכי אשור ובבל אך מופיע תדיר בכתובות נציבי סוחו. ייתכן שהדבר נבע ממקומם בשולי הארץ הנושבת, במקום שחיו בו קבוצות גדולות וקטנות של רועים נוודים ששלטונות המחוז השגיחו היטב על תנועותיהם ומן הסתם אף ניסו ליישבם. כל המעשים הקשורים לייסוד יישוב חדש נזכרים בקטע זה: פעולות תשתית, אכלוס המקום בגרעין ראשון של מתיישבים, נטיעת מטע כדי ליצור מקור פרנסה קבוע, כינון מרכז פולחן, בניית מרכז מִנהל והקמת מעגן סמוך ליישוב. כתובות מלכי אשור ובבל מסוגננות ורשמיות תדיר, ואילו התיאור כאן מצטיין בפירוט רב ובשיקוף מדויק של הצעדים שננקטו לשם הקמת המקום וביסוסו.

אני שַׁמַשׁ־רֵשַׁ־אֻצֻר, נציב הארצות סוחו ומארי, הורדתי מן ההרים של בני חַבְּחַ דבורים אשר יאספו דבש, אשר מימי אבותיי לפנים איש לא ראה ולא הביא לארץ סוחו, והושבתי אותן במטעים של העיר גַּבַּרִ־אִבְּנַ. הן אוספות דבש ושעווה. אני יכול להמס דבש ושעווה, וכן יכולים הגננים. מי שיעלה (לשלטון) בימים יבואו ישאל את זקני ארצו לאמור: 'הנכון הדבר ששַׁמַשׁ־רֵשַׁ־אֻצֻר, נציב ארץ סוחו, הכניס דבורי דבש אל ארץ סוחו?'[37]

הקטע מציג היבט מיוחד במינו בנושא פיתוח הממלכה: הבאת דבורים וביותן בחבל הפרת התיכון. הדבורים הובאו, ככל הנראה, מאזור הרמה האירנית והושמו סמוך למטעי התמרים שנטע הנציב שַׁמַשׁ־רֵשַׁ־אֻצֻר בגַבַּרִ־אִבְּנַ, העיר החדשה שייסד. הנציב מתפאר בידע הקשור להפקת הדבש, וייתכן שגם ידע על הקשר בין הדבורים להפריית עצי התמר. למותר לציין כי לפיתוח החקלאות, הכולל נטיעת מטעי תמרים ביישובים רבים במחוז, נטיעת ערבות לאורך תעלות המים כדי לנצל את הגזעים וביות דבורים כדי להפיק מהן דבש אין זכר בכתובות מלכי מסופוטמיה.[38]

36 פריים (לעיל, הערה 3), עמ' 298, כתובת 2 iii 22–32.

37 פריים (לעיל, הערה 3), עמ' 281–282, כתובת 1 iv 13 – v 6.

38 בכתובות מלכי אשור בראשית האלף הראשון לפסה"נ יימצא מוטיב פיתוח החקלאות אך רק בניסוח כללי מתוך ציון הקשר שבין השימוש במחרשות להגדלת כמות התבואה שנאגרה באסמים. במקרא מוטיב זה מודגש בעיקר בתיאור דברי ימי עוזיהו בספר דברי הימים ב (כו:י).

סיכום

במהלך הדיון ראינו עד כמה חרגו הכתובות של נציבי סוחו מן הדפוסים המקובלים בכתובות מלכים במסופוטמיה. חריגה זו באה לידי ביטוי במבנה הכתובות, בפתיחות, במבחר הנושאים ובמידת הפירוט שבהצגתם וכן בפנייה החוזרת ונשנית אל מי שיעלה על כס הנציבות בעתיד. קריאת הכתובות על רקע הכרת כתובות של מלכי מסופוטמיה מעוררת לעתים תחושה של חוסר ניסיון ואף חוסר תחכום אבל מצד אחר גם תחושת רעננות ואימוץ דרכי ביטוי חדשות.

החריגות הבולטות מן הנורמות של כתובות מלכים מסופוטמיות נובעות ממקומה של סוחו בשוליים של מרכזי התרבות הגדולים של מסופוטמיה ומהעדר מסורת מקומית של כתיבת כתובות רשמיות. הסופרים בסוחו אימצו את הדפוס של כתובות מלכים ומקצת דרכי הביטוי שלהן מתוך סיגולם לכתובות של נציבים, אבל היו משוחררים במידה רבה מן המסורת רבת-השנים של הסופרים באשור ובבבל. לפיכך הרשו לעצמם חירות מרובה וחרגו מן הדפוסים הספרותיים והאידאולוגיים המאפיינים את הכתובות המלכותיות. משום כך יכלו לבחור נושאים ודרכי עיצוב שהתאימו טוב יותר לרעיונות שרצו למסור בכתובותיהם. למותר לציין שכמקורות לחקר ההיסטוריה יש לכתובות האלה משנה-חשיבות דווקא בשל הצגת נושאים שבדרך כלל אינם באים על ביטוים בכתובות בשל הפירוט הרב שבו הם מוצגים ומשום שנציבי סוחו אינם עושים מאמץ להסוות את המניעים למעשיהם. חוסר הניסיון והכתיבה הישירה והגלויה הם דווקא שעושים את כתובות נציבי סוחו למקורות החשובים כל כך לחקר חבל הפרת התיכון בתקופת השפל של ממלכת אשור באמצע המאה השמינית לפני הספירה.

על לידתו ועיצובו של החוג לאשורולוגיה באוניברסיטה העברית בירושלים

מאת

חיים תדמור

ברצוני לגולל לפניכם פרשה ארוכה ומפתיעה – פרשת הקמתם של לימודי המזרח הקדום באוניברסיטה העברית בירושלים או בשם אחר – תולדות החוג לאשורולוגיה. לא ייאמן, אך פרשה זו שזורה כמעט לאורך כל תולדות האוניברסיטה העברית, והיא עולה לפתע ושוב נעלמת לה. נראה שפרנסי האוניברסיטה הראשונים ראו חשיבות יתרה בשילוב לימודי המזרח הקדום בין מקצועות היהדות והמזרחנות ולא היססו לפנות ולהזמין חוקרים שלימים היו טובי המלומדים במקצוע.

בדצמבר 1923 פנה יוליוס לוי, בן למשפחה ציונית מברלין ומרצה צעיר (פריבט־דוצנט) באוניברסיטת גיסֶן, במכתב לאוניברסיטה העברית בירושלים והציע את עצמו למשרת הוראה. וכך כתב: ׳בעידודו של הפרופסור אוטו ורבורג [נשיא ההסתדרות הציונית בגרמניה] אני רוצה במכתב זה להציע את מועמדותי למשרת מרצה בתחום האשורולוגיה, אם תוקם באוניברסיטה העברית מחלקה למזרחנות׳. במכתב פורטו שמות אנשים העשויים להמליץ עליו וצורפו מהלך חיים מפורט ורשימת פרסומים בת חמישה־עשר פריטים. המכתב מסתיים בבקשתו של לוי: אם דרושות עוד תעודות או המלצות, יובא הדבר לידיעתו בהקדם, ׳מפני ששמעתי מפרופ׳ ורבורג שפיתוח אוניברסיטה בירושלים מתקדם במהירות ואוניברסיטה זו תהיה, על שום מקומה בירושלים, מרכז לחקירת כתבי יתדות של המזרח התיכון׳.[1]

ד״ר י״ל מאגנס, שנתמנה זמן קצר קודם לכן לראש המכון למדעי היהדות, ענה ללוי ושאלו אם יוכל ללמד בעברית. בתשובתו מאוקטובר 1924 כתב לוי: ׳רק כעת אני מסוגל לכתוב לך בחיוב על שאלתך, היינו שאהיה מסוגל ללמד ולהרצות בשפה העברית, זאת לאחר שאשהה זמן קצר בארץ ישראל, שכידוע אינה זרה לי׳.[2] כעבור חודשים אחדים, בינואר 1925, פנה לוי שנית לאוניברסיטה ושלח את מסמכיו באמצעות מתווך שלא התברר לי מי היה, וביקש ממנו לדון עם מאגנס ׳על האפשרות לשריין לו מקום בקתדרה למחקר כתבי היתדות בירושלים׳.[3] למכתב שוב צורפו קורות החיים של לוי

1 גנזך האוניברסיטה העברית (להלן: גא״ע), תיק 5 ל, 15.12.1923.

2 שם, 10.10.1924.

3 שם, 19.1.1925.

ורשימת פרסומיו הכתובים בכתב יד יפה ורהוט. מְקורות החיים שלו עולה שלוי התחיל את לימודיו באוניברסיטת לייפציג בשנת 1914, אחר כך התגייס לצבא ושירת עד תחילת שנת 1918. בין השאר היה מתורגמן מתורכית, הוצב בארץ ישראל ובה שירת כשנה.

באותן השנים הייתה האוניברסיטה העברית בשלבי הקמתה הראשונים. באפריל 1922 נבחרה ועדה לייסוד הפקולטה למדעי הרוח. אנשי הוועדה ראו חשיבות יתרה בפיתוח המחלקה המזרחנית, שלימים הייתה למכון למדעי המזרח.[4] בדצמבר 1924 בטקס רב־רושם נחנך המכון למדעי היהדות, ובאפריל 1925 נפתחה ברוב עם והדר האוניברסיטה העברית על הר הצופים. שני מכוני היסוד שלה היו באותה שעה המכון לכימיה ומיקרוביולוגיה והמכון למדעי היהדות.[5]

במרוצת אותה השנה נרקמו יחסים הדוקים בין מאגנס, שנעשה פעיל ביותר בוועדה הירושלמית המנהלת את ענייני האוניברסיטה, ובין יוסף הורוביץ, פרופסור לערבית באוניברסיטת פרנקפורט, שהיה לדמות המרכזית בהקמת המכון למדעי המזרח באוניברסיטה בשנת 1926.[6] הורוביץ היה אדם תקיף ופעיל שעיצב כמעט לבדו את לימודי הערבית באוניברסיטה העברית ואת כיווני ההתפתחות המדעית של המכון. אמנם הוא לא עלה ארצה, אך הוא נטל לידיו את רסן הנהלת המכון בתואר 'מנהל־פוקד' (Visiting Director). מאגנס הביא לפני הורוביץ את פנייתו של יוליוס לוי לפתוח את תחום האשורולוגיה בירושלים. הורוביץ אימץ את הרעיון אך לא את הפונה: לדעתו, המועמד המתאים ביותר היה חוקר יהודי אחר בתחום זה בגרמניה, ד"ר בנו לנדסברגר מאוניברסיטת לייפציג.

מכתביו של לוי לאוניברסיטה נשתמרו ברובם הגדול, ואילו בהתכתבות על אודות לנדסברגר השתמרו רק מקצת מכתביו של הורוביץ אל מאגנס בעניינו ופניות אחדות של מאגנס אל לנדסברגר. מכתבי לנדסברגר אל הורוביץ לא הגיעו לגנזך האוניברסיטה. אפשר להשלים במידת־מה את התמונה באמצעות ידיעות על הנסיבות ועל תולדותיו של לנדסברגר באותן השנים.

בשנת 1926 היה בנו לנדסברגר, מלומד צעיר בן שלושים ושש, מרצה לאשורולוגיה באוניברסיטת לייפציג. הקתדרה לאשורולוגיה הייתה השנייה בחשיבותה בתחום זה בגרמניה אחרי הקתדרה של ברלין. בראשה עמד פרידריך דליטש, ממייסדי מדע האשורולוגיה המודרני. כשעָבר דליטש לברלין ירש ממנו את ראשות הקתדרה בלייפציג תלמידו היינריך צימרן, שגם הוא עמד לצאת לגמלאות באמצע שנות העשרים. תלמידו, בנו לנדסברגר, עמד

4 ח' לבסקי, 'בין הנחת אבן הפינה לפתיחה: ייסוד האוניברסיטה העברית, 1918–1925', בתוך ש' כ"ץ ומ' הד (עורכים), תולדות האוניברסיטה העברית בירושלים: שורשים והתחלות, ירושלים תשנ"ז, עמ' 142–143.

5 שם, עמ' 158–159.

6 מ' מילסון, 'ראשית לימודי הערבית והאסלאם באוניברסיטה העברית', בתוך כ"ץ והד (לעיל, הערה 4), עמ' 577–579.

לבוא במקומו. קתדראות לאשורולוגיה ולשפות שמיות, חידוש אקדמי גדול באותם הימים, נפתחו עוד בכמה אוניברסיטאות ובהן אוניברסיטאות מרבורג, ברסלאו וגיסן שבה, כאמור, לימד יוליוס לוי. בין המלומדים בתחום זה היו אפוא שני יהודים יודעי עברית מקראית. באוניברסיטאות גרמניה הייתה האשורולוגיה ארוגה במארג מפותח של מקצועות קרובים: ערבית, ארמית, סורית, חבשית ועברית מקראית, ואין פלא אפוא שפרופסור הורוביץ, תושב גרמניה, לחץ מאוד שתיקבע משרה לאשורולוגיה במכון ללימודי המזרח באוניברסיטה העברית. הורוביץ נפגש עם לנדסברגר כבר בשנת 1925 ואף דיבר אתו על הכוונה להזמינו לירושלים.[7]

לנדסברגר היה בבחינת אהבה נכזבת של האוניברסיטה העברית. הוא כיהן כפרופסור באוניברסיטת לייפציג למן שנת 1929 ועד לשנים הראשונות לשלטון הנאצי. כיוון ששירת כקצין בצבא האוסטרי, לא פוטר ממשרתו בשנת 1933 עם עליית היטלר לשלטון והוסיף להחזיק בה עוד שנתיים. בשנת 1935 בוטלה הקתדרה שלו והוא הוצא לגמלאות בהיותו בן ארבעים וחמש. באותה שנה הוצעה לו פרופסורה באוניברסיטה החדשה שהקים כמאל אתאטורק באנקרה שבתורכיה. לנדסברגר נענה להצעה, יצא לאנקרה ושם לימד עד לשנת 1948. בשנה זו עבר עם תלמידו וידידו חוקר החִתים האנס גיטרבוק למכון המזרחני הנודע באוניברסיטת שיקגו. לנדסברגר שימש בה יועץ למערכת המילון האשורי (CAD (Chicago Assyrian Dictionary, משרה שהחזיק בה עד מותו בשנת 1968.[8]

שני החוקרים הצעירים מן האוניברסיטה העברית, אברהם מלמט וחיים תדמור, שנשלחו כל אחד בתורו בשנות החמישים להשתלם אצל לנדסברגר, שמעו מפיו לא פעם סיפורים על זיקתו לאוניברסיטה העברית. הוא סיפר, למשל, שרצה לבוא לירושלים בשנת 1935, אך מישהו באוניברסיטה חסם את דרכו, ועוד סיפר כי פנו אליו כשהיה בתורכיה בעיצומה של מלחמת העולם השנייה והזמינו אותו לבוא לירושלים. אמנם הסיפורים הללו אינם מתועדים במסמכים בגנזך האוניברסיטה, ואולם יש בגנזך מסמכים על המגעים הראשונים עמו בשנות העשרים. לנדסברגר חש זיקה עמוקה לאוניברסיטה העברית ובין השאר, מלבד יחסו החם למלומדים הצעירים מירושלים, היא התבטאה בעצם הדבר שאת ספרייתו הוריש בצוואתו לאוניברסיטה העברית. ברבות הימים הייתה ספרייה זו לגרעין הספרייה בחדר הסמינריון של החוג לאשורולוגיה, שהוקם באוניברסיטה לאחר פטירת לנדסברגר.

לעניין מגעיו של לנדסברגר עם הורוביץ בשנים 1925–1926 מתברר שלנדסברגר לא דחה את הצעתו האמורה של הורוביץ, ועל מאגנס הופעל

7 למיטב ידיעתי, מתפרסמים כאן בפעם הראשונה המגעים המוקדמים הללו בין האוניברסיטה העברית ובין בנו לנדסברגר. עד עתה היו כל ידיעותינו על פרשת לנדסברגר בלא סימוכין בכתב.

8 ראה H. Güterbock, *In Memoriam*, *AfO*, 22 (1968/9), p. 203; W. von Soden, 'Landsberger, Benno', *RLA*, 6, 1980–1983, pp. 467–468

אפוא לחץ לשלוח ללנדסברגר מכתב הזמנה רשמי. מאגנס היה מוגבל בתקצוב משרה חדשה, שכן תקציב האוניברסיטה הצעירה היה מצומצם מאוד ואף בקושי הספיק למשרות הקיימות. לכן מיהר לשלוח אל לנדסברגר מכתב התנצלות, וכך כתב:

> אנו חושבים ברצינות להקים מחלקה אשורית־בבלית ובוודאי גם לפנות אליך. טרם עשינו זאת משום שנאלצנו להתמודד עם מצבים קשים מאוד ובלתי צפויים ומפני שעדיין לא הצלחנו להגיע למצב ארגוני וכספי שמאפשר לנו לפנות לבר־אוריין שכמוך. אנו מקווים שבתוך זמן קצר יהיה הדבר אפשרי. מכתב זה נועד אפוא להסביר לך מדוע עדיין לא עשינו זאת.[9]

כעבור חודשים אחדים, באספת מועצת חבר הנאמנים של האוניברסיטה במינכן, הודיע מאגנס שמשרת פרופסור תהיה שמורה באוניברסיטה העברית לבנו לנדסברגר במכון למדעי המזרח על־פי הצעת הורוביץ.[10] מועצת חבר הנאמנים הייתה, כידוע, מועצה מכובדת ביותר שבראשה עמד אז אלברט איינשטיין, ועם חבריה נמנו מרטין בובר, יוסף הורוביץ, חיים ויצמן, אוטו ורבורג, אויגן טויבלר, י׳ לנדאו, זיגמונד פרויד, ארנסט קסירר ואחרים וכן ארבעה נציגים מירושלים: י״נ אפשטיין, יוסף קלוזנר, שמואל קליין ואנדור פודור. ככל הנראה, לנדסברגר היה אז פתוח להצעות, אולם הצעה למשרה בירושלים הגיעה אליו רק אחרי כשנתיים. בקיץ 1928 פנה אליו מאגנס באופן רשמי במכתב:

> מועצת הנגידים של האוניברסיטה העברית בישיבתה מאתמול החליטה ליצור משרת מרצה באשורולוגיה ונתבקשתי לפנות אליך ולשאול אותך אם יהיה לך עניין במשרה זו.
>
> ידוע לנו שב־1925 פנה אליך, לפי בקשתנו, פרופ׳ הורוביץ מפרנקפורט בשאלה אם תהיה מעוניין בקתדרה לאשורולוגיה באוניברסיטה העברית. לצערנו הרב, אחר כך התברר לנו שמצבה הכספי של האוניברסיטה לא אפשר לנו באותה העת לפתח נושא חשוב כאשורולוגיה. עתה שמח אני להודיע לך שהאוניברסיטה מעוניינת מאוד לייסד בה את המדור לאשורולוגיה ומטבע הדברים היא פונה אליך בראש ובראשונה.
>
> משכורת שנתית של מרצה באוניברסיטה העברית היא 400 עד 480 לא״י. האוניברסיטה תשמח, כמובן, להציע לך את הדרגה הגבוהה ביותר האפשרית למרצה. יש גם תוספת משפחה. מתנהל עתה באוניברסיטה תהליך של קביעת מערכת פנסיה לעובדי המוסד ולסגל האקדמי.
>
> בשלב זה אין האוניברסיטה מציעה מחלקה לאשורולוגיה שפרופסור בראשה, שכן עדיין אין היא יכולה להשוות את רמת האשורולוגיה

9 המכתב כתוב גרמנית, מאגנס אל לנדסברגר, גא״ע, תיק 5 ל, 18.4.1926.

10 גא״ע, פרוטוקולים של חבר הנאמנים, 1926, עמ׳ 18–19.

> לזו של ערבית או מדעי היהדות. עם זאת אנו מקווים שלא ירחק היום והאשורולוגיה, על כל המדעים הקשורים בה, תוכל להיות למחלקה שלמה באוניברסיטה. נהיה אסירי תודה אם תואיל להשיב לנו במרוצת השבועיים הקרובים.[11]

בינתיים הוזמן לנדסברגר לכהונת פרופסור מן המניין בקתדרה במרבורג (1928), וכעבור שנה הוזמן לאוניברסיטת לייפציג לכהן בה כפרופסור. להורוביץ היה ברור שלא היה אז כל סיכוי שלנדסברגר יקבל את הצעתו של מאגנס לבוא לאוניברסיטה בירושלים למשרת מרצה.

בראשית יולי 1928 שלח מאגנס מכתב להורוביץ ובו העלה שם אחר: אפרים ספייזר מאוניברסיטת פנסילווניה, שעמו נפגש בירושלים: 'ד"ר ספייזר, שכידוע לך נתמנה לפרופסור עוזר באוניברסיטת פנסילווניה, היה פה אתמול'. מאגנס ציין שספייזר יהיה מוכן לשוב לירושלים בתום שלוש שנות המינוי הראשון בפנסילווניה. מאגנס הוסיף שהרצאות המבוא לפילולוגיה שמית השוואתית שנשא ספייזר בירושלים עוררו עניין רב. המעורבות שלו ברעיון האוניברסיטה העברית וידיעת העברית שלו יעשו אותו מועמד אידאלי, אם לא יקבלו לנדסברגר ולוי את הצעת האוניברסיטה. ועוד כתב: 'טוב היה לחשוב על הזמנת אדם צעיר מבטיח, שרק עכשיו סיים ללמד כעוזר הוראה באשורולוגיה לתלמידי המכון למדעי היהדות והמדרשה למדעי המזרח. הוא יעבוד בפיקוחו של ד"ר ספייזר ובתום שלוש שנים אפשר שספייזר עצמו יבוא הנה'.[12]

אכן, ההצעה בדבר מלומד צעיר מתלמידי ספייזר שיבוא לירושלים ללמד אשורולוגיה יצאה אל הפועל אך באיחור של שלושים וחמש שנה: אהרן שפר, דוקטור צעיר שלמד אצל הפרופסורים אפרים ספייזר וש"נ קרמר, התמנה למרצה לאשורולוגיה באוניברסיטה העברית. הוא הצטרף אל חיים תדמור, תלמידם של בנימין מזר ובנו לנדסברגר, שיסד את לימודי המזרח הקדום באוניברסיטה בשנת 1958.

בראשית ספטמבר 1928 עדיין חיכה הורוביץ לתשובתו של לנדסברגר אף שציפה לסירוב מצדו. בספטמבר כתב הורוביץ למאגנס:

> כשהייתי באוקספורד הייתה לי הזדמנות לפגוש את פרופ' לוי מגיסן. לפני שנים מספר הוא הביע את נכונותו לבוא לירושלים. הוא מוכן לעשות זאת גם כיום. מדבריו ברור לי לחלוטין שלנדסברגר לא יבוא, שכן כל הסיכויים הם שיוזמן למשרת פרופסור מן המניין. לפיכך אני ממליץ בכל לשון של המלצה להזמין את לוי מיד כשתתקבל תשובתו של לנדסברגר.[13]

בינתיים חלפה שנה תמימה ולנדסברגר השיב בשלילה להצעת האוניברסיטה בירושלים. מאגנס חזר אפוא למועמד האחד שהיה לו: יוליוס לוי מגיסן,

11 המכתב כתוב באנגלית, מאגנס אל לנדסברגר, גא"ע, תיק 5 ל, 6.6.1928.

12 מאגנס אל הורוביץ, שם, 1.7.1928.

13 הורוביץ אל מאגנס, שם, 9.9.1928.

שהועלה בינתיים לדרגת פרופסור שלא מן המניין. הדבר לא מנע את מאגנס מלהציע ללוי משרת מרצה.

מאותם ימים נשתמרה חליפת מכתבים מעניינת ביותר בין הורוביץ למאגנס. וכך כתב הורוביץ בראשית ספטמבר 1929: 'אני שולח לך בזה את התשובה שנתקבלה מפרופ' לוי, שממנה אתה למד שהוא מוכן לקבל את המינוי המוצע בתנאי שתתקבלנה הבקשות שלו. אין ספק שכפרופסור שלא מן המניין הוא המועמד הטבעי לקתדרה זו כאשר מצבה הכספי של האוניברסיטה יאפשר לפתוח אותה'.[14] בנובמבר השיב מאגנס להורוביץ: 'אני שמח לבשר עתה שהצלחנו להשיג את האמצעים בתקציב הבא להזמנת פרופ' לוי מסמסטר הקיץ 1930'.[15] בהמשך דן מאגנס בשתי שאלות שהעלה לוי: שאלת מעמדו ושאלת משכורתו. אשר לראשונה, הכוונה היא למנות את לוי למעין פרופסור חבר בתקן של מרצה, כלומר הוא ייחשב מרצה לכל דבר, אך ביחסי חוץ ייחשב לפרופסור חבר. עם זה החברות במועצת הפרופסורים בירושלים איננה אוטומטית לבעלי מינוי מעין זה. לשאלה השנייה בעניין משכורתו כמרצה, הרי המקסימום בדרגתו הוא ארבעים לא"י בחודש יותר ממשכורתם של רוב המרצים. תוספת משפחתית של עשרים לא"י לשנה תגדיל את המשכורת לחמש מאות לא"י לשנה. כעשרה ימים בלבד לאחר מכתבו של מאגנס הגיעה תשובתו של לוי להורוביץ:

> לצערי הרב, לא אוכל להיענות להצעות לבוא לירושלים, כפי שכתבתי בארבעה בספטמבר. תנאי למשא ומתן בעתיד הוא שהעבודה בירושלים תהיה זהה לעבודתי בגיסן. כאן אני מנהל באופן עצמאי סמינר בפקולטה והנני בעל מושב וקול בסנט. יתרה מזו, גם ההסדר הכספי שד"ר מאגנס מציע אינו מספק. על-פי המידע שברשותי לא אוכל, בהיותי נשוי, לשמור על רמת החיים שהורגלנו אליה כאן בגרמניה בשכר של 500 לא"י לשנה.[16]

מדוע שינה לוי את נימת מכתבו למאגנס לפסקנית וחריפה? נראה לי כי לוי נעלב מן הסידור המוזר שהציעה לו האוניברסיטה: פרופסור חבר לעומת דרגתו ומעמדו אז בתחומו. זאת ועוד: בחמש השנים מאז פנה בפעם הראשונה לאוניברסיטה העברית השתנו מאוד מעמדו ותנאי עבודתו, והובטח לו, כנראה, מעמד של פרופסור מן המניין. ואכן, הוא קיבל אותו בשנת 1930. ואולם מפתיעה מאוד עמדתו בעניין המשכורת: הצעת האוניברסיטה הייתה נדיבה ביותר, שהרי משכורתו של מורה בבית ספר תיכון בעל תואר דוקטור בארץ ישראל באותה התקופה הייתה כרבע מן המשכורת שהוצעה ללוי ופחותה הרבה יותר הייתה משכורתו של פועל. משכורת זו הייתה נדיבה מאוד גם בגרמניה של אותם הימים, ודומני שלוי העלה טענה זו

14 הורוביץ אל מאגנס, שם, 5.9.1929.

15 מאגנס אל הורוביץ, שם, 18.9.1929.

16 לוי אל הורוביץ, שם, 28.11.1929.

משום שחש עלבון מהתנהגות האוניברסיטה. על כך הגיב מאגנס במכתב אל הורוביץ:

> קיבלתי את תשובתו של פרופ׳ לוי אליך מ־6 בדצמבר. הופתעתי ללמוד ממנה שהתנאים שהצענו לו במכתבנו נתקבלו בזעזוע.
> כאשר נאלצנו לוותר על מועמדותו של פרופ׳ לנדסברגר הדגשנו שמוצעת כעת משרת מרצה, והבנו שפרופ׳ לוי, למרות משרתו בגיסן, היה מוכן לשקול משרה זו בירושלים ורק ביקש שהתואר שלו יישמע טוב יותר. לכן חשבתי שמשכורת של 500 לא״י לשנה ותואר אישי של פרופסור חבר ללוי יפתרו לגמרי את הבעיה. כרגע אין זה משנה אם פרופ׳ לוי לא הבין את מהות הצעתנו או אם שינה את דעתו מאז. ברור ששוב איננו מועמד לתנאים שהאוניברסיטה מסוגלת להציע לו. אני מציע עכשיו שתעשה סקר של מלומדים הבאים בחשבון למשרת מרצה באשורולוגיה כדי שנוכל להציע אותו לפני הפגישה הבאה של המועצה האקדמית. נצטרך בוודאי לחפש אדם צעיר יותר שעדיין לא קיבל תואר פרופסור.[17]

העניין המובא בסיומו של המכתב, שעל האוניברסיטה העברית לפנות לאדם צעיר יותר שעדיין איננו פרופסור, נשאר בגדר משאלה בלבד. נושא האשורולוגיה באוניברסיטה בירושלים ירד אפוא מן הפרק עד שהבשילו התנאים לחזור ולדון בו. האוניברסיטה העברית שוב לא הציעה הצעות ללוי, וסיפור הזמנתו נגנז ונשכח. אף אינני בטוח אם בנימין מייזלר (לימים מזר), שסיים את לימודיו אצל לוי וקיבל תואר דוקטור באשורולוגיה ולימודי המזרח הקדום, ידע על כל הפרשה.

מעניין ביותר האפילוג בפרשת לוי. עם עליית הנאצים לשלטון בשנת 1933 הוא פוטר ממשרתו בגיסן ויצא לצרפת לחפש משרה. בסוף 1933 או בתחילת השנה שלאחריה הגיע ארצה לביקור קצר אצל אביו, ד״ר בנו לוי, שעלה והתיישב בחיפה. בהזדמנות זו שוב פנה לוי לאוניברסיטה.[18] מאגנס, הנגיד הכול יכול, היה באותה העת טרוד בענייני ועדת הסקר של חבר הנאמנים, הידועה בכינויה ׳ועדת הרטוג׳ על שם יושב הראש שלה, סר פיליפ הרטוג. בדין וחשבון של הרטוג הוטחה, כידוע, ביקורת חריפה במנהיגותו של מאגנס והוצע לבטל את משרת הנגיד, לייסד משרת נשיא ולכונן סנט של פרופסורים ובראשו רקטור. לענייננו יש להזכיר את ההצעה בהמלצות האקדמיות בדוח הנוגעת ללוי: ׳אנו מצטרפים לדעה שהביע ראש המכון ללימודי המזרח בתזכיר שהגיש, והיא שרצוי להרחיב את מאגר ההוראה במכון באופן שיכלול, למשל, פילולוגיה שמית השוואתית והיסטוריה של המזרח הקדום. האדם המתאים ביותר לשני הנושאים

17 מאגנס אל הורוביץ, שם, 6.12.1929.

18 K. Hecker, 'Julius Lewy', in H. Gundel, P. Moraw & V. Press (eds.), *Giessener Gelehrte in der ersten Hälfte d. 20 Jaarhundert*, Marburg 1982, pp. 626–633; idem, 'Lewy, Julius', *RLA*, 6, 1980–1983, pp. 608–609

גם יחד יוכל להיות פרופ׳ לוי מגיסן, פליט גרמני השוהה כעת בפריז׳.[19] בתשובתו לדוח הרטוג הסכים מאגנס להקמת מסלול הוראה בהיסטוריה של המזרח הקדום, אך בסגנונו החד והסרקסטי שאל: ׳מניין יבוא התקציב למשרה זו?׳ הוא הוסיף והעיר שפילולוגיה שמית השוואתית היא תחומו של פרופסור נ״ה טורטשינר (לימים טור־סיני), ואין צורך להוסיף על כך, ועוד אמר שלוי היגר בינתיים לארצות הברית.[20] כידוע, לוי היה פרופסור אורח באוניברסיטת ג׳ונס הופקינס וכעבור זמן־מה נתמנה לפרופסור לאשורולוגיה ב׳היברו יוניון קולג׳׳ (HUC) בסינסינטי, ושם עבד עד שנפטר בשנת 1963.

הזכרת שמו של טורטשינר כמי שנועד ללמד בירושלים פילולוגיה שמית השוואתית יש לה חשיבות מיוחדת: היא בישרה את הקמת החוג לבלשנות שמית, שבשעתו היה קשור בשמו של לוי, אלא שכאן לא דובר בהזמנת אשורולוג שזה תחום התמחותו. אמנם טורטשינר היה בנעוריו אשורולוג מקצועי[21] שלמד אצל דליטש בברלין בשנת 1908, כתב עבודת דוקטור על תעודות הענקה מבבל בתקופת השושלת הכשית (ספרו זה התפרסם בווינה בשנת 1914), אך בעשרים וחמש השנים שבאו אחר כך לימד מקרא בבית הספר הגבוה למדעי היהדות בברלין, הרצה על שפות שמיות וחיבר ספר מקורי על הנושא. בשנת 1933 עלה ארצה והתקבל לאוניברסיטה כפרופסור ללשון עברית בקתדרה על שם ביאליק. תחום אחר שלימד בו שעות מעטות ביותר באוניברסיטה העברית היה שפות שמיות.[22] בתכנית הלימודים משנות השלושים וראשית שנות הארבעים הוא מופיע כמלמד אשורית למתחילים ולמתקדמים בהיקף של שעה עד שעתיים בשבוע.[23] ידיעת האשורית שלו

19 P. Hartog, *Report of the Hebrew University Survey Committee*, Jerusalem 1934, p. 213, §18

20 J.L. Magnes, *Reply to the Report of the Survey Committee of the Hebrew University*, Jerusalem 1934, pp. 13, 199

21 קורות חייו, בלא תאריך, ראה גא״ע, תיק אישי טורטשינר. המסמך נתחבר סמוך לעלייתו ארצה בשנת 1933.

22 בשנת תרצ״ו לימד טורטשינר תחום זה בלא ציון שם החוג. באמצע אותה שנה אושרה הקמת החוג לשפות שמיות בוועידה העשירית של חבר הנאמנים, שהתכנס בציריך באוגוסט 1936 (גא״ע, תיק חבר הנאמנים, 1936, עמ׳ 101). במערכת השיעורים משנת תרצ״ז מופיע פירוט לימודי החוג ולימודי ההשלמה. חוג זה כלל את השיעורים בסורית ובחבשית ולימודי השלמה, בעיקר בערבית, שהורה יעקב פולוצקי. מורה צעיר זה היה למלומד דגול ומורה מרכזי בחוג לשפות שמיות. הוא עלה ארצה מגרמניה באותן השנים ונתקבל לאוניברסיטה העברית להיות בה אגיפטולוג וחוקר שפות שמיות. במרוצת השנים נוסף מורה שלישי בלימודי החוג, הוא ד״ר מאיר מאכס בראפמן, שעבד בירושלים במכון ללימודי המזרח. עליו הוטל בשנת 1947 ללמד אשורית למתחילים, אך בשנת 1951 התפטר מן האוניברסיטה ויצא לארצות הברית.

23 בשנת 1935 ביקש טורטשינר להקל על עצמו והציע לשתף עוד מורה בהוראת האשורית. כך יוכל הוא עצמו ללמד שיעור למתחילים מדי שנה בשנה ולא אחת לשנתיים. המורה המוצע היה פרופסור חיים פיק, מראשי תנועת המזרחי בארץ ישראל. הוא עלה ארצה בראשית שנות העשרים וישב בירושלים. פיק למד כתבי יתדות אצל דליטש בברלין, היה מומחה למגעים שבין האכדית ובין הארמית, ובנושא

באה לידי ביטוי קבוע בפרשנות המקרא שלו אך לא הייתה סוגיה העומדת בפני עצמה. מאגנס ביקש מטורטשינר להורות אשורית וכך מילא את הצורך, לשיטתו, להזמין מרצה מיוחד לתחום זה.

ועדת הרטוג המליצה, כאמור, גם על הוראת ההיסטוריה של המזרח הקדום. למעשה היה בירושלים מועמד מצוין לתחום זה והיה אפשר להזמינו למשרה האמורה: ד"ר בנימין מייזלר, שהציע פעמים אחדות את מועמדותו לאוניברסיטה העברית אך נדחה שוב ושוב בטענה שאין לכך תקציב. מייזלר היה צעיר בעשר שנים מלוי מורו. ידיד המשפחה, הרב יחיאל וויינברג, שישב בגיסן והכיר יפה את משפחת מייזלר, התרשם מכישרונותיו של בנימין הצעיר, השפיע על אביו להוציאו מבית הספר בוורשה, שלשם היגרה המשפחה מרוסיה, ולשלוח אותו ללמוד בגרמניה.[24] בתוך כשנתיים השלים מייזלר את לימודיו בגימנסיה הרוסית בברלין, קיבל תעודת בגרות ונרשם לאוניברסיטת גיסן ללימודי המזרח הקדום ושפות שמיות. בשנת 1928, והוא בן עשרים ושתיים, סיים מייזלר בהצלחה רבה את לימודיו והגיש את עבודת הדוקטור שלו.[25] הוא נסע לבקר את משפחתו שבינתיים עלתה ארצה והתיישבה בחיפה. בעת ביקורו בארץ, בשנת 1929, פנה במכתב לד"ר לוי ביליג, סגן המנהל הממונה מטעם פרופסור הורוביץ במכון למדעי המזרח בירושלים. וכך נאמר במכתבו: 'מקצועי אשורולוגיה והיסטוריה אוריינטלית עתיקה [...] משאלת לבי היא לפעול באוניברסיטה העברית בירושלים, והנני מרשה לעצמי לפנות לכבודו בבקשה להודיע למקומות המוסמכים באוניברסיטה העברית בדבר הצעתי לקבלת העסקה באוניברסיטה בשדה האשורולוגיה, היסטוריה וארכיאולוגיה אוריינטלית עתיקה'.[26] המכתב נושא תוספת של רישום בעיפרון אדום באנגלית: 'מר גינזברג יראיין אותו ויאמר לו: "אין לנו קרנות כרגע, רוצה הייתי לפגוש אותו לאחר מכן"'. לפי הכתב מתברר שמאגנס כתב את ההערה, אך אין לנו כל מידע אם נפגש מאגנס עם מייזלר וכיצד התרשם ממנו. מכל מקום המועד היה גרוע למייזלר, שכן במאי 1929 עדיין התנהל משא ומתן עם לוי, והאוניברסיטה ציפתה שהוא יקבל את תנאיה.

חמש שנים חלפו, ובשנת 1934 שוב פנה מייזלר לאוניברסיטה.[27] במכתבו מסר שהסיבה לפנייתו הייתה תכנית שהציע חבר פרופסורים המבקש לייסד דוצנטורות פרטיות בפקולטה למדעי הרוח. הוא מציע אפוא את מועמדותו במקצוע ההיסטוריה העתיקה של ארץ ישראל והמזרח הקדמון. הקורס

זה אף פרסם כמה רשימות קצרות בעיתונות המקצועית בראשית המאה העשרים. הצעת טורטשינר נבחנה בוועדה של חברי הפקולטה למדעי הרוח, ולבסוף החליטו שאין לה מקום (גא"ע, מועצת הפקולטה למדעי הרוח, ישיבה כט, 14.6.1935).

24 מלכה פלס (מייזלר), 'ויהי ...', חיפה תשמ"ה, עמ' 101.

25 *Untersuchungen zur alten Geschichte und Ethnographie Syriens und Palästinas*, I, Giessen 1930

26 מייזלר אל ביליג, אע"ג, תיק אישי מזר, א, 1.5.1929.

27 אע"ג, תיק אישי מזר, א, 25.2.1934.

לא יעלה כסף לאוניברסיטה. במכתב זה תיקן מייזלר למעשה את הצעתו המקורית להתמנות לתחום האשורולוגיה והתכוון למיזוג שני התחומים: היסטוריה קדומה של ארץ ישראל והמזרח הקדמון. התברר שבחמש השנים שעברו מאז מכתבו הראשון התמקד מייזלר בהיסטוריה ובארכאולוגיה של ארץ ישראל בהשראת ו״פ אולברייט, מלומד דגול שישב באותן השנים בירושלים.[28]

בשנת 1937 חידש מייזלר את פנייתו לאוניברסיטה והציע שיהיה מורה מן החוץ לנושא ארץ ישראל העתיקה והארצות השכנות (במסגרת תרבויות המזרח הקדמון). קורס זה נחלק לשניים: (1) ׳הרצאה על תולדות הארץ ותרבותה מהימים הקדומים ביותר עד חורבן בית ראשון׳; (2) ׳עמי המזרח הקדמון (בבלים, אשורים, תושבי סוריה ואנטוליה), שהשפיעו על הארץ השפעה מדינית, כלכלית ותרבותית׳.[29] למעשה זו הפעם האחרונה שמייזלר הציע לאוניברסיטה קורס בתולדות המזרח הקדום. מכאן ואילך התרכז אך ורק בתולדות ארץ ישראל בתקופה הקדומה. רצה הגורל ושערי האוניברסיטה נפתחו לפני מייזלר כאשר בשנת 1940 נפטר פרופסור שמואל קליין. ידיעת ארץ ישראל, מקצוע שקליין לימד, נשאר מיותם. בשנת 1941 החליט הסנט להזמין את מייזלר ללמד גאוגרפיה היסטורית של ארץ ישראל (שם חדש שהציע ב־1940) במחצית המשרה, ובמחצית האחרת – ללמד היסטוריה של עם ישראל בימי הבית הראשון.[30] החלטה זו אושרה בוועד הפועל של האוניברסיטה בשנת 1943 ומייזלר הוזמן לפתוח בהוראה בשנת הלימודים תש״ד.[31]

נושא המזרח הקדום, לימודי האשורולוגיה, ירד לכאורה מעל סדר היום של האוניברסיטה העברית. עם זאת שב הנושא לחלחל ולבעבע במחצית השנייה של שנות הארבעים בזכות כוח ההוראה בעלת ההשראה של מייזלר ובזכות יזמות חדשות שלו. הן בהוראת ההיסטוריה של עם ישראל הן בגאוגרפיה היסטורית הדגיש מייזלר בעצמה את תולדות המזרח הקדום: הוא ראה בתולדות ארץ ישראל חלק בלתי נפרד מן ההיסטוריה של ארצות הקשת הפורייה, ואת תולדות עם ישראל ראה נטועים ומשולבים בתולדות עמי המזרח הקדום. בסמינריונים שלו, למשל, עסק מייזלר בתעודות נוזי, מארי ואוגרית שנעשו נושאים לגיטימיים

28 B. Mazar, 'Autobiographical Reflections of a University Teacher', in M. Cogan & I. Ephʿal (eds.), *Ah, Assyria...: Studies in Assyrian History and Ancient Near Eastern Historiography, Presented to Hayim Tadmor*, Jerusalem 1991, pp. 332–334

29 גא״ע, תיק אישי מזר, א, 7.9.1937. רקטור האוניברסיטה פרופסור שמואל הוגו ברגמן הגיב על מכתבו של מייזלר (שם, 5.5.1938), אך דחה למעשה את ההצעה, שתמכו בה שבעה מורים בכירים בפקולטה (שובה, טורטשינר, קאסוטו, קליין, מאיר, סוקניק ואפשטיין). חברים אלו שלחו מכתב תמיכה מיוחד בתכניתו של מייזלר ללמד את תולדות ארץ ישראל כמורה מן החוץ (שם, 26.10.1939), אך גם פנייתם הושבה ריקם בנימוק של חוסר משאבים (סנטור אל מייזלר, שם, 23.11.1939).

30 גא״ע, תיק מזר, א, 19.9.1940.

31 שם, שם, חומר לישיבת הוועד הפועל, 7.5.1943.

לחוקרי ההיסטוריה המקראית. הדגש בכל הסוגיות האלה היה היסטורי, אינטגרטיבי־תרבותי ולא פילולוגי.

אני, שהתחלתי ללמוד בשנת תש"ד, גיליתי במרוצת הזמן עניין רב במקורות לכרונולוגיה של המזרח הקדום, בעיקר בכרונולוגיה האשורית־בבלית, ולאט לאט עברתי לסוגיות של מחקר מקורות וביקורת מקורות, ושם מן הדין נדרשה ידיעת האכדית. את החלל בהשכלתי מילאתי בשנת השתלמות כשנשלחתי לאנגליה בסוף שנת 1951 בעת כתיבת הדוקטורט על בעיות בכרונולוגיה של המזרח הקדום. סידני סמית', החוקר הדגול שנסעתי להשתלם אצלו ב־School of Oriental and African Studies בלונדון, הודיע לי בזו הלשון: 'אינני מלמד השנה קורס למתחילים. יש לי רק קורס למתקדמים, שמשתתפת בו תלמידה אחת, ואנו קוראים את עלילות גילגמש. אתה מוזמן להצטרף לקורס בתנאי שתבוא בעוד שבועיים לאחר שתכין בעצמך את סימני היתדות, דקדוק וחמישים שורות ראשונות מעלילת גילגמש ביתדות'. האתגר היה קשה, אולי מן הקשים בחיי, והייתי חייב להיענות לו. אחרי גילגמש קראנו את כתובות סנחריב בכמה מהדורות ובהן המהדורה של המסע הראשון שפרסם סמית' בנעוריו. השלב הבא, שלב מתקדם הרבה יותר בלימודי האכדית, היה בשיקגו בשנים 1957–1955 כשנסעתי להשתלם אצל בנו לנדסברגר, גדול האשורולוגים בדורנו. באותה הזדמנות למדתי גם בשיעורים של מלומדים נודעים אחרים: א"ל אופנהיים ואיגנאץ ג' גלב (טקסטיים אכדיים), תורקילד יעקבסן (שומרית) והאנס גיטרבוק (חִתית).

בשנים שנעדרתי מן הארץ, בהיותי בלונדון ואחר כך בשיקגו, התרחשו עוד שתי אפיזודות חדשות בחבלי הלידה הארוכים של החוג לאשורולוגיה: הזמנת כורש הרצל גורדון ואחר כך הזמנת ג'קוב ג' פינקלשטיין לשמש מורים בכירים בלימודי המזרח הקדום בירושלים, שהיו אמורים להיפתח עם בואם. אעבור אפוא לתאר אפיזודות אלו בפירוט, ואתחיל בפרשת גורדון.

כורש גורדון, יליד 1908, היה מדען נודע שלימד באותן השנים בדרופסי קולג' בפילדלפיה. הוא היה המלומד הבולט בחקר לשון אוגרית והטקסטים המיתולוגיים שלה. גורדון למד בשעתו אצל אולברייט באוניברסיטת ג'ונס הופקינס, השתתף בחפירות ארכאולוגיות, ישב זמן־מה בירושלים והתיידד עם בנימין מזר. בשנת 1950, כאשר יצא מזר לשבתון הראשון שלו במכון המזרחני בשיקגו והוא כבר פרופסור מן המניין, ביקר אצל גורדון בפילדלפיה והזמין אותו לאוניברסיטה העברית. מיד בשובו מן השבתון פתח מזר בפעילות מסועפת לייסוד חוג חדש – 'לימודי המזרח הקדמון'. לפי הפרוטוקול של הוועדה המתמדת של הסנט, שלפניה הובאה ההצעה בסוף דצמבר 1951, כך הציג מזר את התכנית:

> דרוש כוח ראשי במשרה שלמה אשר יקיף את התרבות הרוחנית של אשור ובבל והסביבה ויהיה בקי בכתב היתדות, ולידו שני כוחות עזר כמורים מן החוץ אשר ישלימו את ההוראה בשפה ובתרבות החומרית

של המזרח הקדמון. המועמד למשרה הראשית הוא פרופ׳ כורש גורדון שיש לו כל הנתונים הדרושים למשרה זו, הוא יודע גם את השפה העברית על בורייה ומעוניין לבוא אלינו. הוא מומחה חשוב באוגריתית וענף זה התייתם עכשיו עם פטירתו של פרופ׳ קאסוטו. האדונים ייבין ובן־דור ממחלקת העתיקות בירושלים מתאימים למתן ההוראה המשלימה.

מזר הוסיף כי יש לראות את העניין דחוף ביותר, שכן עלינו לשלוח הזמנה לפרופסור גורדון בשבועות הקרובים כדי שיוכל להשתחרר בשנת תשי״ג. יש לנצל את נכונותו של האיש לבוא, ׳שהוא מלומד גדול במקצועו ומקומו הטבעי בינינו׳.[32]

ההצעה לפתיחת החוג החדש הובאה לפני ועדת הקבע של הוועד הפועל של האוניברסיטה העברית בראשית 1952, ושם הוצע להמליץ על יצירת החוג ׳המזרח הקדמון׳.[33] הבעיה היא שיושב ראש הוועד הפועל ד״ר ורנר סנטור, סגן הנשיא האקסקוטיבי של האוניברסיטה, התנגד להצעה והודיע ש׳הוא נאלץ להשתמש בסמכות הניתנת לו ע״י החוקה, זכות הווטו, לעכב לפי שיקול דעתו כל החלטה שנתקבלה ע״י הוועד הפועל, עד שיידון הדבר בחבר הנאמנים׳. לפיכך נדחה הדיון עד לחודש יוני הקרוב. סנטור כתב לגורדון מכתב ובו הסביר את מגמת האוניברסיטה לפתוח בלימודי המזרח הקדמון, אלא שלפי שעה הנסיבות הכספיות של האוניברסיטה אינן מאפשרות לעשות זאת.[34] בינתיים, ביוני 1952, נבחר בנימין מזר לרקטור, ובמועצת הפקולטה למדעי הרוח בראשית שנת הלימודים תשי״ג אושרו הן הקמת החוג ללימודי המזרח הקדמון הן ההצעה להזמין את כורש גורדון להיות בו פרופסור מן המניין.[35] כעבור כשבועיים ניסח ד״ר סנטור מכתב הזמנה רשמי לכורש גורדון, אך מכתב זה נשאר בגדר טיוטה ומשום־מה לא נשלח.[36]

בשנת 1953 נבחר בנימין מזר גם לנשיא האוניברסיטה והמגעים עם גורדון נפסקו לזמן־מה. רק בשנת 1955 נתחדשו המגעים כאשר יעקב פולוצקי, דיקנה החדש של הפקולטה למדעי הרוח, כתב לגורדון וחידש את ההזמנה לייסד באוניברסיטה העברית מחלקה ללימודי ארצות המזרח התיכון הקדום ולעמוד בראשה. פולוצקי הודיע לו שאת הלשונות אכדית ואוגריתית

32 גא״ע, תיק הוועדה המתמדת, תשי״ב, 27.12.1951.

33 גא״ע, תיק הוועד הפועל, תשי״ב, 14.2.1952.

34 גא״ע, תיק כורש גורדון, 9.3.1952. מכתב זה נתחבר על־פי הטיוטה שניסח מזר לפי בקשת סנטור, הצמודה למכתבו אל גורדון. במסמך זה הביע מזר את השקפת עולמו בכל הנוגע ללימודי המזרח הקדום באוניברסיטה: ׳היה בדעתנו לקבוע את לימודי המזרח הקדמון, ובכללם הלשון הבבלית־האשורית ותולדות המזרח הקדמון כחוג ראשי ולקושרו ללימודי אגיפטולוגיה הניתנים ע״י פרופ׳ פולוצקי׳.

35 גא״ע, תיק מועצת הפקולטה למדעי הרוח, תשי״ג, 10.12.1952.

36 גע״א, תיק כורש גורדון, 31.12.1952.

ילמד במחלקה לבלשנות, שזה עתה נוסדה ופולוצקי עמד בראשה.[37] במכתב רשמי מטעם הנשיא פירט מזר את תנאי המשכורת של גורדון, שכירת דירה בירושלים ופרטים אחרים הקשורים למשרתו באוניברסיטה.[38] תשובת גורדון לא נשמרה בארכיון, אך מתברר שהייתה מורכבת, שכן הוא דרש תנאים כספיים טובים יותר. מזר לא ענה למכתבו והמגע עם גורדון כמעט נותק. במאי 1956 הודיע גורדון למזר שהוא מבין משתיקתו של מזר שאין באפשרותה של האוניברסיטה להיעתר לדרישותיו, וכיוון שהוא חייב לעזוב את דרופסי קולג׳ בהקדם האפשרי, קיבל הצעה לפרופסורה באוניברסיטת ברנדייס.[39] בעצם גורדון קיבל ראשות של מחלקה חדשה – ׳לימודי הים התיכון׳ – ובה לימד עד שיצא לגמלאות בשנת 1973.

היה שלב שני בפרשת גורדון וגם הוא לא התגשם. בשנת 1961 ביקש מזר מגורדון לבוא לאוניברסיטה העברית כפרופסור אורח על חשבון קרן פולברייט וללמד את לשון אוגרית וספרותה.[40] בהמשך נשלחה הזמנה רשמית מן האוניברסיטה לגורדון,[41] אך בשלב זה התגלעו קשיים, שכן גורדון ביקש שהאוניברסיטה העברית תשלם בעד כרטיסים לכל משפחתו – אישה וחמישה ילדים – ותדאג למגורים מתאימים למשפחה בת שבע נפשות.[42] בהתניה זו לא יכלה האוניברסיטה לעמוד והזמנת גורדון לא יצאה אל הפועל.[43]

הפרשה האחרונה ברשימת חיזוריה של האוניברסיטה אחרי מלומדים נודעים מחוץ לארץ היא פרשת הזמנתו של ג׳קוב פינקלשטיין. פינקלשטיין היה אז בראשית דרכו אחרי שהשלים דוקטורט על תעודות מתל בילה בהדרכת פרופסור ספייזר בפילדלפיה. הוא נפגש עם פרופסור מזר בביקורו בארצות הברית ובפגישה דובר על האפשרות למנותו לחוג למזרח הקדום באוניברסיטה העברית.[44] באותה העת, מאי 1954, היה פינקלשטיין עוזר מחקר באוניברסיטת ייל. אחרי חליפת מכתבים בינו ובין המזכיר האקדמי מר אדוארד פוזננסקי והנשיא פרופסור מזר הוחלט שיש מקום להקצבה כספית מיוחדת להזמנת פינקלשטיין לחודש ימים לירושלים, ואף נקבע נושא הרצאותיו – ׳חוקי אשור, בבל והעמים השכנים׳.[45] פינקלשטיין הגיע לארץ בדצמבר 1955 וניהל שיחות רציניות מאוד על קבלת משרה בלימודי

37 שם, 3.7.1955.
38 שם, 4.7.1955.
39 שם, 10.5.1956.
40 על־פי ציטוט בתזכיר של גורדון לקרן פולברייט, שם, 29.9.1961.
41 מר אדוארד י״י פוזננסקי, המזכיר האקדמי, שם, 17.4.1962.
42 שם, 23.4.1962.
43 מברק של הנשיא אליהו אילת אל גורדון, שם, 30.4.1962.
44 פולוצקי אל פינקלשטיין, גע״ע, תיק פינקלשטיין, 2.5.1954.
45 גא״ע, תיק פינקלשטיין: פוזננסקי אל מזר, 6.2.1955; מזר אל פינקלשטיין, 20.3.1955; פינקלשטיין אל מזר, 5.4.1955; פינקלשטיין אל פולוצקי, 28.4.1955; פוזננסקי אל הגזברות, 24.11.1955; פוזננסקי אל פינקלשטיין, 27.11.1955; פינקלשטיין אל פוזננסקי 30.11.1955.

המזרח הקדום באוניברסיטה העברית. אולם בשיחות האלה התברר שהיה קושי גדול בתכנית להזמנתו, שכן הוא התנה את בואו במתן משרה גם לגב׳ דבורה מטליצקי (שכבר שימשה לפני שנים אחדות מורה בחוג לאנגלית באוניברסיטה), שעמה עמד להתחתן בקרוב. תנאי זה לא היה מקובל על אנשי החוג לאנגלית בירושלים.[46] לפיכך בחר פינקלשטיין לקבל את ההצעה מאוניברסיטת ברקלי בקליפורניה למשרה באשורולוגיה בשנת 1956/57 ולדחות את הזמנת האוניברסיטה העברית למשרת מרצה בכיר לאותה שנה.[47] חליפת המכתבים המפורטת בינו ובין כל הגורמים באוניברסיטה העברית ובייחוד עם הפרופסור מזר שרדה במלואה.

לימים קיבלה האוניברסיטה את ספרייתו של ג׳קוב פינקלשטיין, אחרי שנפטר בדמי ימיו בשנת 1974. ההחלטה להעניק את הספרייה לחוג לאשורולוגיה שנוסד בינתיים בירושלים הייתה של אחיו ואחותו. הספרייה צורפה לספריית לנדסברגר בחדר הסמינריוני של החוג.

יחסיי עם ג׳קוב פינקלשטיין היו קרובים. הכרתיו בפעם הראשונה בכנס American Oriental Society בבולטימור בשנת 1956, בתקופת לימודיי בשיקגו. התיידדנו, וקצת אחר כך הוא הזמין אותי למלא את מקומו באוניברסיטת ברקלי בשנת 1963, שנת השבתון שלי. זו הייתה הזמנה שלא יכולתי לקבלה מפני שהתנגשה בתכנית המחקר שלי, לבלות אותה שנה בעבודה על כתובות מלכי אשור במוזאון הבריטי. הידידות שלנו נמשכה גם אחרי שעבר פינקלשטיין לאוניברסיטת ייל. הוא הזמין אותי למלא את מקומו בהוראה בשנת 1971. זאת עשיתי ברצון ואותה שנה הייתה לאחת השנים החשובות בשבילי מכוח השתתפותם של מלומדים צעירים מעולים בסמינריון שלי. אחד התלמידים באותו הסמינריון היה פיטר משיניסט, המלמד כיום באוניברסיטת הרווארד, והאחר היה פיוטר מיכלובסקי, המלמד כיום באוניברסיטת מישיגן, אן־ארבור.

בפרשת הזמנתו של ג׳קוב פינקלשטיין, שלא יצאה לפועל, תמו ניסיונות האוניברסיטה העברית לייסד את החוג על־ידי הזמנת חוקר מחוץ לארץ, ניסיונות שכאמור, נמשכו עשרות שנים.

הודעה ברורה ומחייבת על הכוונה לשלוח אותי להשתלם בהיסטוריה של המזרח הקדום מסר לי רשמית בנימין מזר בשנת 1954 אחרי שסיימתי את עבודת הדוקטור שלי. נקראתי לפגישה בחדרו, חדר הנשיא, ונאמר לי שעליי לצאת להשתלמות נוספת באוניברסיטת שיקגו, במכון המזרחני, ושבשובי אקלט בהוראה בהיסטוריה של המזרח הקדום.

46 גא״ע, תיק פינקלשטיין: פינקלשטיין אל מזר, 13.4.1956 (המכתב מזכיר את הפגישה הראשונה עם חיים תדמור בכנס מדעי); מזר אל פינקלשטיין, 10.5.1956, ובו הצעה למשרה למטליצקי בלימודי היסוד באנגלית.

47 גא״ע, תיק פינקלשטיין: מברק ממזר אל פינקלשטיין, 4.5.1956, ובו הצעה למשרת מרצה ללימודי המזרח הקדום בירושלים; מכתב אל פינקלשטיין, 10.5.1956, החוזר על ההצעה למשרה בירושלים; מכתב של פינקלשטיין אל מזר, 20.6.1956, ובו פינקלשטיין דוחה את ההצעה למטליצקי ומודיע לו שקיבל משרה באוניברסיטת ברקלי בקליפורניה.

מאותה תקופה שרד מסמך מעניין למדיי, והוא מכתב שכתבה גב׳ טובה וגר (וילק), מזכירת ההנהלה באוניברסיטה, למזכיר הפקולטה למדעי הרוח, מר יוסף אבירם, וזו לשונו:

> למר אבירם,
> בקשר עם המזרח הקדמון הוחלט בישיבה שהתקיימה בזמנו עם הפרופסורים גויטיין ופולוצקי:
> 1. להזמין לשנה הבאה את ד״ר פינקלשטיין לכשיתברר – מה שקרוב לודאי – כי גורדון לא יבוא.
> 2. למנות את פרומשטיין (תדמור) להיסטוריה של המזרח הקדמון (על דרגה לא דובר).
> 3. במרוצת הזמן יש למצוא מורים להיסטוריה וארכיאולוגיה של מצרים.[48]

מזר חזר לעניין קליטתי באוניברסיטה העברית בעת ביקורו בשיקגו במרוצת שנת 1956. נושא זה חזר ועלה בחליפת המכתבים ביני ובין יוסף אבירם, מזכיר הפקולטה למדעי הרוח. על סמך חליפת מכתבים זו ערכנו את תכניותינו לשוב לישראל בסוף הקיץ של 1957. בינתיים דנה ועדת ההוראה בהצעות השיעורים שלי לשנת תשי״ח.[49] הצעות אלו כללו שיעור באכדית למתחילים, שיעור בהיסטוריה מסופוטמית ותרגיל בכרונולוגיה של המזרח הקדמון – תחום עבודת הדוקטור שלי. בשובי התחלתי ללמד לפי תכנית זו, והשיעורים שלי נרשמו כיחידה העומדת ברשות עצמה בכותרת ׳קורסים (או שיעורים) במזרח הקדמון׳.[50] שיעורים אלו נחשבו ללימודי השלמה בחוגים להיסטוריה של עם ישראל בתקופת המקרא ולארכאולוגיה.

מתברר שפתיחת מסלול לימודים זה בהוראה בפקולטה למדעי הרוח היה בו חידוש גדול, שכן ללימודים אלו נמשכו תלמידים מתקדמים בהיסטוריה של עם ישראל ובמקרא, בשלבי דוקטורט.

הקורס ההיסטורי שנתתי היה בנוי על-פי דגם הלימודים בהיסטוריה הקלסית, כדרכו של מורי אביגדור צ׳ריקובר, שהקיף בשלוש שנים את תולדות יוון ורומא. בדומה לזה לימדתי שנה שלמה את תולדות שומר ובבל הקדומה; השנה השנייה התרכזה בתקופה למן נפילת בבל באמצע האלף השני לפסה״נ ועד לעליית הממלכה האשורית, והשנה השלישית יוחדה לתולדות האימפריה האשורית וממלכת בבל החדשה. במרוצת הזמן התברר שקורס מפורט כל כך – שברבות השנים היה לסקירה בת ארבע שנים – אינו ניתן בשום מחלקה ממחלקות לימודי המזרח הקדום באוניברסיטאות אירופה וארצות הברית.

48 המכתב מיום 25.1.1956 שרד בגא״ע בשני עותקים, האחד בתיק פינקלשטיין והאחר בתיק המזרח הקדמון.

49 גע״א, תיק ועדת ההוראה למדעי הרוח, תשי״ז, 8.5.1957.

50 גא״ע, רשימת השיעורים תשי״ח, עמ׳ 68; תשי״ט, עמ׳ 70; תש״ך, עמ׳ 70; תשכ״א, עמ׳ 73; תשכ״ב, עמ׳ 82; תשכ״ג, עמ׳ 83.

הוראת האכדית כפי שלימדתי, הייתה מכוונת מעיקרה להיסטוריונים, והדגש היה פילולוגי־היסטורי. הצד הבלשני המשווה לא הודגש בדרך כלל. גם בקורס למתקדמים בחרתי בטקסטים היסטוריים כגון כתובות המלכים של סנחריב, אסרחדון ואשורבניפל. במרוצת השנים עסקתי גם בסוגיות של סגנון ועריכה, של הרכב הטקסט, זמן חיבורו ורקעו וכן המסר האידאולוגי של הטקסט. קורסים אלו, שניתנו כסמינריונים למתקדמים, משכו תלמידים מן הארץ וממרכזי מחקר חשובים בעולם. כעבור שנים השתתפו בקורס גם מורים – עמיתיי באוניברסיטה. כיוון שכך, נדרשו ממני הכנה רבה והכרח מתמיד לחדש ולהימצא בקדמת חזית המחקר.

כאן עליי לומר כמה מילים כדי להסביר את הדגשתה היתרה של הוראת ההיסטוריה המסופוטמית. בראש ובראשונה אני היסטוריון שבמרוצת לימודיו קנה תורה אצל ריכרד קבנר ואביגדור צ׳ריקובר בחוג להיסטוריה כללית, וכן אצל יצחק בער, גדליהו אלון ובנימין מזר בחוג להיסטוריה של עם ישראל. שפות קלסיות למדתי אצל משה שוובה ויוחנן לוי. אולם בחוג להיסטוריה כללית בירושלים התחיל רצף ההיסטוריה העולמית והוא מתחיל עד היום ביוון העתיקה, לפי המסורת האירופית המקובלת. על אף ניסיונות אחדים שניסיתי נשארה ההיסטוריה של המזרח הקדום מחוץ לרצף זה. רק באוניברסיטת בר־אילן נקלט עמיתי פנחס ארצי בחוג להיסטוריה כללית.

כל העת היה לי ברור שלימודי המזרח הקדום לא יהיו לחוג בלי מינויו של מלומד נוסף, פילולוג, המומחה באכדית בצד הספרותי ובעל ידע בשומרית. ואכן, מלומד כזה נמצא בשנת 1962: אהרון שפר, יליד טורונטו בקנדה, שעמד לסיים אז את הדוקטורט אצל הפרופסורים אפרים ספייזר וש״נ קרמר באוניברסיטת פנסילווניה בפילדלפיה. הוא ואשתו אתל, שבאה ממשפחה ציונית, רצו לעלות ארצה ולהיקלט בה. זו הייתה אפוא התאמה אידאלית בין המועמד ובין צורכי האוניברסיטה. בהתכתבות בינינו הביע שפר רצון להשתלם בשיקגו בשנה שאחרי הדוקטורט ולעבוד במילון האשורי, ואת ההוראה בירושלים להתחיל בשנת 1964 לאחר שאחזור גם אני משנת עבודה במוזאון הבריטי. כך נפתח שלב אקדמי חדש בהיריון הארוך שקדם ללידתו של החוג.

בתחילה נתבקשתי להגיש הצעת תכנית מפורטת לחוג לימודי המזרח הקדום. זאת עשיתי כשישבתי בלונדון. אחר כך נתמנתה ועדת משנה מצומצמת מטעם ועדת ההוראה של הפקולטה לדון בהצעת התכנית הזאת.[51] בדיונים בוועדת המשנה נתגלו כמה מגמות: האחת – זו של פרופסור פולוצקי שלדעתו, לא היה מקום לשם ׳מזרח קדום׳ ולמגמה התרבותית־היסטורית המודגשת בו. הוא הציע את השם ׳אכדית׳ במקביל למצרית – החוג שבראשו עמד כל השנים. את העמדה האחרת הציג פרופסור מזר בהציעו

51 גא״ע, תיק ועדת הוראה למדעי הרוח, תשכ״ד, 13.11.1963. חברי הוועדה היו הפרופסורים מזר, פולוצקי, מלמט, ידין, וירשובסקי ותדמור (ששהה כל השנה בלונדון).

לקרוא לחוג החדש בשם 'אשורולוגיה', שם שהיה מקובל באירופה ויכול להקיף את מכלול ההוראה של כתבי היתדות ושל התרבות וההיסטוריה של מסופוטמיה ושכנותיה. מיהרתי אפוא לשלוח הצעת תכנית מתוקנת לחוג החדש. אכן, בוועדת ההוראה של הפקולטה ובמועצת הפקולטה, שבה הציג עמיתי פרופסור אברהם מלמט את התכנית, היו ויכוחים סוערים על שם החוג, והיו שביקרו את השם ההיברידי ('אשורולוגיה') שבינתיים היה לשם דבר. החוג אושר במועצת הפקולטה ובסנט בלא בעיות.[52] למרבה התדהמה, התברר שלא מעטים מן הפרופסורים בפקולטה למדו בצעירותם אשורית, ובזכות זה ראו עצמם רשאים להביע דעה על פרטי התכנית ועל תכניה. דרך אגב, אפילו היו חברי כנסת שלמדו אשורית, כגון יוסף בורג, ואלימלך רימלט אף כתב בשעתו דוקטורט באשורולוגיה.

לחוג החדש לא היה מגע עם לימודי המצרית באוניברסיטה. ואמנם במרוצת השנים שונה שם הלימודים האלה ל'אגיפטולוגיה', והחוג שבראשו עמדה אז פרופסור שרה גרול, תלמידתו של פולוצקי, שמר למרות שינוי השם על אופיו הבלשני המובהק.

מכאן ואילך נפתחה הדרך להוראה במתכונת שלמה בחוג לאשורולוגיה. הוראה זו נמשכה למן שנת 1964 כשלושים שנה עד ליציאתי לגמלאות בשנת 1992. בתקופה זו לימדו בחוג דרך קבע עוד מורים: צבי אבוש, אשורולוג[53] וגלינה קלרמן,[54] חִתיתולוגית. תוספת לימודי חִתית הרחיבה את קשת האינטרסים של החוג והייתה בה תרומה מיוחדת ללימודי הארכאולוגיה. חבל מאוד שגלינה קלרמן עזבה את החוג ואין לה מחליף. כמו כן לימדו בחוג פרופסורים אורחים נודעים שבאו לשנה או לשנתיים: ש"נ קרמר לימד שומרית[55] ותורקילד יעקובסן לימד שומרית, אכדית ואמנות המזרח הקדום.[56] יעקובסן אף קיבל תואר דוקטור לשם כבוד מטעם האוניברסיטה העברית.[57] מורה אורח היה גם פיטר משיניסט – אף הוא היה פעמיים, והאחרונה בהן הייתה בשנה שעברה.[58] מלבדם לימדו בחוג במרוצת השנים מורים אורחים פרקי זמן שונים בדרגות אקדמיות למיניהן.[59]

52 גא"ע: תיק ועדת ההוראה למדעי הרוח, תשכ"ד; תיק הפקולטה למדעי הרוח, תשכ"ד, עמ' 60–61, 154–155; תיק אשורולוגיה, עמ' 188; תיק סנט, תשכ"ד, ישיבה ט, 27.6.1964.

53 גא"ע, שנתון הפקולטה למדעי הרוח, בשנים תשל"ד-תשל"ו.

54 שם, בשנים תשל"ח-תשמ"ד.

55 שם, בשנת תשל"ג.

56 שם, בשנים תשל"ד, תשל"ז, תשמ"ו.

57 טקס הענקת התואר היה ביום 15.6.1988.

58 גא"ע, שנתון הפקולטה למדעי הרוח, תשמ"א, עמ' 387; תשס"ג, עמ' 370.

59 מורים אלו לימדו אכדית בכל מיני רמות או נתנו תרגילים בהיסטוריה מסופוטמית: פיליפ אברהמי , שושנה ארבלי, אביגדור הורוויץ, ג'ואן וסטנהולץ, מרדכי כוגן, דינה כץ, מאיר מלול, יונתן ספרן, טרי פנטון, יחזקאל קוטשר; שומרית לימדו רפאל קוטשר, יעקב קליין, צ'לסו ג'ו, טקיושי אושימה; אלכסנדר אוצ'יטל לימד חתית היירוגליפית; עמיתיי ראובן ירון וריימונד וסטברוק לימדו משפט מסופוטמי; אמנות מסופוטמיה

מורי החוג כיום, הנושאים בעול ההוראה הם: נתן וסרמן ואלנתן וייסרט, שקנו את השכלתם באשורולוגיה בירושלים, וויין הורוביץ, תלמידו של פרופסור למברט באוניברסיטת ברמינגהם.

אזכיר כאן את מורי החוג להיסטוריה של עם ישראל בתקופת המקרא בירושלים: ישראל אפעל, מרדכי כוגן ונילי ואזנה, העוסקים במחקריהם בסוגיות מתחום האשורולוגיה, וכך עושים גם המורים לתולדות עם ישראל בתקופת המקרא באוניברסיטת תל־אביב: נדב נאמן ורן צדוק וכן המורים באוניברסיטת חיפה: גרשון גליל ודנאל קאהן – כולם תלמידי החוג שלנו בעבר.

רבים מן המורים בחוג למקרא ובארכאולוגיה מקראית בירושלים ובעת האחרונה המרצה החדשה באמנות של המזרח הקדום טלי אורנן למדו בחוג שלנו באוניברסיטה העברית. ראובן ירון, פרופסור למשפט רומי ומשפט של המזרח הקדום, החל את לימודיו באשורולוגיה בחוג שלנו. בחוג למדו שלושה דורות של תלמידים מיפן – קויצ׳ירו גוטו, טומואו אישידה וייטקה איקדה וכן שיגאו ימאדה, נציג הדור השלישי, שאף הוא קנה את השכלתו האשורולוגית אצלנו.

בדצמבר 1994 פנה עמיתי ישראל אפעל במכתב מפורט לדיקן הפקולטה למדעי הרוח מנחם מילסון והציע להקים מסגרת משותפת ללימודי אשורולוגיה, אגיפטולוגיה והחטיבה למזרח הקדום שתכלול את לימודי השפות השמיות העתיקות. במכתבו ציין שבכל אחת מן היחידות הנזכרות התרחשו שינויים אישיים מרחיקי לכת, המורים הבכירים באשורולוגיה ובאגיפטולוגיה פורשים לגמלאות, ואילו בחוג לשפות שמיות נפטרו שני מורים בכירים, משה גושן־גוטשטיין ויונה גרינפלד, ופרש לגמלאות יוסף נוה.[60] בשנת 1996 החליטה הוועדה המרכזת של האוניברסיטה להקים מסגרת חוגית אחת שתכלול את החוג לאשורולוגיה ואת החוג לאגיפטולוגיה וכן את הצירוף הבין־חוגי לימודי המזרח הקדום. הוחלט שהיא תיקרא ׳החוג ללימודי המזרח הקרוב הקדום׳. החוגים הנפרדים יוסיפו להתקיים במסגרת המשותפת החדשה.[61] כך בעצם חזרה האוניברסיטה לתכנית המרבית של המזרח הקדום שחלם עליה בנימין מזר, ואולם הדרך למיצוי אקדמי הולם של המסגרת הזאת על כל השוני בין רכיביה עדיין ארוכה.

הרשוני לסכם. נוכחנו לדעת שהעיסוק בלימודי האשורולוגיה ימיו כימי האוניברסיטה העברית. במרוצת השנים היו מועמדים אחדים ללמד בחוג,

---

לימדה איירין וינטר; ועמיתיי מאוניברסיטת תל־אביב איתמר זינגר, נדב נאמן ואהרן קמפינסקי מילאו את מקומי בהוראה של תולדות מסופוטמיה בתקופות השבתון שלי.

60 אפעל אל מילסון, 23.12.1994.

61 גא״ע, תיק המזרח הקדום (2264), מכתב של הדיקן מילסון מיום 21.1.1996 אל ראשי החוגים אשורולוגיה, אגיפטולוגיה, שפות שמיות עתיקות ומורי תקופת המקרא בהיסטוריה של עם ישראל בצירוף העתקים לנשיא, לרקטור ולמזכיר האקדמי. במכתב מצוין שפרופסור אפעל הסכים לשמש ראש החוג החדש. ההחלטה הובאה לידיעת הוועדה המתמדת של הסנט; גא״ע, תיק הוועדה המתמדת, תשנ״ו, ישיבה יא, 22.2.1996; שם, ישיבה כה, 31.7.1996.

מהם גדולי עולם, אבל הם לא באו הנה ולא חשוב במי האשם. ולבסוף, ארבעים שנה לאחר ייסוד האוניברסיטה העברית נוסד המקצוע בידי כוח מקומי בשיתוף הדוק עם עולה מאוניברסיטת פנסילווניה.[62] האבות המייסדים של האוניברסיטה העברית היו בוודאי נחרדים אילו שמעו את הסִסמה 'מי צריך אשורולוגיה?' שהושמעה במרוצת השנים, והיא צצה ועולה מדי פעם בפעם. כעת, אחרי התמורות שחלו בחוג, נמצא השרביט בידי דור ההמשך. שמרו־נא על ה'אשורולוגיה' והעבירו אותה בהוקרה ובחיבה גם לבאים אחריכם.

62 פרופסור אהרן שפר פרש לגמלאות בשנת 1997 ונפטר בט"ז בניסן תשס"ד (7 באפריל 2004), בשנת השבעים לחייו.